CRITICAL INVESTIGATION OF DOMESTIC TERRORISM IN NIGERIA

Peter Okoro Nwankwo, L.L M; Ph D

Albany State University

Create Space Publishers

ISBN-13:978-1500209391

ISBN-10:1500209392

Create Space Publishers

CONTENTS

ABSTRACT

I examine and analyze domestic terrorism in Nigeria. I used data from the Global Terrorism Database (GTD) at http://www.start.umd.edu/gtd/. Each recorded attack was described with date of occurrence, the city in which it occurred, who was blamed for the attack, the number of people killed and the number of people injured during the attack, weapons used in the attack, and the target of the attack. The dependent variable, Severity, was constructed from the number of people killed or injured. See appendix B. Sixteen independent variables were constructed as dichotomous variables based on who was blamed for the attack, who was targeted, and what weapons were used. Two additional variables, longitude and latitude of the city in which the attack occurred, were added from independent source. I used multiple linear regression analysis. All of my significant dichotomous variables described targets of the attack The targeted groups that were significant with respect to the number of people killed were (1) citizens,(2) businesses,(3) churches, and (4) Police. I concluded that the target of the attack is the essential distinguishing feature of domestic terrorism. Any proposed solution to domestic terrorism must start with analysis of who is being attacked and why.

KEYWORDS: Boko Haram, business, citizen, church, Efik/Ibibio, ethnic, Hausa, Ibo, MEND, military, police, religion, target, Terrorism, Yoruba

INTRODUCTION

Nigeria is a multi-ethnic country with about two hundred and fifty dialects spoken by different ethnic groups. In Nigeria, three dominant groups account for nearly sixty percent of the country's population. These are Ibos in the Southeast, Yorubas in the Southwest, and Hausas in the North. There are other smaller, but important groups scattered all over the country. This multi-ethnic nature of Nigeria is one of the critical conditions in Nigeria that is relevant in analysis of terrorist attacks.

This research examines severity of Domestic Terrorism. Domestic Terrorism severity is measured by the number of people killed plus .001 * the number injured. I make severity my dependent variable. My independent variables are dichotomous variables constructed from the GTD data. I also add longitude and latitude as independent variables to test if location of the attack is related to the severity of the attack. Because ethnicity in Nigeria is highly localized, location is a proxy for ethnicity.

RESEARCH QUESTIONS AND ANSWERS:

How has the rate of terrorist attacks changed in recent years?

See Appendix A.
The years 2006 to 2011, showed an irregular trend toward increased number of terrorist attacks in Nigeria.. The year of most attacks was 2011. 175 attacks occurred in 2011.

The year with the second most attacks was 2008. 81 attacks were recorded for 2008. More terrorist attacks were reported in Nigeria in the 3 years from 2009 to 2011, than in the thirty-three years from 1976 to 2008.

What conditions caused or is causing incident attacks?

Some suggested answers are in the literature review. Corruption, poverty, Economic discrimination, Moslem tradition, and conflicts with western technology have been suggested. I found that the severity of the terrorism depends not on who the terrorist is, but on who the target is. Therefore, the focus should be not so much on conditions of the terrorists , but on why the target is the target.

What type of weapons did the terrorists use in Nigeria?

Weapons used were:
Chemical, Explosives/Bombs/Dynamite, Firearms, Incendiary, Melee, Sabotage Equipment

Were there any suicide bombing that occurred in any of the named incident attack occurrence?

Approximately a third of the terrorist attacks involved bombs. The GTD does not report on which bombings were suicide bombings.

What type(s) of properties were destroyed?

Church owned buildings, shopping centers, parking lots, some villages in Northern Nigeria, oil wells, and oil pipelines.

Had there been negotiations between the Nigerian government and the terrorist?

In the oil industry conflict in the Niger Delta, the Nigerian government has generally taken the side of the oil companies. Because of this stance, it is unlikely that the Nigerian government would be interested in negotiations with the terrorists.

Were there any terrorist group that was suspected to have performed these acts of terrorism in Nigeria?

There are two major terrorist groups: Boko Haram and Movement for the Emancipation of the Niger Delta (MEND). In addition there are 49 smaller terrorist groups active in Nigeria. Of the 602 G.T.D. reported terrorist acts in Nigeria, 299 of them were by persons or groups unknown.

Why are borders more vulnerable to terrorists?

"Nigeria's shares 773km border stretch with Benin Republic, 87km with Chad and then an entire stretch of 1,049km with Niger republic and 1,690km with Cameroon. The

Nigeria Immigration Service, NIS announced there are about 1,487 illegal routes to Nigeria through these porous borders.
"http://www.nigeriavillagesquare.com/forum/main-square/76383-boko-haram-foreign-terror-via-nigeria-s-porous-borders-urgent-matter-national-security.html

It is believed that since Nigeria has very porous borders, that foreign agents can easily enter the country and persuade local citizens to take up terrorist activities.

Were the attacks transnational, or domestic?

Some believe that Boko Haram is both. Foreign agents have persuaded citizens of Nigeria to do the terrorist activities of "Boko Haram".

Some local citizens responsible for terrorists attacks were deported to neighboring countries. After they were deported, they still organized terrorist attacks, but from a base in the neighboring country.

Why have economically developed countries become the target of terrorists?

People unable to get the justice they need from peaceful channels are likely to resort to violence. Economically developed countries are more likely to have treated unfairly those people not protected by rule of law.

What are the four phases of management models in the preparation for attack by the terrorists?

Emergency management in the United States has been described for the past three decades as a "four phase" process, involving:

- Mitigation
- Preparedness
- Response
- Recovery

Mitigation refers to activities that are designed to:
Reduce or eliminate risks to persons or property, or
Lessen the actual or potential effects or consequences of an incident.

Preparedness is defined as the range of deliberate, critical tasks and activities necessary to build, sustain, and improve the operational capability to prevent, protect against, respond to, and recover from domestic incidents. Preparedness is a continuous process involving efforts at all levels of government and between government and private-sector and nongovernmental organizations to identify threats, determine vulnerabilities, and identify required resources.

Response begins when an emergency event is imminent or immediately after an event occurs. Response encompasses the activities that address the short-term, direct effects of an incident. Response also includes the execution of EOPs and of incident mitigation activities designed to limit the loss of life, personal injury, property damage, and unfavorable outcomes.

The goal of recovery is to return the community's systems and activities to normal. Recovery begins right after the emergency. Some recovery activities may be concurrent with response efforts.

Who are potential targets for terrorist attacks in Nigeria?

Business, Educational Institution, Government, Journalists & Media, Maritime, Military, NGO, Police, Private Citizens, Property, Religious Figures/Institutions, Telecommunication, Transportation, Utilities, Violent Political Party

What are the assumptions in regard to the causes of Domestic terrorism in Nigeria?

In the case of MEND, the assumption is that the oil companies are damaging the living environment of the people. In the case of Boko Harram, the assumption is that Christians and Muslims are ignorant of each other's religion, and each group is being taught to be intolerant of the other.

What are the strategies for counter attacks, if any?

One strategy for schools is listed at the web site
http://www.vanguardngr.com/2014/02/boko-haram-attacks-counter-terrorism-guidance-schools/

A discussion from the government's point of view is at the web site
http://en.wikipedia.org/wiki/State_Security_Service_(Nigeria)

Why are terrorist acts different than acts committed by other organized criminals?

In fact, if terrorists need money to finance their terrorism, then they will probably engage in criminal activity, such as kidnapping for ransom.

Despite the difficulty in articulating an acceptable definition, terrorism does have several key features that distinguish it from other types of violence (Boylan, 2009). First, it is planned and calculated (Enders and Sandler 2002; 145; Krueger 2007; 14). Terrorism is not spontaneously executed, but rather "premeditated and purposeful" (Crenshaw (1983,

2). Terrorists devote much time, consideration, and care to the preparation process in order to increase the impact of their attacks (Boylan, 2009).

Are Muslims responsible for all the terrorism in Nigeria?

No. Boko Haram is the group associated with Muslims. In addition to Boko Haram, there is also the following terrorist groups: Fulani Militants (suspected); Modakeke Ethnics; Ijaw militants; The Joint Revolutionary Council; Movement for the Emancipation of the Niger Delta (MEND); and may other smaller groups.

At most, about 1/4 of total attacks and 3/8 of total fatalities could be attributed to Boko Haram. It is true that Boko Haram is the largest terrorist group in Nigeria. The second largest terrorist group is MEND which is responsible for at most about 1/9 of the attacks and almost 1/7 of the fatalities.

If not, where do the other terroristic acts occur?

The Terrorist group MEND has attacked in the cities of Abia, Abuja, Agoro, Awoba, Bayelsa, Beniboye, Bonny, Bonny Channel, Bugama, Buruto, Delta, Escravos, Forcados, Kula, Lagos, Nembe Creek, Nembe Oil Field, Okono/Okpoho, Okrika, Onitsha, Penington (Estuary), Port Harcourt, Riverine Area, Sand fill, Tarkwa, Tebidaba, Utorogu, Warri, and Yenagoa.

Who are the targets of terrorism?

Terrorists have targeted Religious Figures/Institutions ,Business, Educational Institutions, Journalists & Media, Maritime targets, Military, Police, Private Citizens & Property, Government, Telecommunication equipment, Transportation facilities, and Utilities.

Which terroristic acts resulted in the most fatalities?

On February 19th, in 1992, in the city of Utan Brama, a group called Effiat ethnic roup or Jbibio Peoples staged an Armed Assault on Private Citizens & Property and killed 80 people.

What are methods and weapons used by the terrorists?

Terrorists have used Chemical weapons, Bombs, Dynamite, Firearms, Incendiary weapons, Melee, and Sabotage Equipment.

This study is a case study, an empirical and literature search inquiry to investigate domestic terrorism. Domestic Terrorism is a contemporary phenomenon. Its context is not evident, due to its complexity, including but not limited to economic, political and Religious Phenomena. The cases under investigation would be terrorist attacks in Nigeria. The severity of the terrorist incidents would be the dependent variable. The independent variables would be determined by the data available in the Global Terrorism

Database. There is no assurance that the available data could capture all the causes of terrorism. Terrorists have two targets, a direct target, and an indirect target. In the case of terrorism against tourists, the direct target is the tourist, and the indirect target is the economy of the country being visited by the tourists. From the analysis of the G.T.D data I concluded that the causes of terrorism generally will be found in the indirect targets, not in the terrorists.

The unit of analysis is the terrorist attacks in Nigeria. The scope is interval of time covered by the attacks reported in the G.T.D. The problem that this research investigates is the relationship of the target, location, and type of attack for terrorist attacks in Nigeria to the severity of the attack.

Before September 11, 2001 attack on the twin towers in New York, U.S. research on terrorism had been very scarce. After the attacks, terrorism research increased significantly, but focused on only transnational terrorism (Cronin, 2002; Enders and Sandler, 202; Sandler 2003; and Li and Schaub, 2004; Rosendorff and Sandler 2005; Chald, 2007 and Boylan, 2009).

Examples of domestic terrorist organizations are the Corsican National Liberation Front (FLNC) in France, Revolutionary Armed Forces of Columbia (FARC), Liberation Tiger Tamil Felam (LTTE) IN Sri Lanka; Lord's Resistance Army (LRA) in Uganda and Boko Haram (BHN) in Nigeria (ARTICLE | 19 DECEMBER 2011 - 12:44PM. Think Africa Press).

It is evident that research that investigates transnational, and Domestic terrorism jointly is ineffective and opinionated in understanding how domestic terrorist activity differ from transnational terrorism, and how terrorism in general differs from other forms of political violence. Not distinguishing transnational terrorism from domestic terrorism conflates some conditions and Mechanisms that are unique and motivational to each form of terrorism i.e. to say that what motivates domestic terrorism in a specific country may not be the same to transnational type of terrorism. Example is found in the September 11 attacks on the U.S. That is the say that transnational and domestic terrorism have certain distinct features that are overlooked when they are studied together.

TERRORISM DEFINED

Terrorism is a difficult term to define due to its political, legal, and complex nature (Boylan, 2009. Many disagree over qualifying motivations, tactics, targets, and consequences. Writing about the concept thirty years ago, Brian Michael Jenkins (1980;1) states that terrorism has no exact or accepted definition. And in the years since, it appears as though scholars, governments, and organizations have still not been able to reach a consensus. As Schmid and Jongman (2008;1) put it, "The search for an adequate definition of terrorism is still on."

Despite the difficulty in articulating an acceptable definition, terrorism does have several key features that distinguish it from other types of violence. First, it is planned and calculated (Enders and Sandler 2002; 145; Krueger 2007; 14). Terrorism is not spontaneously executed, but rather "premeditated and purposeful" (Crenshaw (1983, 2). Terrorists devote much time, consideration, and care to the preparation process in order to increase the impact of their attacks.

Again, terrorism is intrinsically violent (Enders and Sandler 2002, 145; Hoffman 2006, 40). Louise Richardson (2007, 4) argues, "If an act does not involve violence or the threat of violence, it is not terrorism." Often, the use of violence is a trait that distinguishes the terrorist group from the political party that supports it. For example, Sinn Fein has not been violent itself, but has supported the Provisional IRA, a group that has used violence in its irredentist campaign.

Terrorism is a political act (Hoffman 2006, 40; Richardson 2007, 5; Krueger 2007, 14). If a premeditated, violent act does not have a political dimension, such as a bank robbery, it is not terrorism. Terrorism seeks to manipulate political standpoints rather than conquer an opponent (Crenshaw 1983, 2). Fernando Reinares (2005, 120) contends that, "Terrorism becomes political when it intends to affect the distribution of power and social cohesion within a given state jurisdiction or in a wider, international scenario."

Terrorists design their attacks to have prolonged psychological effects beyond the immediate victims (Bjørgo 2005, 2; Hoffman 2006, 40). Terrorism is effective when it generates an atmosphere of fear. The shock of the incident, compounded by continuous media coverage, conveys a message that no one is safe until the political environment changes. For Reinares (2005; 120), "an act of violence is to be considered as terrorist when its psychical effects within a certain population or social aggregate, in terms of widespread emotional reactions such as fear and anxiety, are likely to condition attitudes and behavior in a determined direction." Fifth, terrorists communicate a message to an audience (Victoroff 2005; 4; Hoffman 2006, 40-41). In many cases, the target of the attack does not have much value to the perpetrators. Instead, terrorists intend their attacks to convey statements to governments, citizenries, or rival groups (Boylan, 2009). Michel Wieviorka usefully distinguishes between primary and secondary audiences (Wieviorka 1995, 599). Terrorists may carry out an attack in order to influence a primary audience, such as a government, so that it adopts (or stops) a certain course of action. However, at the same time, the attack may send a signal to a secondary audience, such as a funder. Hezbollah's attacks against Israeli and Western targets, for example, not only demonstrate the organization's resolve in fighting against those that it believes are invaders but also aim to convince Iran and Syria that the group is competent in carrying out these regimes' objectives in the region, thus securing their funding.

It is noted that, a defining characteristic is the deliberate targeting of civilians (Richardson 2007; 6) or non-combatants (Bjørgo 2005; 2; Victoroff 2005; 4). This is a controversial point and many scholars consciously do not include this facet in their definition of terrorism. However, the deliberate targeting of civilians (or non-combatants) is a defining feature that separates terrorism from other forms of political violence, especially insurgency. Insurgents wish to overthrow their government using armed conflict, but they do not explicitly target civilians for this purpose – though they may kill civilians in the process of their campaigns. Phil Williams (2008, 14) notes, "For terrorist organizations . . . the use of indiscriminate violence against civilian targets is not only central to their strategy but is also their defining characteristic." Terrorism comes in several varieties. It is useful to think about "terrorisms" rather than "terrorism" (Miller 2007). This differentiation is helpful in understanding transnational and domestic forms. For a terrorist incident to be transnational, it must involve at least two countries. Walter

Enders and Todd Sandler (1999, 149) write, "Whenever a terrorist incident in one country involves victims, or targets, or institutions of another country, then the incident is characterized as transnational." The attacks on September 11, 2001 in the United States, and March 11, 2004 in Madrid are well-known examples of transnational terrorism. Domestic terrorism, in contrast, is terrorism that nationals carry out against their own country, including their government or their fellow countrymen and women. It does not involve foreign victims, targets, or institutions. Sandler (2003, 781) notes, "Domestic terrorism is home grown and has consequences for only the host country, its institutions, people, property, and policies." Much of the terrorism that occurs in Thailand and Sri Lanka, for example, is domestic in nature. However, the type of domestic terrorism discussed in this dissertation is more complex, due to the conditions of Nigeria.

It can be difficult to differentiate domestic terrorism from other forms of violence, such as civil war, insurgency, and organized crime, but some defining traits stand out. Domestic terrorism can resemble civil war when it takes the form of a protracted campaign. Even when this is the case, however, it is a tactic employed as part of a larger violent movement. Terrorism can take place within the context of civil war, but the two types of violence are not identical. Unlike civil war, domestic terrorism also includes isolated incidents that do not occur in conjunction with civil conflict, such as the Oklahoma City Bombing. Moreover, both domestic terrorist campaigns and insurgencies carry out violence against the state, but terrorists explicitly target civilians and civilian infrastructure as part of their strategy; casualties during insurgencies are usually a byproduct of violence. Finally, unlike organized criminals, domestic terrorists seek to draw public attention to their cause and to broadcast a message to their audience. In contrast, criminals use private bribery and extortion for financial gain, rather than seek public power, as noted by Boylan above.

Terrorism is not new; it has been used since the beginning of recorded history. It is relatively hard to define. Terrorism has been described and defined by different scholars as both a tactic, and strategy; and also as a crime and a Holy duty; a justified reaction to oppression and an inexcusable abomination. However a lot of these depend on whose point of view is being represented. Terrorism has been an effective tactic for the weaker side in a conflict. It is an asymmetric form of conflict. It confers coercive power with many of the advantages of military force at a fraction of the cost. Due to the secretive nature and small size of terrorist organizations, they often offer opponents no clear organization to defend against or to deter .That is why prevention is so important. In some cases, terrorism has been a means to carry on a conflict without the adversary realizing the nature of the threat, mistaking terrorism for criminal activity. Because of these characteristics, terrorism has become increasingly common among those pursuing extreme goals throughout the world.

Terrorism is a nebulous concept. Even within the ongoing fighting against terrorism, people use different definitions. The United States Department of Defense defines terrorism as "the calculated use of unlawful violence or threat of unlawful violence to inculcate fear; intended to coerce or to intimidate governments or societies in the pursuit of goals that are generally political, religious, or ideological." Within this definition, there are three key elements, violence, fear, and intimidation, and each element produces terror in its victims. The FBI defines "Terrorism as the unlawful use of force and violence against or to coerce a government, the civilian population, or any segment thereof, in furtherance of political or social objectives." The U.S. Department of State defines terrorism to mean "premeditated politically-motivated violence perpetrated against non-combatant targets by sub-national groups or clandestine agents, usually intended to influence an audience."

Outside the United States Government, there are greater variations in what features of terrorism are emphasized in definitions. The United Nations produced this definition in 1992; "An anxiety-inspiring method of repeated violent action, employed by (semi-) clandestine individual, group or state actors, for idiosyncratic criminal or political reasons, whereby – in contrast to assassination – the direct targets of violence are not the main targets." The most commonly accepted academic definition starts with the U.N. definition quoted above, and adds two sentences totaling another 77 words on the end; containing such verbose concepts as "message generators" and 'violence based communication processes." Less specific and considerably less verbose, the British Government definition of 1974 is "the use of violence for political ends, and includes any use of violence for the purpose of putting the public, or any section of the public, in fear."

Terrorism is a criminal act that influences an audience beyond the immediate victim. The strategy of terrorists is to commit acts of violence that draws the attention of the local populace, the government, and the world to their cause. The terrorists plan their attack to obtain the greatest publicity, choosing targets that symbolize what they oppose. The effectiveness of the terrorist act lies not in the act itself, but in the public's reaction to the act. For example, in 1972 at the Munich Olympics, the Black September Organization killed 11 Israelis. The Israelis were the immediate victims. But the true target was the estimated 1 billion people watching the televised event.

It is acknowledged that the Black September Organization used the high visibility of the Olympics to publicize the plight of the Palestinian refugees. Similarly, in October 1983, terrorists bombed the Marine Battaloin Landing Team Headquarters at Beirut International Airport. Their immediate victims were the 241 U.S. military personnel who were killed and over 100 others wounded. Their true target was the American people and the U.S. Congress. Their act of violence influenced the United States' decision to withdraw the Marines from Beirut and therefore became a terrorist success.

Statement of the Problem

What do we know about the causes of terrorism? How may we prevent it? Religions differ from groups to groups such as Islamic religion, Christianity, and African traditional religion and various rituals. Boundary disputes resulting in civil unrest or riots are common. In addition, there are problems between social classes in relation to income. The financial problems are disturbing because few people control the wealth and income. Political rancor also abounds, a few ethnic groups compete to dominate others through electoral frauds, for both the national, state and local governments. In Nigeria, there are a lot of corruptions, fraud, swindles, scams, and organized white collar crimes. There are almost two hundred universities and polytechnics, including teacher colleges in Nigeria, turning out or graduating thousands of bachelors, masters, and doctorate degree holders yearly but there is lack of industries or other employable opportunities to absorb these applicants. Almost 60% of Nigerians are unemployed (Nairaland Forum, June 2014).

There are also indigenous young men and women who are out to form gangs or to terrorize the entire population due to anger, hunger, starvation and frustration. Most of the young men and girls devise means to leave the country. If they can migrate to other countries, they can hope to get jobs and survive. Sometimes the Nigerian government itself is unfair to its citizens. One example was, in past years when the government made irregular payment of teacher salaries to public school teachers (Adelabu, 2005).

A contemporary problem now in Nigeria is domestic terrorism, which is defined sometimes as the "unlawful use of force against persons or property to intimidate or coerce a government or civilian population, or any segment thereof, in the furtherance of the social, political or religious objectives" of the terrorist

Purpose of the study.

The purpose of this investigation is to develop a conceptual framework, and the theoretical models, that are applicable to the problems described above, in Nigeria, and to solve the problem of why and how Domestic terrorism occurs. Another purpose of this investigation is to design a resourceful mechanism for dealing with these problems for the well-being of the people of Nigeria and the entire government, whether national, state, or local. A quantitative analysis of the data from the Global terrorism database will be applied toward these purposes.

Significance of the study.

There are several significant theoretical points in this study. Do Nigerian conditions represent a unique sub-set of transnational terrorism, or is it domestic terrorism which is different from racism or hate crime? I view it as domestic terrorism. I am restricting my study to terrorism in Nigeria in order that only one type of terrorism be included in the study. Hate crimes and crimes of racism do not qualify to be called domestic terrorism.

Suggestions to Nigerian policy makers are made in this study. The primary suggestion is for policy makers to adhere to the rule of law. This study documents that the cause of terrorism lies not in the terrorist, but in their targets. Suppose you ask, "Why is Boko Haram terrorizing the country?" The Muslims are used to being in charge of government. Now that the Nigeria has a Christian President, some Muslims feel that their privilege to have a voice in Nigerian government have been taken away from them. Instituting a rule of law could re-assure the Muslims that their religious and political privileges will not be taken away from them. Instituting a rule of law will go far to removing the cause of their terrorism. If you ask, "Why is MEND terrorizing the oil companies polluting their neighborhood?" you will see that you have already answered your question. Instituting the rule of law will help make the oil companies responsible for the environmental damage they cause, and thus remove the cause for MEND doing those terroristic acts. Democracy and the rule of law go hand in hand. Instituting the rule of law will support democratic practice and instituting democratic practice will enable the rule of law.

THEORETICAL FRAMEWORK

Introduction:

This article explores, and seeks to explain and describe Domestic terrorism in Nigeria.

This includes describing the motivations and conditions that lead to terrorism. It is hoped that the description will enable the researcher to frame a comprehensive counter terrorism strategy. Terrorists are not a homogenous group (O'Connor,2011). They differ from country to country or from place to place. Most, if not all the terrorists see themselves as legitimate geopolitical actors, while others are nothing more than gang or thrill-kill cults.

Theoretical efforts at understanding terrorism come from the sub-field of collective violence in the field of political science. It is prior to the emergence of Criminal Justice as a separate discipline in the early 1970's (O'Connor,2011) Political science enjoys a near monopoly over the theories of terrorism. Runners up are the disciplines of religion and economics. Sociological, psychological and criminological theories have also certainly had a role to play with some relevance in connection with terrorism.

The investigator sees that political theories often blame the form of governance for terrorism. It makes sense that political theories would naturally relate the subject matter of the theory to the form of governance. With the other theories, the researcher may find a number of sub-cultural or psychological factors at work. From the sociological view, the interplay between social movements and social responses may explain terrorism. Being theoretical is more than the study of motive. In criminology, theories tend to take on more than the explanation of offender mind sets and behavior. Criminologists do often tackle issues, such as victim status and criminal justice response. Most of the time, motive is frequently ignored in the prosecution of terrorists (smith, 1994: smith, Damphouse, Jackson and Karlson , 2002). Understanding their motive is the most important tool available for dealing with terrorists.

This study uses the Terrorism START Global Terrorism Database to decide which aspects of the terrorisms are the most revealing of their many causes.

Theory of anarchism as a theory of terrorism

Terrorism is definitely not a form of governance, but anarchism is (O'Connor,2011). Anarchism justifies terrorism as a form of criminal action that attacks the values of an organized complacent society (O'Connor,2011). Anarchism, being a theory of governance, rejects any form of central or external authority. It prefers instead to replace it with alternative forms of organization, such as shaming, cursing songs, rituals for deviants, mutual assistance pacts between citizens syndicalism or (any non-authoritarian organizational structure that gives the greatest freedom for workers,) iconoclasm (the destruction of cherish beliefs) liberalism, (a belief absolute liberty and plain old rugged individualism. Anarchism is often assigned to be the nineteenth century roots of terrorism. He contends that the term was first introduced in 1840 by Pierre-Joseph Proudhon. Then later he defines anarchism as the rejection of the state or of any form of coercive government, domination, and exploitation. It is the notion of free and equal access to all the word's resources to enable positive freedom (freedom to) in place of negative freedom from, as the basis of most constitutional rights).

As a theory, anarchism holds a unique place in history because it was the first revolutionary movement to come up with systematic ideas about the purpose of agitation. You'll recognize some of these ideas as terrorist tactics, but it's important first to understand them in the context of anarchism. Proudhon contributed the idea of finding the "moment" as in when the moment is ripe for revolutionary action. Another anarchist, Mikhail Bakunin, popularized the idea of "propaganda by deed" or letting your actions speak for themselves, which was a theory originally developed by Carlo Pisacane, an Italian revolutionary who argued that ideas spring from deeds and not the other way around. Over the years, this notion has evolved into a fairly competent philosophy of the bomb as part of a propaganda campaign to stimulate awareness and sympathy with the cause, and in this respect has been noted as a defining feature of terrorism (Georges-Abeyie & Hass 1982). Bakunin's ideas strongly influenced anarchism because his concept of propaganda by deed also included a prohibition against large scale group action (it being better, he thought, for anarchist action to be individualized or done in small groups). Most anarchists operate on the principle of leaderless resistance, or acting on your own, with little knowledge or support of the groups they may belong to (O'Connor,2011). Another anarchist, Sergei Nachaev, who was an associate of Bakunin, glorified the "merciless" aspect of destruction, but it was Bakunin who laid out the six steps necessary to destroy a social structure, as paraphrased below:

- *Kill the intelligentsia* (kill those who are intelligent and most energetic in society)
- *Kidnap the rich and powerful* (those who will yield the biggest ransoms)
- *Infiltrate the politicians* (to find out their secrets and discredit them)
- *Help the guilty criminal* (to confuse society over justice and punishment)
- *Defend the loudmouths* (those who make dangerous declarations)
- *Nurture the supporters* (help fellow travelers who believe in societal destruction)

It is acknowledged that major anarchist figures, like Karl Heinzen and Johann Most, contributed the idea that murder, especially murder-suicide, constituted the highest form of revolutionary struggle. Both advocated the use of weapons of mass destruction. Other anarchists, contributed different ideas, such as Peter Kropotkin's notion of "propaganda by word" or radicalizing the public by use of subversive publications (O'Connor,2011). Anarchism has also had some influential female figure, and Emma Goldman (1849-1940) comes to mind as a early founder of free speech (the ACLU) and sexual freedom movements. Minor figures in the history of anarchism, like Charles Gallo, Auguste Vailante, Emile Henry, and Claudius Konigstein advocated the idea that to have the most effect, the targets must be innocents (in places such as crowded dance halls or shopping centers) or symbols of economic success (like banks and stock exchanges).

Between 1875 and 1912, anarchists alone or in small groups managed to assassinate or attempt to assassinate the leaders of nine (9) different countries, including the U.S. (with President William McKinley in 1901)(Ferrell, J.,1991). These crimes were just the most well-known acts of anarchism, as anarchists were involved in numerous ordinary crimes such as theft, robbery, murder, kidnapping, assault, and bombing. The most famous incident was the Haymarket riot in Chicago in 1886. During these peak years for classic anarchism, *"May Day" celebrations,* became famous as all-out crime-rampant days. Police departments around the world became convinced there was an international conspiracy, and in many countries, they locked up hundreds of suspicious foreigners. Perfunctory trials were held, and many defendants were hanged or deported. The most famous of these trials was the 1920 case of Sacco and Vanzetti who were more antiwar and labor activists than anarchists. Classic anarchism started to break up during the Russian Revolution, when something called "anarcho-communism" (also called "libertarian communism") came about. Peter Kropotkin) is generally regarded as the most important theorist of this strand, but charismatic figures in the 1920s such as Nestor Makhno were just as important. Anarcho-communism (as opposed to collectivist anarchism) totally rejects the idea of ownership in favor of the idea of usage. They also believe in spontaneous satisfaction of bodily needs and urges. Twentieth-century terrorist groups which later claimed an ancestrywith anarchism include: the Japanese Red Army, the British Angry Brigade, the German Baader-Meinhof Gang, the Weatherman in the United States, and the Mexican Zapatista movement (Kushner 2003). During the Spanish revolution of 1936, something called anarcho-syndicalism came about, which best describes a loose confederation of various protest groups. For example, those who call themselves anarchists today (see Purkis & Bowen 1997) are somewhat likely to be environmentalists, survivalists, alternative currency traders, and/or part of the anti-globalization movement who hate institutions such as the World Bank, International Monetary Fund, World Trade Organization. Anarchists are not inherently antagonistic toward Jews, their anti-Semitism being constrained by the fact they don't believe in pogroms (race riots) (O'Connor,2011).

For purpose of balance, it is important to point out that anarchism today does not support terrorism (Crenshaw 1995). It has historically supported terrorism and even today might support some acts of terrorism, but there are only weak theoretical links between the two, most strongly with the propaganda by deed concept. Anarchists hold to a doctrine that anarchy must be created in the act of self-liberation from oppressive and coercive relationships. You don't blow up the relationship as terrorists do; instead, you convince others that grounds for the existing relationship must be blown up. Anarchism is not really about mad bombing or chaos. *Terrorist target people; anarchists target things* such as institutions and structures. Bakunin did not want the death of people but the destruction of things and positions of authority (Robertsfool, 2012). Only a small minority of terrorists have ever been anarchists, and only a small minority of anarchists have ever been terrorists. Anarchists of almost all stripes do not believe in prisons or keeping prisoners in cells.

In fact, there is an area of study called anarchist criminology; a controversial subfield of critical criminology which celebrates the difficulties anarchism has had finding a workable definition (Tifft 1979; Ferrell 1997). Anarchist criminology advocates the abolishment of criminal justice systems. It argues that much harm has been committed in the name of reasonableness, and anarchist critical criminology is committed to promoting the unthinkable and unreasonable. Like other subfields of critical criminology, anarchist criminology views the state as an inherently oppressive entity, and anarchist justice not only promotes social justice (equal access to all resources), but protects diversity and difference among people (Ferrell 1999).

The Political Theory of Fascism

Fascism is the one form of government with the most disagreement about a definition for it. Passmore (2002) attempts a definition as the consolidation of an ultranationalist ideology that is unabashedly racist. The word comes from the Latin "fasces" which means to use power to scare or impress people. It refers to the consolidation of all economic and political power into some form of super-patriotism that is devoted to genocide or endless war with one's enemies. Benito Mussolini, who practically invented the term in 1922, said "it is the merger of state and corporate power." Mussolini's version of fascism was based on the idea of an indomitable power and an attempt to resurrect imperial Rome. Adolf Hitler said "fascism is the clever and constant application of propaganda, so that people can be made to see paradise as hell, and the other way around." Hitler's brand of fascism drew upon philosophical reflections by Spengler, Hegel, and Nietzsche, and drew upon Nordic old romance from Wagner to Tacitus. Japanese fascism involved a mixture of Bushido, Zen and Shinto Buddhism, racism, fanaticism, historical destiny, emperor worship, and past samurai legends.

The so-called Islamo-Fascism can be traced to the time period of the birth of Nazi "national socialist" fascism in 1928 when the Muslim Brotherhood (Al Ikhwan Al Muslimun), parent organization of numerous terrorist groups, was formed in reaction to the 1924 abolition of the caliphate by the Turks. Islamo-fascism draws heavily upon the Muslim Brotherhood pamphleteers, but also upon on the Koran, the career of Saladin, and the tracts of Nasserites and Baathists. The term, "Islamic Fascism" is a better term to use, best describing the agenda of contemporary radical Islam. It captures the twin thrusts of reactionary fascism today. In one sense, fascism in born out of insecurity and a sense of failure, but in another sense, fascism thrives in a once-proud, humbled but ascendant, people. Envy and false grievance are the trademarks of such reactionary fascism. Believers are subject to all kinds of conspiratorial delusions that setbacks were caused by others and can be erased through ever more zealotry. Fascist leaders love conspiracies and lies; nothing they say should be trusted.

Fascism supports terrorism at home and abroad. Charismatic leaders are usually given supreme powers to stop by force dissidents, peacemakers, and anyone who doesn't abide by the "cult of the individual" which worships a He-man mentality and the party line. With the frequent wars and militaristic ventures that come with fascism, an effort is made to demonize the enemy as sub-humans who deserve extinction. These enemies, according to O'Connor, are also made into scapegoats for all the past problems a country has had. Fascism appeals to the frustrations and resentments of a race of people who think they ought to have a bigger place at the global table. Combined with an anti-western slant fascism becomes a means of social identity (Pan-Africanism, Pan-Arabism, Islamo-Fascism) as well as a facilitator of terrorism.

O'Connor notes that frustrated fascists who fail to gain control in their own countries have historically turned to terrorism. They are most likely to turn to domestic terrorism since fascists do not believe that citizen rights are bestowed merely because someone inhabits a country. Nor do they believe that all human beings are possessed of equal rights. Fascists usually target "Foreign" families and businesses (as they define them) for extermination. The enemies who are seen as the greatest threat are usually those who fascists see as corrupting or poisoning family and property relations.

Fascism is full of ironies and contradictions. On the one hand, it is anti-modern in its glorification of the land, a return to country life, and its fascination with peasant dress or costume. On the other hand, it is pro-modern in its worship of military technology, favoritism of big business, mass mobilization of people, promotion of commercialized sport, and its surprisingly liberal attitude toward the involvement of women in the movement (Deborah, 1983). Science and scholarship also take on interesting twists under fascism. "Hard" sciences like biology and chemistry usually advance significantly, especially in areas such as genetic research. "Soft" sciences like sociology and psychology usually become usurped into mumbo-jumbo pseudoscientific ideas about a glorified fold culture and reasons for hating the enemy (Deborah, 1983).

Just as anarchists have their May Day (May 1st) celebrations, fascist also tend to celebrate anniversaries. Many terrorists, of course, have been known to time their attacks to coincide with the date for an historical event or the birthday of someone special to them. For example, with eco-terrorism, that day is October 19, which coincides the United Nation's World Food Day, and is usually when McDonald's restaurants are targeted for vandalism. However, *the most important date in the study of terrorism is April 19.* A number of significant events have happened on that date. Right-wing domestic terrorist groups call it "Militia Day" because it was when the siege at Waco ended, it was when surveillance began at the Ruby Ridge compound in Idaho, and it marks the anniversary of the Oklahoma City bombing of the federal building. Neo-Nazi fascist groups celebrate April 19 because it was the day German Nazis started wiping out Jewish ghettos across Europe, as well as the following day being Adolf Hitler's birthday. Internationally, terrorist groups who regard themselves as "freedom fighters" and trace at least part of this justification to the American Revolution, take heart in the fact that the American Revolution started on April 19, 1775 at the Battle of Lexington. It remains to be seen if September 11 will replace April 19 as the most popular date for terrorism.

Religion as an explanation of Terrorism

More than one criminologist has pointed out that the disciplines of theology, religion, and philosophy have had important things to say about terrorism (Stitt 2003; Kraemer 2004). It is also a fact that about a quarter of all terrorist groups and about half of the most dangerous ones on earth are primarily motivated by religious concerns (Hoffman 1993). They believe that God not only approves of their action, but that God demands their action. Their cause is sacred, and consists of a combined sense of hope for the future and vengeance for the past. Of these two components, the backward-looking desire for vengeance may be the more important trigger for terrorism because the forward-looking component (called apocalyptic thinking, or eschatology) produces wild-eyed fanatics who are more a danger to themselves and their own people. The trick to successful use of terrorism in the name of religion rests upon convincing believers or converted that a "neglected duty" exists in the fundamental, main stream part of the religion. Religious terrorism is therefore, not about extremism, fanaticism, sects, or cults, but is instead all about a fundamentalist or militant interpretation of the basic tenets. Most religious traditions are filled with plenty of violent images at their core, and destruction or self-destruction is a central part of the logic behind religion-based terrorism (Juergensmeyer 2001). Evil is often defined as malignant narcissism from a theological point of view, and religion easily serves as more cover for self-centered terrorists and psychopaths (Stitt, 2003). Religion has always absorbed or absolved evil and guilt in what is called theodicy, or the study of how the existence of evil can be reconciled with a good and benevolent God. Most religions theorize evil away as: (1) functional to let people learn right from wrong; (2) a test of faith; (3) a product of free will, or (4) part of God's plan. Terrorists easily make use of these established theodicies or critiques of them (Kraemer 2004).

To be sure, the usual pattern in religious-based terrorism is for a psychopathic, spiritual leader to arise that is regarded as somewhat eccentric at first (a tendency toward messianic regard). But then, as this leader develops their charisma, they tend to appear more and more mainstream and scholarly. They begin to mingle political with religious issues (a tendency toward the theocracy), and little-known religious symbols or pieces of sacred text take on new significance. Quite often, these symbols are claimed to be an important part of that religion's history that has somehow been neglected. The stage is then set for blaming somebody for the betrayal of this sacred heritage. First, the politicians in one's own country are blamed, but soon a foreign influence, like secularization or modernization is blamed. Militant religions quickly move to blaming a foreign influence for at least three reasons. First, it doesn't serve the religion's survival interests to blame a homeland. Second, it makes use of a long history of competition, animosity, and war among the many world religions'. Third, any blaming to be done must occur on the symbolic or cosmic level, which is to say that the enemy cannot have a face, but must be some impersonal, evil-like force or influence. Hence, the most specific enemy a militant religion can have is some global trend like secularization, modernization, or Westernization. The strength of fundamentalism is its ability to guarantee a radical change is coming without specifying exactly what it will look like. However, once a semi-vague enemy has been identified, the religious movement borrows the idea of "sovereignty" from the political realm and begins to see itself as the legitimate defender of the faith and legitimate restorer of dignity to the homeland. Most importantly, such "defenders" justify terrorist action in their accountability only to God, for God has chosen them for this sacred mission in history (Juergensmeyer 2001).

Juergensmeyer (2001) notes that the most interesting aspect of religion as a theory of terrorism is how a devout believer could come to mix politics and religion in such a way. The answer is in the conception of worship. Most of us associate worship with dressing up, the ringing of church bells, and one-way communication with God (human to God) But worship is not just about the liturgy of church ritual. Worship is part of service to God and all of humanity on behalf of God (striving to receive instructions from God). Politics is also about service, especially public service. So-called "liberation theology" that permeates Latin America has always had a handle on this aspect of worship as service which is intended to bring about the emancipation of the poor. Antonio Gramsci

(1891-1937), a founder of the Italian communist party who is best remembered for the concept of hegemony (Bocock 1986), or the idea of an all-encompassing world-view, also postulated a model of worship as opposition. To engage in any sort of enterprise involving service to God, humanity, or social justice, each group of devout worshippers must see through their religious culture toward political goals. It is not so much as using religion to achieve secular ends, but the transformation of theology to create "free spaces" that permit creative action consistent with that religion's view on the needed transformation of society. A key theological transformation that supports terrorism would be the notion that communal violence, even though violence is despised, is still a form of worship that may help discover the true nature of God and open up two-way communication with God (God to human) (Bocock 1986).

Religious terrorism can be quite extreme in its tactics. Not only does it strive to avenge a long history of persecution and injustice, but it frequently carries out preemptive attacks. This is because a high level of paranoia is usually maintained about the actual degree of threat that the enemy trend poses. Rarely are religious terrorists swayed by secular sources of information about the degree of actual threat, but instead are driven by doctrinal differences of opinion over interpretation of Holy Scriptures. As a consequence of this there is: (1) a rather non-selective targeting pattern lashing out blindly, often harming innocents; and (2) the creation of numerous offshoot, spin-off, or fringe groups who believe they are commanded to follow a different mission imperative. Add to this, Most adherents have already long felt like alienated and marginal members of society, and you've got a recipe for perhaps the most dangerous or prolific kind of terrorism in the world today.

Most religious terrorist groups can trace their origin to key historical events. Institutional memory is long, as the example of Irish terrorism points out, and it is not uncommon for the group to conduct rituals designed to "never forget" some long-ago grievance. In one sense, this is why religious terrorism is popular, because political terrorism, like politics, has a much shorter memory. Another variety of religious terrorism has its roots in millenarianism, where the key event is some doomsday or apocalyptic date where something was supposed to happen. I know from studies of UFO cults that such groups are often more dangerous after an event fails to happen because for cognitive dissonance, which forces a rearrangement of attitudes and beliefs that are frequently more rigid and fantastic. However, political events also serve as the catalyst for religious terrorism, and these are usually tied into whatever messianic traditions the religion has. For example, the rise of al-Ikhwan Muslim militancy can be traced to a date in 1979 (during the Islamic year 1400) when the return of the prophet Madhi was anticipated at the Grand Mosque in Mecca. Adherents of the belief stormed the mosque by force, which happened to coincide with a time for pilgrimage and the height of the tourist season. The government reacted by forcing the militants out, cementing forever a date of infamy in which the group became certain that the homeland needed rescuing from secularization. Religious terrorists also typically have "mourning periods" or dates such as "anniversary of the martyrs" because these activities are important ways the group recruits true believers from those who have been standing on the sidelines. Recruitment generally is followed by a reeducation program that changes the way a person thinks about good and evil. Anything foreign, secular, or modern without question becomes evil; and anything supporting and all-out, uncompromising struggle with the enemy, including the killing of innocents, becomes good. The only exceptions are when the group has freed up some nonviolent avenues of experimentation.

It is important that you understand the practice of martyrdom in the terrorist context. Not only does a martyr serve recruitment and other purposes after their death, but a whole mythology develops around them, which might be called a process of martyrology (Ranstorp 1996). *Targets are chosen not for strategic purposes, but for symbolic purposes, and the repercussions of an attack are managed as well.* The idea is to produce an impression that the group is larger and more powerful than it actually is. This feeling of power is enhanced by the use of anonymity, whereby the martyr goes through an indoctrination process where they are stripped of their real identity and provided with a false background history. The process goes much further than establishing a cover story in case of capture. The process involves changing the family name and home town the martyr came from, so that any repercussions or reactions to the terrorist event can be channeled toward another family or town. In some cases, the cover story is used to direct government counterterrorism toward the wrong target (especially if the martyr's family is well known and the town is small). In other cases, it is used to give the impression that dozens of martyrs are coming from the same town, when in fact they are not.

In all fairness, it should be said that most militant religious groups only adopt terrorism as a tactic of last resort. We, (the terrorists contend) have not discussed Just War Doctrine here, but ethics and/or fair play are integral parts of most religions, and there are usually unwritten rules for when the cosmic struggle (as Juergensmeyer 2001 calls it) spills over into political struggle. Religious terrorists demonstrate marvelous ingenuity in means, methods, and timing, but their targeting is flawed, and one can only wonder how strategically effective is their "symbolic" success from "striking at the heart of the infidels." Perhaps the whole reason for it is to bolster their reputation among other religious communities. This would be supported by the fact that some terrorist's acts are scheduled on dates specifically designed to desecrate a competitor's religious holidays and sacred moments.

Rational Choice as a Theory of Terrorism

The discipline of economics has many concepts that are relevant to an understanding of terrorism—supply and demand – costs and benefits, etc. Fully-developed economic or econometric models of terrorism are quite rare, however, and often involve such things as "physic" costs and benefits (Nyatepe-Coo 2004). More practical economic theories can be found in the literature on deterrence. Rational choice theory, in particular, has found a place in criminology. It holds that people will engage in crime after weighing the costs and benefits of their actions. They arrive at a rational choice about motivation after perceiving that the chances of gain outweigh any possible punishment or loss. Criminals must come to believe their actions will be beneficial – to themselves, their community, or society – and they must come to see that crime pays, or is at least a risk-free way to better their situation. This idea in criminology is illustrated by routine activities theory (Cohen and Felson 1979), which postulates that three conditions must be present in order for a crime to occur: (1) suitable targets or victims who put themselves at risk; (2) the absence of capable guardians or police presence; and (3) motivated offenders or a pool of the unemployed and alienated. Other rational choice theories exist which delve further into models of decision-making. In the few models of collective violence that have found their way into criminology, the Olson hypothesis (source unknown) suggests that participants in revolutionary violence predicate their behavior on a rational cost-benefit calculus to pursue the best course of action given the social circumstances.

Rational Choice theory, in political science holds that people can be collectively rational, even when making apparently irrational decisions for them as individuals, after perceiving that their participation is important and their personal contribution to the public good outweighs any concerns they may have for the "free rider" problem (Muller and Opp 1986). For those unfamiliar with it, the "free rider" problem is a classic paradox in social science and economics, which asks why anybody should do something for the public good when most likely someone else will get credit for it and most everybody else will benefit merely by sitting idly and doing nothing. Perhaps the most eloquent spokesperson for rational choice ideas in the field of terrorism is Wesleyan professor Martha Crenshaw (1998), whose writings inform my remarks below.

Let's take, for example, a typical terrorist event that involves hostage-taking and all-to-frequent hostage-killing. From an individualist rational point of view, the best choice would be to keep at least some of the hostages alive in order to bargain with the government for leniency. Yet, often a collectivist rational mentality sets in, and the group choice (or groupthink) is to kill all the hostages. Is this killing senseless, the product of deranged minds, or an example of mob behavior? The answer is NO on all points from a rational choice point of view. It may be a reasonable and calculated response to circumstances. It may involve a collective judgment about the most efficient course of action that has the most lasting impact on observers (for social learning purposes). And most importantly, the senselessness of it all may be just what the group needs to make their ideological point that they are terrorists, not just ordinary criminals.

Terrorism is not a pathological phenomenon; the resort to terrorism is not an aberration. The central focus of study ought to be on why some groups find terrorism useful, and in standard control theory fashion, why other groups do not find terrorism useful. Some groups may continue to work with established patterns of dissident action. Other groups may choose terrorism as an early choice because they have learned from the experiences of others, usually through the news media, and Crenshaw (1998) calls this the contagion effect, and claims it has distinctive patterns similar to the copycat effect as in other theories of collective violence (Gurr 1970). There may be circumstances in which the terrorists group wants to publicize its cause to the world, a process Crenshaw (19950 calls the globalization of civil war.

Factors that influence the rational choice of terrorism include place, size, time, and the climate of international opinion. A terrorist plot in a democratic society is less likely to involve senseless violence than a scheme hatched under an authoritarian regime because under the latter, terrorist realize they have nothing to lose with the expected repercussions. Size is important because a small elite group is more likely to resort to terrorism when the population is passive. This means that more senseless acts of violence mat occur in a stable society rather than one on the verge of collapse. Time constraints are important because the terrorist group may be competing with other groups or attempting to manage a tit-for-tat strategy with counterterrorism. The climate of international opinion, if low for the problems of the host country, may force the terrorists to take action that risks a repressive counterterrorist reaction, in hopes that their suffering will capture public attention. In short, terrorism is an excellent tool for managing the political agenda on a world stage.

Globalization contributes to dreams, fantasies, and rising expectations, but at the same time, it leads to dashed hopes, broken dreams, and unfulfilled achievements. Terrorism breeds in the gap between expectations and achievements. The thinking is very similar to strain theory in criminology or the rising expectations theory of prison riots, and about the only thing unique about globalization theory is that it adds a rich-poor dichotomy. Rich people (or nations) are seen as wanting power and wealth, and poor people (nations) are seen as wanting justice. From this perspective, then, rich people are part of the causal factor or root cause of terrorism, since they contribute to the conditions which give rise to it. Perpetrators of "terrorism" (always treated as an ill-defined concept in globalization theory) are never seen as born or raised with any specific predispositions toward it. In brief, globalization theory holds that if the oppressed and disgruntled poor people of the world were simply given the chance to find peaceful means for achieving justice, terrorism would not thrive.

Globalization theory is further tied into the ideas about colonialism, imperialism, and neocolonialism. The first two words are often used interchangeably to describe a set of conditions (technically, extensions of sovereignty) where the mores, values, and beliefs of the colonizers are considered superior to those of the colonized. However, when the assumption is made that (imperial) power is a necessary thing to maintain cultural superiority; this is the usual meaning of imperialism. Neocolonialism is a concept developed by Marxists and holders of certain conspiracy theories to refer to allegations about First World nations, international organizations, and /or multinational corporations employing economic, financial and trade policies to dominate less powerful countries. Onwudiwe (2001) is typical of the criminological approach taken when globalization ideas are incorporated into theories about terrorism, and it is probably safe to say that the approach remains relatively underdeveloped.

REVIEW OF THE LITERATURE

Introduction

Oyeniyi (2007) published an article entitled "A Historical Overview of Domestic Terrorism in Nigeria." The paper is not considered a scholarly work per se because it has no structure of a scholarly article. However, he considered colonial rule as domestic terrorism. He pointed out that colonial rule was the cause of civil war in Nigeria because the colonialists lumped the entire Nigeria into an entity, which would have been three countries based on clear boundaries, ethnic differences, cultural difference etc. The colonialist did that for easy administration. His writing lacks empiricism.

Over a decade has passed since the horrible events on 11 September 2001 made the world acutely aware of the significant threat posed by terrorism. Even though transnational terrorism had plagued the world after 1967, no event before these four hijackings caused so many casualties or had such a profound influence on the global awareness of terrorism risks. The events on that fateful day induced an inflow of government spending into counter-terrorism activities in many at-risk countries (Enders & Sandler, 2006).

Since 11 September 2001, scholars in economics, political science, and other disciplines have devoted much effort to the study of terrorism and its impact on the economy and society. Some studies have investigated the reverse impact – i.e. the influence of the economy and social grievances on terrorism (Abadie, 2006; Blomberg, Hess & Weerapena,2004). In recent years, scholars have applied both empirical and theoretical methods to the study of terrorism. The former has been facilitated by increased availability of data on terrorist events – e.g. *International Terrorism: Attributes of Terrorism Events* (ITERATE) and *Global Terrorism Database* (GTD) (Boylan, 2009). The development for new econometric techniques involving time series and panel estimations also bolstered novel empirical studies on terrorism (Boylan, 2009). On the theory side, many recent theoretical articles have used game theory (Arce & Sandler, 2005; Sandler & Siqueira, 2009). As a theoretical tool, game theory is particularly appropriate because it accounts for interactive rational choice, where adversaries (e.g. terrorists and governments) or allies (e.g. commonly targeted governments or different factions in a terrorist group) must take actions, while accounting for the anticipated responses of others. Moreover, these actors realize that their counterparts are also trying to anticipate their responses. In the study of terrorism, game theory has provided important insights in understanding bargaining in hostage negotiations (Lapan & Sandler, 1988) the recruitment of terrorists (Bueno de Mesquita, 2005), the practice of counter-terrorism (Enders & Sandler, 1993), and the structure of terrorist networks (Enders & Jindapon, 2010). The game theory did not tell us anything about the conditions of a particular country or answer the question of why terrorists attack. Enders & Sandler, (1993); Zussman & Zussman, (2006) have made empirical studies to analyze the effectiveness of counter-terrorism policies. Blomberg, Hess & Orphanides, (2004); Keefer & Loayza, (2008) have examined the macroeconomic consequences of terrorism. Drakos, Konstantinos and Ali M. Kutan (2003); Enders, Sandler & Parise (1992) studied the sectoral effects of terrorism. Krueger & Maleckova, (2003) discussed the root causes of terrorism. Piazza, (2008) discussed the role of failed states. Finally, Brandt, Santifort, & Sandler, (2012) studied the dynamics of terrorist attacks.

These and other studies generated policy insights – e.g. metal detectors in airports induced terrorists to substitute into other kinds of hostage taking attacks. Recently, scholars have turned their attention to the study of suicide terrorism (Pape, 2005; Wintrobe, 2006), the strategic analysis of terrorist organizations (Feinstein Kaplan, 2010), the optimal allocation of defensive resources (Powell, 2007), and the use of foreign aid for counter-terrorism purposes (Azam & Thelen, 2010). Many other terrorism topics are being pursued. All these researchers did not focus on Domestic terrorism, but transnational terrorism.

The purpose of this special issue of the *Journal of Peace Research* is to present new scholarship on the impact of terrorism on myriad concerns including trust, interrogation techniques, foreign assistance, economic growth, and security choices. Economic discrimination and poverty are the root causes of domestic terrorism.

Some preliminaries

Terrorism is the premeditated use or threat to use violence by individuals or subnational groups to obtain a political or social objective through the intimidation of a large audience beyond that of the immediate victims. The key ingredients in this definition concern the political or social objective, the non-state perpetrator, and the need for a large audience. Violence for non-political goals – e.g. a kidnapping for ransom, not intended to promote a political agenda – is a crime, but is not terrorism. If the perpetrator is a state, then state terrorism results. Although state terrorism is an important concern, it is not the terrorism that is addressed in the current investigation. Finally, terrorists want a large audience to feel at risk so that public pressures are applied to officeholders or rulers to concede terrorists; demands for change. To create this general atmosphere of fear, terrorists engage in various types of operations – kidnappings, bombings, assassinations, hijackings, and armed attacks – in a seemingly random fashion so that everyone feels in jeopardy. That randomness is the glaring gap that this research intends to fill by knowing the condition that triggers the attack. However, in fact, these attacks are not random. Instead, terrorists trade off risk and return when choosing their targets. Soft, high-valued targets are particularly attractive. Terrorism is a tactic of the weak to deploy against the strong. With a carefully planned and executed campaign, small groups of extremists may effectively use violence to gain a presence. Even though governments seldom cave in to terrorist demands, these campaigns can still have many deleterious effects – e.g. a general sense of fear or restrictions on civil liberties – on targeted societies. Governments may have to spend heavily on counter-terrorism measures that raise taxes and divert public moneys from more productive activities. Counter-terrorism can be damaging to the society in general. It is necessary to research why given targets are chosen and to figure out which condition triggers terrorist attacks.

An important distinction is domestic versus transnational terrorism. Domestic terrorism involves perpetrators, targets, victims, venues, and audience in the same country. The kidnapping of a local politician by a domestic terrorist group to promote political change at home is an example of domestic terrorism. The present investigation focuses on domestic terrorism, using the variables, conditions and various attacks on a country by citizens of the same country. Domestic terrorist events far outnumber transnational terrorist incidents (Enders, Sandler & Gaibulloev, 2011). Countries are motivated to address domestic terrorism because the associated benefits or costs of doing so are solely gained or borne at home. Counter-terrorism actions taken by other countries do not curb domestic terrorism in this country. The best way to go is to reduce the causes of the attack, in order to reduce the attacks. As we discover the causes of the most severe attacks, we can prevent them. I find it reasonable to hope that preventing the most severe attacks will also prevent all the other terrorist attacks.

Through perpetrators, victims, institutions, governments, or implications, transnational terrorism concerns more than one country. A letter bomb sent for political purposes, by a terrorist group, in country *A*, to intended targets in country *B*, constitutes a transnational terrorist incident. The downing of Pan Am flight 103 over Lockerbie, Scotland, on 21 December 1988, was a transnational terrorist incident because the victims were from a number of countries, the perpetrators were foreigners (neither American nor British), and the bomb was transferred in London from a flight originating in Malta. The takeover for the US embassy in Tehran of 4 November 1979 by radical Islamic students was another instance of transnational terrorism. Transnational terrorism is more difficult than domestic terrorism to address owing to the need for international cooperation, which faces many roadblocks – e.g. the unwillingness of nations to sacrifice their autonomy and control over national security matters.

Another distinction germane in this current investigation concerns the two types of counter-terrorism policies that have been commonly used (e.g. Arce, Croson & Eckel, 2001; Enders, Sandler & Gaibulloey, 2011). Defensive policy involves hardening targets through protective measures that make it more costly for terrorists to attack successfully. Defensive measures also limit the damage in case of an attack. Often, defensive measures are reactive – e.g. checking shoes at airport security after the shoe bomber, or deploying full-body imagers after the underwear bomber. In the case of transnational terrorism, defensive measures can give rise to targeted countries engaging in a 'protection race' in the hopes of transferring attacks abroad. This inclination is attenuated if a country has assets and citizens abroad, because the transfer can jeopardize the country's own interests abroad.

The same inducement to transfer attacks to other venues is not a concern for domestic terrorism insofar as a central government oversees such defensive decisions, unlike the case of transnational terrorism, and does not gain from such transfers.

The other category of counter-terrorism commonly used consists of offensive measures, which seek to limit or destroy terrorist resources. Offensive responses involve the infiltration of terrorist groups, the collecting of intelligence, the curbing of terrorist finances, and the destroying of terrorist training camps. For transnational terrorism, there is a marked tendency to do fewer offensive operations, because one country's offensive actions in another country would be viewed as an invasion by that other country. Iraq and Afghanistan illustrate this point very well.

Third category of counter-terrorism

What counter-terrorism actions are neither offensive or defensive? It is necessary that we focus on preventive actions. Preventing terrorism from occurring by removing all the perceived injustices will be much more effective than either standard defensive or offensive measures.

Application of game theory

The Enders & Jindapon (2011) article applies game theory to contrast two alternative strategies of detainees, which may include terrorists or soldiers, in the 'war on terror'. One strategy – **Big 4** – requires a prisoner to provide only his or her name, rank, serial number, and birth date, while the other strategy – **Little Fish** – allows a prisoner to give useful verifiable information. In the latter case, this information causes limited harm to the detainee's group or government; nevertheless, the information demonstrates that the prisoner is cooperating. If this strategy works and more extreme interrogation methods are not subsequently applied, then the detainee and the interest that he or she represents may be protected , because more damaging information may not be extracted under duress. In contrast, the **Big 4** strategy will result in harsher interrogation measures being applied by the captors. Enders & Jindapon construct two game structures to show that the **Little Fish** game may Pre-dominate the **Big 4** game, so that all interests – those of the detainee, the interrogator, and society – are made better off. Society may gain because it does not necessarily impose extreme interrogation measures that tarnish its reputation and create backlash attacks.

The Enders & Jindapon article contains a number of findings. First, it shows that game theory may disclose novel insights. Second, the article offers perspectives on an important debate that was raised by the Bush administration's claims that torture may protect against future terrorists acts, so that the ends justify the means. The game-theoretic analysis here casts serious doubts on this assertion insofar as terrorists playing Little Fish are not really giving up very valuable information. Moreover, harsh interrogation methods may motivate new terrorist acts that greatly harm the government and society. Third, the article puts forward an analytic structure that captures the conflict between human interrogation methods compared with **Big 4**. This finding indicates that standard operating procedures for captive soldiers are not optimal. Fourth, their model may be applicable to other strategic interactions with asymmetric information. Finally, the method may be applied in the future to uncover strategies to prepare detainees to play a strategy better than **Little Fish** or **Big 4**.

The Bapat (2011) article represents another application of game theory in the study of counter-terrorism. This article asks the question of why a rich targeted country supplies proactive military aid to countries with a resident terrorists group when past studies have shown this aid to be ineffective or even counter-productive. The author puts forward a game with three active players – the U.S. government, the host state (H), and the anti-American terrorist group (T) – that operates in the host country. The US government moves first by offering its aid to country H, which then negotiates with the terrorists, takes defensive measures, or engages in offensive measures. In the case of negotiations or defensive measures, the terrorists must accept or reject H's bribe to not attack the United States government. Other choices may follow at later points in the game.

Bapat shows that US military aid can create a moral hazard problem for country H, since its aid ends once the terrorists disband or are defeated. Consequently, H has little incentive to eliminate the resident terrorists, if it wants to keep its aid; thus, H takes defensive measures against the resident terrorists. This response is hypothesized to lengthen the duration of terrorist groups in countries receiving US military assistance to counter a resident terrorist threat. Country H must, however, worry about the terrorists gaining strength and support over time with their longevity. Although the terrorist group may exist for a longer time because of aid, in dollars by the USA may gain from the reduced incentive of country H to negotiate with the anti-American terrorists group.

Thus, the USA may profit even though its military assistance keeps the terrorist group around for longer. Bapat applies a hazard model to show that US military assistance to the host country increases significantly the duration of a resident terrorist group.

With the wide release of GTD, researchers now have access to a long dataset (currently, in Nigeria, terroristic events from 1976 to 2011) that records numerous variables for terrorist incidents. Variables include, among others, the incident date, country of location, mode of attack, terrorist group responsible, and the number of casualties. Researchers are flocking to the data without questioning its strengths, shortfalls, or properties. Although GTD includes domestic and transnational terrorist incidents, GTD does not explicitly distinguish between the two types of terrorist incidents. This distinction is essential for some analyses – for example, the Gaibulloey & Sandler (2011) article finds that only transnational terrorist incidents harmed income per capita growth in Africa. Moreover, the root causes for domestic terrorism may be quite different from those for transnational terrorism. In addition, foreign assistance may be more easily justified by targeted countries to support a recipient country's efforts to curb transnational, rather than domestic, terrorism. A comparison and contrast between domestic and transnational terrorism is missing from the literature; Enders, Sandler & Gaibulloey (2001) provide this analysis.

Their article serves many proposes. First, it devises a method for partitioning GTD into three types of events: domestic, transnational, and unknown.

Second, Enders, Sandler & Gaibulloey (2011) put forward a calibration method based on ITERATE transnational terrorist incidents to overcome reporting problems in GTD stemming from undercounting and over counting terrorist incidents.

Third, the article identifies research questions where investigators should use either domestic or transnational terrorism data. In some instances, both types of terrorism data are required. Fourth, Enders, Sandler & Gaibulloey (2010) investigate the co-movements (if any) between domestic and transnational terrorist events, the correlations between specific kinds of terrorist incidents, and the composition of attack modes. Fifth, these authors apply vector auto regression (VAR) techniques to investigate shock-induced impulse response, variance decomposition, and Granger-causality test. The authors find that shocks to domestic terrorism spill over to affect transnational terrorism; however, there is no evidence of reverse causality. (Gaibulloey and Sandlers, 2011).

RESEARCH METHOD

Data Collection:

I downloaded the data from the START Global Terrorism Database. Then I re-formatted it to create dependent and independent variables to be used in a multiple linear regression.

Data Analysis

The categories in the Global terrorism base were :
Date of the terroristic event,
What region the terroristic act occurred in,
Country where the terroristic act occurred,
City where the terroristic event occurred,
Who committed the terroristic act,
How many people were killed in the terroristic act,
How many people were injured in the terroristic act,
What type of terroristic act occurred,
and What types of weapons were used in the terroristic act.
From this data I created variables
Severity = dependent variable = number of fatalities + number injured / 1000
Longitude = longitude of the city in which the terroristic act occurred
Lattitude = latitude of the city in which the terroristic act occurred
Boko Harem = dichotomous variable to signify whether Boko Haram committed the terroristic act
MEND = dichotomous variable to signify whether MEND committed the terroristic act
Unknown Perpetrator = dichotomous variable to signify whether the perpetrator of the terroristic act was known
Citizen = dichotomous variable to signify whether the terroristic act targeted citizens
Business = dichotomous variable to signify whether the terroristic act targeted businesses or other independent organization
Government = dichotomous variable to signify whether the terroristic act targeted government
Utilities = dichotomous variable to signify whether the terroristic act targeted Utilities
Police = dichotomous variable to signify whether the terroristic act targeted Police
Church = dichotomous variable to signify whether the terroristic act targeted religious leaders or institutions
Military = dichotomous variable to signify whether the terroristic act targeted the military
Armed Assault = dichotomous variable to signify whether the terroristic act used Armed Assault
Bomb = dichotomous variable to signify whether the terroristic act used bombs

Hostage = dichotomous variable to signify whether the terroristic act took hostages

Assassination = dichotomous variable to signify whether the terroristic act used Assassination

Infrastructure = dichotomous variable to signify whether the terroristic act attacked the facilities or infrastructure

Research Unit of Analysis

The unit of analysis was one individual terroristic act at a given place and time.

Study Timeline

The Global Terrorism Database contains Nigerian events from 1976 through Dec 2011. Although I used all the data available in the regression analysis, I find it important to point out that half of the recorded fatalities occurred in the years 2008 to 2011. Also, active work to prevent terrorism must focus on events that occurred only in recent years. In this sense, I say that the scope of my investigation is from 2008 to 2011.

Research Limitation

Not every terroristic act got recorded in the Global Terrorism Database. However, that database does provide a reasonably random sample of the population of terroristic events.

Assumptions

Nigeria is unique in several ways:

Multiple religions, cultures and Ethnicities:

Bribery and corruption have become the culture of the nation

No middle class between rich and poor

Tribalism: Individual tribes want to control all else

Poor infrastructure: few paved roads, lack of piped water, unstable electric power, no welfare system to help the poor, no public respect for senior citizens, no medical insurance to help pay medical expenses,

Universities and colleges turn out students but those students have no place to work

Multiple regression is a commonly used technique to confirm or disconfirm causal relationships.

METHODOLOGY:

The method used is Multiple Regression Analysis.

In the Global Terrorism Database,

it gives location of the terrorist attack,

who did it,

who the target was, and

what weapons were used or

what type of attack it was..

Each of these types of data were considered as possible contributions to severity of any particular terrorist attack.

The location of the attack is represented by longitude and latitude.

Who did the attack is represented by dichotomous variables.

Each variable is set to 1 for the cases blamed for that particular group.

Otherwise, the variable is set to default of zero.

The target of the attack is represented by dichotomous variables such as Citizen, Business, Government, Police, etc.

The type of weapons used is represented by dichotomous variables such as Bomb, or ArmedAssault,

The type of attack was represented by dichotomous variables such as Hostage, or Assassination.

ECONOMETRIC ISSUES AND DATA SOURCES

Data was retrieved from the Global Terrorism Database (GTD) at http://www.start.umd.edu/gtd/

In the GTD, each attack was described with date of occurrence, country where the attack occurred, the city in which it occurred, who was blamed for the attack, the number of people killed and the number of people injured during the attack, weapons used in the attack, and the target of the attack. The dependent variable, Severity, was constructed from the number of people killed or injured. 16 independent variables were constructed as dichotomous variables based on who was blamed for the attack, who was targeted, and what weapons were used. Two additional variables, longitude and latitude of the city in which the attack occurred, were added from independent sources.

I named my variables as follows:

VARIABLES

SEVERITY

is my dependent variable. It is defined as the number of people killed + .001 * the number injured. Since the largest number of people injured during any one attack was 200, Severity is approximately equal to the number of people killed during the attack.

LONGITUDE

is the longitude of the city in which the attack occurred. If the severity of the attack depended on location, then Longitude would have captured the east west component of the location.

LATTITUDE

is the latitude of the city in which the attack occurred. If the severity of the attack depended on location, then latitude would have captured the north south component of the location.

BOKOHAREM

is the name of one of the two major groups of domestic terrorists in Nigeria. This dichotomous variable is set to 1 is Boko haram is blamed for that particular attack. Otherwise, it is set to 0.

MEND

is the name of the other major domestic terrorist group in Nigeria. Their main focus is to free the Niger Delta from foreigners. Their main concern are the oil companies that are polluting the environment while removing oil. Mend has been blamed for attacking the Shell Oil Company pipelines.

UNKNOWNPERPETRAT

is a dichotomous variable created to capture those cases in which it was not known who did the attack.

CITIZEN

is a dichotomous variable created to capture whether or not the attack targeted citizens.

BUSINESS

is a dichotomous variable created to capture whether or not the attack targeted businesses.

GOVERNMENT

is a dichotomous variable created to capture whether or not the attack targeted government.

UTILITIES

is a dichotomous variable created to capture whether or not the attack targeted utilities.

POLICE

is a dichotomous variable created to capture whether or not the attack targeted police.

CHURCH

is a dichotomous variable created to capture whether or not the attack targeted churches or church members.

MILITARY

is a dichotomous variable created to capture whether or not the attack targeted the military.

ARMEDASSAULT

is a dichotomous variable created to capture whether or not the terrorists used armed assault as the method.

BOMB

is a dichotomous variable created to capture whether or not the terrorists used bombs in their attack.

HOSTAGE

is a dichotomous variable created to capture whether or not the terrorists took hostages.

ASSASSINATION

is a dichotomous variable created to capture whether or not the terrorists assassinated anyone as part of their attack.

INFRASTRUCTURE

is a dichotomous variable created to capture whether or not the terrorists ....

Of my 18 independent variables, 16 of them are dichotomous. This is because of the format of the data available to us from the Global Terrorism Database. Dichotomous variables are acceptable in multiple regression as independent variables.

EMPIRICAL RESULTS

The dependent variable is Severity.

Dependent Variable	SEVERITY
Usable Observations	478
Degrees of Freedom	460
Centered R^2	0.1399268
R-Bar^2	0.1081415
Uncentered R^2	0.2287123
Mean of Dependent Variable	2.7428807531
Std Error of Dependent Variable	8.0928035617
Standard Error of Estimate	7.6427028271
Sum of Squared Residuals	26869.016992
Regression $F(17,460)$	4.4022
Significance Level of F	0.0000000
Log Likelihood	-1641.2119
Durbin-Watson Statistic	1.0272

Variable	Coeff	Std Error	T-Stat	Signif
1 Constant	1.453622658	2.404014521	0.60466	0.54569996
2. LONGITUDE	-0.119053228	0.215521609	-0.55240	0.58094551
3. LATTITUDE	0.032394438	0.225918421	0.14339	0.88604499
4. BOKOHAREM	-0.808189922	1.674792119	-0.48256	0.62963679
5. MEND	-2.977326642	1.694102423	-1.75747	0.07950364
6. UNKNOWNPERPETRAT	-2.679268770	1.198472805	-2.23557	0.02585904

7.	CITIZEN	5.761709140	1.018961993	5.65449	0.00000003
8.	BUSINESS	4.417988746	1.168062596	3.78232	0.00017587
9.	GOVERNMENT	2.001752090	1.248920878	1.60279	0.10966845
10.	UTILITIES	1.705835097	1.674332670	1.01881	0.30882637
11.	POLICE	3.922482706	1.258349240	3.11717	0.00194039
12.	CHURCH	4.415801641	1.516904821	2.91106	0.00377695
13.	MILITARY	2.246290696	1.822195212	1.23274	0.21830288
14.	ARMEDASSAULT	1.082387216	1.201554037	0.90082	0.36815394
15.	BOMB	-0.245028711	1.363385740	-0.17972	0.85745094
16.	HOSTAGE	-2.826230345	1.326740169	-2.13021	0.03368460
17.	ASSASSINATION	-0.521864890	1.900628881	-0.27457	0.78376616
18.	INFRASTRUCTURE	-2.098339179	1.395017251	-1.50417	0.13322458

Armed assault was not significantly more severe that other forms of attack.

The attacks against citizens, Business, Police, and church were more severe than attacks against government, utilities, military, or other.

The ranking of targets by severity is

Citizen

Business

Church

Police.

The Effects of the independent variables

The variables that were Significant at .05 level variables are:				
UNKNOWNPERPETRAT	-2.679268770	1.198472805	-2.23557	0.02585904
CITIZEN	5.761709140	1.018961993	5.65449	0.00000003
BUSINESS	4.417988746	1.168062596	3.78232	0.00017587
POLICE	3.922482706	1.258349240	3.11717	0.00194039
CHURCH	4.415801641	1.516904821	2.91106	0.00377695
HOSTAGE	-2.826230345	1.326740169	-2.13021	0.03368460

The dependent variable is Severity, which is nearly the same as the number of people killed. Why is unknown perpetrator a significant independent variable? It is because nearly half of the terrorist attacks were by persons unknown.

Why is Citizen a significant independent variable? It is because on the average, 5.14 citizens were killed per attack on private citizens or property. Contrast this with attacks on government, in which the average number of people killed per attack is 1.03.

Why is Business a significant independent variable? It is because the average number of people killed in an attack on business is 1.55.

Why is Police a significant independent variable? It is because the average number of people killed in an attack on the police is 2.15.

Why is Church a significant independent variable? It is because the average number of people killed in an attack on a religious figure or institution is 3.17.

Why is Hostage a significant independent variable? Note that the coefficient for Hostage is negative. This means that attacks involving hostages tend to be less severe in the sense of number of fatalities. This is borne out by the average number of fatalities per hostage attack being 0.51. Out of 137 attacks involving hostages, there were 70 Fatalities.

CONCLUSION

Except for Hostage and Unknown Perpetrator, the significant independent variables indicated the target of the terrorism. Therefore to reduce the severity of the terrorism, and possibly to prevent terrorism, we should focus on who is the target of the terrorism, and why they are the target.

REFERENCES

Arce, D. G.; Croson, R. TA.; Eckel, C. C. (2011). *Terrorism experiments*. Journal of Peace Research May 2011 vol. 48 no. 3 383-398.

Azama, JP; Thelenb, V. (2010). *Terrorism and Policy: Introduction.* Journal of Conflict Resolution April 2010 vol. 54 no. 2 203-213

Abadiea, A., Gardeazabal, J. (2007). Terrorism and the world economy. European Economic Review 52 (2008) 1–27.

Adelabu, M. A. (2005) *"Teacher Motivation and Incentives in Nigeria".* Retrieved from http://www.eldis.org/vfile/upload/1/document/0709/teacher_motivation_nigeria.pdf

Arce M., Daniel G., and Todd Sandler. 2005. *Counterterrorism:A game-theoretic analysis*. Journal of Conflict Resolution 49 (2): 183-200.

Arendt, Hannah. (1951). *The origins of totalitarianism*. NY Harcourt, Brace & Co.

Arrigo, B. (ed.) *Social justice/Criminal justice*. Belmont, CA: Wadsworth.

Bapat, N. A. (2011). *Transnational terrorism, US military aid, and the incentive to misrepresent*. Journal of Peace Research May 2011 vol. 48 no. 3 303-318

Bjørgo, T. (2005). *"Introduction." in Root Causes of Terrorism: Myths, Reality, and Ways Forward*. London: Routledge.

Blomberg, S. Brock; Hess, Gregory D.; Orphanides, Athanasios (2004). *The Macroeconomic Consequences of Terrorism*, CESifo Working Paper, No. 1151

Boylan, B. M. (2009). Economic Development, *Religion, and the Conditions for Domestic Terrorism*. Public and International Affairs. University of Pittsburgh.

Brandt, P.;Santifort, C.; Sandler, T (2012). *Terrorist attack and target diversity: Changepoints and their drivers*. School of Economic, Political & Policy Sciences. University of Texas at Dallas.

Jenkins, B. M. (1980). *The Study of Terrorism: Definitional Problems*. The Rand Corporation. Santa Monica, California.

Bell, Bowyer. (1982). *"Psychology of leaders of terrorist groups."* International journal of group tensions, 12: 84-104.

Bocock, R. (1986). *Hegemony*. London: Tavistock.

Borradori, G. (2003). *Philosophy in a time of terror: Dialogues with Habermas and Derrida*. Chicago: Univ. of Chicago Press.

Burton, Anthony. (1978). *Revolutionary violence: The theories*. NY: Crane, Russak.

Cohan, A.S. (1975). *Theories of revolution*. NY: Wiley.

Cohen, Lawrence & Marcus Felson. (1979). "*Social change and crime rate trends: A routine activities approach*." American sociological review 44: 588-608.

Crenshaw, Martha. (1981). "*The causes of terrorism*." Comparative politics 13: 379-99.

Crenshaw, Martha, (ed.) (1995). *Terrorism in context*. University Park: Pennsylvania St. Univ. Press.

Crenshaw, Martha. (1998). "*The logic of terrorism: Terrorist behavior as a product of strategic choice*," in Walter Reich (ed.) *Origins of terrorism*. NY: Woodrow Wilson Center Press.

Drakos, Konstantinos and Ali M. Kutan (2003), "*Regional Effects of Terrorism on Tourism in Three Mediterranean Countries*," Journal of Conflict Resolution, 47(5), 621-41.

Daly, M. & Wilson, M. (1994). "*The evolutionary psychology of male violence*." Pp. 253-288 in J. Archer (ed.), *Male violence*. London: Routledge Kegan Paul.

Enders, W. & Jindapon, P. (2010). "*Network Externalities and the Structure of Terror Networks*," Journal of Conflict Resolution, Peace Science Society (International), vol. 54(2), pages 262-280, April.

Enders, W.; Jindapon, P. (2011). *On the economics of interrogation: the Big 4 versus the Little Fish game*. Journal of Peace Research May 2011 vol. 48 no. 3 287-301

Enders,W., and Sandler, T.(1993). *The effectiveness of anti-terrorism politics: Vector-autoregression intervention analysis*. American Political Science Review 87 (4): 829-44.

Enders, W. and Sandler, T. (1999). "*Transnational Terrorism in the Post-Cold War Era*." International Studies Quarterly. 43:1, pp. 145-67.

Enders, W. and Sandler, T. (2000). "*Is Transnational Terrorism Becoming More Threatening*." Journal of Conflict Resolution. 44:3, pp. 307-32.

Enders, W. and Sandler, T. (2001). "*Patterns of Transnational Terrorism*, 1970-99: Alternative Time Series Estimates." unpublished manuscript.

Enders, W. and Todd Sandler (2002). "*Patterns of Transnational Terrorism*, 1970-1999: Alternative Time-Series Estimates." International Studies Quarterly. 46(2), 145-165.

Enders, Walter and Todd Sandler (2006), *The Political Economy of Terrorism* (Cambridge: Cambridge University Press)

Enders, W.; Sandler, T.; Gaibulloev, K. (2011). *Domestic versus transnational terrorism: Data, decomposition, and dynamics.* Journal of Peace Research May 2011 vol. 48 no. 3 319-337

Feinstein, J. S.; Kaplan, E. H. (2010). *Analysis of a Strategic Terror Organization.* Journal of Conflict Resolution January 11, 2010 (on line first).

Reinares, F. (2005). *Conceptualising International Terrorism. Real Instituto Elcano. Area: International Terrorism* - ARI N 82/2005 (Translated from Spanish)

Ferracuti, Franco. (1982). "*A sociopsychiatric interpretation of terrorism.*" P. 129-41 in *Annals of American academy of political & social science*, 463: 129-41.

Ferrell, J. (1997). "*Against the law: Anarchist criminology,*" In Brian D. MacLean and Dragan Milovanovic (eds.) *Thinking critically about crime.* Richmond, British Columbia: Collective Press.

Ferrell, J. (1999). "*Anarchist criminology and social justice,*" Pp. 91-108 in

Freilich, J. (2003). *American militias: State-level variations in militia activities.* NY: LFB Press.

Frey, B. (2004). *Dealing with terrorism: Stick or carrot?* Northhampton, MA: Edward Elgar.

Gaibulloev, K.; Sandler, T. (2011). *The adverse effect of transnational and domestic terrorism on growth in Africa.* Journal of Peace Research May 2011 vol. 48 no. 3 355-371

Georges-Abeyie, D. & Hass, L. (1982). "*Propaganda by deed: Defining terrorism.*" The justice reporter 2: 1-7.

Goldman, Emma. *Anarchism and Other Essays.* 3rd ed. 1917. New York: Dover Publications Inc., 1969. ISBN 0-486-22484-8

Dearn, M. (2011). *Boko Haram: Nigeria's Terrorist Insurgency Evolves.* ARTICLE | 19 DECEMBER 2011 - 12:44PM. Think Africa Press.

Galvin, Deborah. (1983). "*The female terrorist: A socio-psychological perspective.*" *Behavioral science & law* 1: 19-32.

Georges-Abeyie, D. & Hass, L. (1982). "*Propaganda by deed: Defining terrorism.*" *The justice reporter* 2: 1-7.

Gibbs, Jack (1989). "*Conceptualizations of terrorism.*" *American sociological review* 53(4): 329-40.

Gurr, Ted. (1970). *Why men rebel*. Princeton: Princeton University Press.

Hacker, Frederick. (1996). *Crusaders, criminals, crazies: Terror and terrorists in our time*. NY: Norton.

Hanson, V. (2001). *A war like no other: How the Athenians and Spartans fought the Peloponnesian war*. NY: Random House. [author's website]

Hoffman, B. (1993). *Holy terror*. Santa Monica: RAND.

Hoffman, B. (2006). *Inside terrorism*. Edition 2, Columbia University Press, 2006. ISBN 0-231-12699-9, ISBN 978-0-231-12699-1.

Hubbard, David. (1983). "*The psychodynamics of terrorism*," Pp. 45-53 in Y. Alexander et. al. (eds.) *International violence*. NY: Praeger.

Hudson, Rex. (1999). *Who becomes a terrorist and why*. Guilford, Ct: Lyons Press.

Jenkins, J. (1983) "*Resource mobilization theory and the study of social movements*." *Annual review of sociology* 9: 527–53.

Juergensmeyer, M. (2001) *Terror in the mind of God: The global rise of religious violence*. Berkeley: Univ. of California Press. [sample pages]

Kaplan, A. (1981). "*The psychodynamics of terrorism*." Pp. 35-50 in Y. Alexander & J. Gleason (eds.) *Behavioral and quantitative perspectives on terrorism*. NY: Pergamon.

Keefer, Loayza P., and Loayza, N. eds. (2008). *Terrorism, Economic Development, and Political Openness*. Cambridge: Cambridge University Press.

Kraemer, E. (2004). "*A philosopher looks at terrorism*." Pp. 113-131 in Nyatepe-Coo, A. & Zeisler-Vralsted, D. (eds.) *Understanding terrorism*. Upper Saddle River, NJ: Prentice Hall.

Krueger, Alan. 2004. *What Makes a Terrorist: Economics and the Roots of Terrorism*. Princeton: Princeton University Press.

Krueger, Alan, and David Laitin. 2008. "*Kto Kogo? A Cross-Country Study of the Origins and Targets of Terrorism*." In Philip Keefer and Norman Loayza, eds., Terrorism, Economic Development, and Political Openness. Cambridge: Cambridge University Press.

Krueger, Alan, and Jitka Maleckova. 2003. "*Education, Poverty and Terrorism: Is There a Causal Connection?*" Journal of Economic Perspectives 17, no. 4: 119–44.

Krueger, Alan, and Jorn-Steffen Pischke. 1997. "*A Statistical Analysis of Crime against Foreigners in Unified Germany.*" Journal of Human Resources 32, no. 1 (Winter): 182–209

Kushner, Harvey. (2003). *Encyclopedia of terrorism*. Thousand Oaks, CA: Sage Publications.

Landes W. M. , 1977. "*An Economic Study of U.S. Aircraft Hijacking*, 1960-1976," NBER Working Papers 0210, National Bureau of Economic Research, Inc.

Landes, W. M, 1978. "*An Economic Study of U.S. Aircraft Hijacking*, 1961-1976," Journal of Law and Economics, University of Chicago Press, vol. 21(1), pages 1-31, April.

Lapan, Harvey E & Sandler T. (1988) *To bargain or not to bargain?*: That is the question. American Economic Review 78(2): 16–20.

Laqueur, Walter. (1999) *The new terrorism*. NY: Oxford Univ. Press.

Leeman, Richard. (1991). *The rhetoric of terrorism*. NY: Greenwood Press.

Li, Q.; Schaub, D. (2004). *Economic Globalization and Transnational Terrorism A POOLED TIME-SERIES ANALYSIS*. JOURNAL OF CONFLICT RESOLUTION, Vol. 48 No. 2, April 2004 230-258 DOI: 10.1177/0022002703262869 © 2004 Sage Publications

Long, David. (1990). *The anatomy of terrorism*. NY: Free Press.

Miller, G. (2007). *Confronting Terrorisms: Group Motivation and Successful State Policies*: Terrorism and Political Violence. Volume 19 : 331-350

Margolin, J. (1977). "*Psychological perspectives in terrorism.*" In Y. Alexander and S.

M. Finger (eds.), *Terrorism: Interdisciplinary perspectives*. New York: John Jay Press.

Martic, Milos. (1975). *Insurrection: Five schools of revolutionary thought*. NY: Dunellen Publishing.

Marty, Martin & & R. Scott Appleby, eds. (1993). *Fundamentalism and the state*. Chicago: Univ. of Chicago Press.

Merari, A. (1990). "*The readiness to kill and die: Suicidal terrorism in the Middle East.*" In W. Reich (Ed.), *Origins of terrorism*. Cambridge: Cambridge University Press.

de Mesquita, E. B. (2005). *The Quality of Terror*. American Journal of Political Science, Vol. 49, No. 3, July 2005, Pp. 515–530.

Muller, Edward & Karl-Dieter Opp. (1986). "*Rational choice and rebellious collective action,*" *American political science review* 80: 471-87.

Nairaland Forum (June 2014). "*60% Of Nigerian Graduates Are Unemployed*". Jobs/Vacancies (1) - Nairaland" retrieved from http://www.nairaland.com/1104008/60-nigerian-graduates-unemployed/1

Nassar, J. (2004). *Globalization and terrorism.* Lanham, MD: Rowman & Littlefield.

Neiberg, M. (Ed.) (2006). *Fascism.* Burlington, VT: Ashgate.
Onwudiwe, I. (2001). *The globalization of terrorism.* Andershort: Ashgate Press.

Nyatepe-Coo, A. (2004). "*Economic implications of terrorism,*" Pp. 77-89 in Nyatepe-Coo, A. & Zeisler-Vralsted, D. (eds.) *Understanding terrorism.* Upper Saddle River, NJ: Prentice Hall.

Nyatepe-Coo, A. (2004). "*Economic implications of terrorism,*" Pp. 77-89 in Nyatepe-Coo, A. & Zeisler-Vralsted, D. (eds.) Understanding terrorism. Upper Saddle River, NJ: Prentice Hall.

Oyeniyi, B. A. (2007). *A historical overview of domestic terrorism in Nigeria.* Institute for Security Studies. DOMESTIC TERRORISM IN AFRICA: DEFINING, ADDRESSING AND UNDERSTANDING ITS IMPACT ON HUMAN SECURITY. Seminar Report.

O'Connor, T. (1994) "*A neofunctional model of crime and crime control*" Pp. 143-58 in G. Barak (ed.) *Varieties of criminology.* Westport, CT: Greenwood Press.

O'Connor, T. R. K. (2011). *THEORIES AND CAUSES OF TERRORISM.* Retrieved from http://www.drtomoconnor.com/3400/3400lect01a.htm

O'Kane. R. (Ed.) (2005). *Terrorism, Vol I-II.* Northhampton, MA: Edward Elgar.

OLSON, M. (1965). *The Logic of Collective Action.* Cambridge: Harvard University Press.

OLSON, M. (1982). *The Rise and Decline of Nations.* New Haven: Yale University Press.

Onuoha F. C. (February 2, 2011). *Nigeria's Vulnerability to Terrorism: The Imperative of a Counter Religious Extremism and Terrorism (CONREST) Strategy.* Peace and Conflict Monitor. Retrieved from http://www.monitor.upeace.org/innerpg.cfm?id_article=772

Oots, K. & Wiegele, T. (1985). "*Terrorist and victim: Psychiatric and physiological approaches,*" *Terrorism: An international journal* 8(1): 1-32.

O'Sullivan, N. (1986) *Terrorism, ideology, and revolution*. Boulder, CO: Westview.

Pape, Robert A (2005) *Dying to Win: The Strategic Logic of Suicide Terrorism*. New York: Random House.

Piazza, James A (2008) *Incubators of terror: Do failed and failing states promote transnational terrorism?* International Studies Quarterly 52(3): 469–488.

Passmore, K. (2002). *Fascism: A very short introduction*. NY: Oxford University Press.

Post, J. (1984). "*Notes on a psychodynamic theory of terrorist behavior.*" Terrorism 7:241-56.

Post, J. (1990). "*Terrorist psycho-logic: Terrorist behavior as a product of psychological forces,*" Pp. 25-40 in W. Reich (ed.) *Origins of terrorism*. Cambridge: Cambridge Univ. Press.

Powell, Robert (2007) *Defending against terrorist attacks with limited resources*. American Political Science Review 101(3): 527–541.

Purkis, J. & Bowen, J. eds. (1997) *Twenty-first century anarchism*. London: Cassell.

Ranstorp, Magnus. (1996). "*Terrorism in the name of religion,*" Pp. 121-36 in Russell Howard & Reid Sawyer (eds.) *Terrorism and counterterrorism*. Guilford, CT: McGraw-Hill.

Rapoport, David & Yonah Alexander, eds. (1982). *The morality of terrorism: Religious and secular justifications*. NY: Pergamon Press.

Rapoport, David. (1984). "*Fear and trembling: Terrorism in three religious traditions.*" *American political science review* 78(3): 668-72.

Reinares, F. (2005). *Nationalist Separatism and Terrorism in Comparative Perspective. in Root Causes of Terrorism: Myths, Reality, and Ways Forward*. London: Routledge.

Research and Citation. Purdue University Retrieved from https://owl.english.purdue.edu/owl/resource/560/08/

Richardson, L. (2007). *What Terrorists Want: Understanding the Enemy, Containing the Threat*. Random House Trade Paperbacks. ISBN-10: 0812975448 ISBN-13: 978-0812975444

Robertsfool (2012). *THE POLITICAL THEORY OF ANARCHISM AS A THEORY OF TERRORISM*. Retrieved from http://robertnyakundi.wordpress.com/2012/06/25/the-political-theory-of-anarchism-as-a-theory-of-terrorism-2/

Ross, Jeffrey Ian. (1996). "*A model of the psychological causes of oppositional political terrorism*" *Peace and conflict: Journal of peace psychology* 2-11.

Ross, Jeffrey Ian. (1999). "*Beyond the conceptualization of terrorism: A psychological-structural model*" in C. Summers & E. Mardusen (eds.) *Collective violence*. NY: Rowen & Littlefield.

Ruby, Charles. (2002). "*Are terrorists mentally deranged?*" *Analyses of social issues and public policy* 2(1): 15-26.

Ruggiero, V. (2005). "*Political violence: A criminological analysis.*" Pp. 35-41 in M. Natarajan (ed.) *Introduction to international criminal justice*. NY: McGraw Hill.

Russell, Charles & Bowman Miller. (1977). "*Profile of a terrorist.*" *Terrorism: An international journal* 1(1): 17-34.

Sandler, T. and Parise, G. F.; Enders, W.;   (1992), "*An Econometric Analysis of the Impact of Terrorism on Tourism*," Kyklos, 45(4), 531-54.

Sandler, T., & Siqueira, K. (2006). *Global terrorism: Deterrence versus pre-emption.* Canadian Journal of Economics, 39(4), 1370-1387

Siqueira, K. (2005). *Political and militant wings within dissident movements and organizations.* Journal of Conflict Resolution, 49(2), 218-236.

Siqueira, K., & Sandler, T. (2006). *Terrorists versus the government*: Strategic interaction, support, and sponsorship. Journal of Conflict Resolution, 50(6), 878-898.

Siqueira, K., & Sandler, T. (2007). *Terrorist backlash, terrorism mitigation, and policy delegation.* Journal of Public Economics, 91(9), 1800-1815.

Siqueira, K. & Sandler, T. (forthcoming). *Defensive counterterrorism measures and domestic politics.* Defence and Peace Economics, 19.

Sandler, T. (2003). "*Collective Action and Transnational Terrorism.*" The World Economy. 26(6). 779-802.

Sandler, T. ; Enders, W. (1999). Retrieved from (http://www.utdallas.edu/~tms063000/website/complete-terror02.pdf

Schmid, A. P.; and Jongman, A. J (2008). *Political Terrorism: A new Guide to Actors, Authors, Concepts, Databases, Theories and Literature*. New Brunswick: Transaction Publishers.

Simonsen, C. & Spindlove, J. (2007). *Terrorism today: The past, the players, the future, 3e*. NJ: Prentice Hall.

Smith, B. (1994). *Pipe bombs and pipe dreams: Terrorism in America*. Albany: SUNY Press.

Smith, B. & Damphousse, K. (1998). *"Terrorism, politics, and punishment: A test of structural contextual theory and the liberation hypothesis." Criminology* 36(1):67-92.

Smith, B., Damphousse, K., Jackson, F. & Karlson, A. (2002). *"The prosecution and punishment of international terrorists in federal court: 1980-1999." Criminology and public policy* 1(3):311-338.

Snowden, L. & Whitsel, B. (Eds.) (2005). *Terrorism: Research, readings, and realities*. NJ: Prentice Hall.

Start:National Consortium for the Study of Terrorisms and Responses to Terrorism. http://www.start.umd.edu/

Stitt, B. Grant. (2003). *"The understanding of evil: A joint quest for criminology and theology."* Pp. 203-218 in R. Chairs & B. Chilton (eds.) Star Trek visions of law & justice. Dallas: Adios Press.

Stern, Jessica. (1999). *The ultimate terrorists*. Cambridge: Harvard University Press.

Strentz, Thomas. (1988). *"A terrorist psychological profile," Law enforcement bulletin* 57: 11-18.

Taylor, Maxwell. (1988). *The terrorist*. London: Brassey's.
Tifft, Larry. (1979). "The coming redefinition of crime: An anarchist perspective." *Social problems* 26: 392-402.

Victoroff, J. (2005). *"The mind of a terrorist: A review and critique of psychological approaches." Journal of conflict resolution* 49(1): 3-43.
Wardlaw, Grant. (1989). *Political terrorism: Theory, tactics, and counter-measures*. Cambridge Univ. Press.

Wieviorka, M. (1995). *"Terrorism in the Context of Academic Research."* in Terrorism in Context. Martha Crenshaw (ed). University Park, PA: The Pennsylvania State University Press.

wikipedia.org (2014). *Igbo People*. Retrieved from http://en.wikipedia.org/wiki/Igbo_people

Williams, P. (2008). *"Violent Non-State Actors and National and International Security."* International Relations and Security Network. Zurich, Switzerland: Swiss Federal. Institute of Technology.

Wintrobe, R. (2006) *Extremism, suicide terror, and authoritarianism.* Public Choice 128(1): 169–195.

White, Jonathan. (2006). *Terrorism and homeland security.* Belmont, CA: Wadsworth.

Wilson, E. (1975). *Sociobiology: The new synthesis.* Cambridge: Harvard Univ. Press.

Young, Jock. (1999). *The exclusive society.* Thousand Oaks, CA: Sage. [sample articles by author]

Zussman, Asaf & Noam Zussman (2006) *Assassinations: Evaluating the effectiveness of an Israeli counterterrorism policy using stock market data.* Journal of Economic Perspectives 20(2): 193–206.

APPENDIXES

Questionnaires: when answered will be attached here. The research questions will also be attached and other printouts from logistic regression analysis will also be attached if needed.

Appendix A

Year	Number of attacks in year
1976	1
1977	0
1978	0
1979	0
1980	1
1981	0
1982	0
1983	3
1984	0
1985	0
1986	0
1987	0
1988	2
1989	0
1990	0
1991	4
1992	16
1993	0
1994	9
1995	1
1996	11
1997	20

1998   3

1999   19

2000   10

2001   6

2002   6

2003   9

2004   6

2005   10

2006   37

2007   63

2008   81

2009   44

2010   65

2011   175

Appendix B

Global Terrorism Data Base at time of research

1	1	DATE	1/17/1980
1	2	COUNTRY	Nigeria
1	3	CITY	Kaduna
1	4	PERPETRATOR	Zimbabwe Patriotic Front
1	5	FATALITIES	Unknown
1	6	INJURED	Unknown
1	7	TARGET TYPE	Government (Diplomatic)
1	8	REGION	Sub-Saharan Africa
1	9	ATTACK TYPE	Unknown
1	10	WEAPON TYPE	Unknown
1	11		
2	1	DATE	11/11/1983
2	2	COUNTRY	Nigeria
2	3	CITY	Unknown
2	4	PERPETRATOR	Unknown
2	5	FATALITIES	0
2	6	INJURED	1
2	7	TARGET TYPE	Government (General)
2	8	REGION	Sub-Saharan Africa
2	9	ATTACK TYPE	Assassination
2	10	WEAPON TYPE	Unknown
2	11		
3	1	DATE	11/27/1983
3	2	COUNTRY	Nigeria
3	3	CITY	Lagos
3	4	PERPETRATOR	Gang
3	5	FATALITIES	1
3	6	INJURED	0
3	7	TARGET TYPE	Government (General)
3	8	REGION	Sub-Saharan Africa
3	9	ATTACK TYPE	Assassination
3	10	WEAPON TYPE	Unknown
3	11		
4	1	DATE	11/29/1983
4	2	COUNTRY	Nigeria
4	3	CITY	Ikoyi
4	4	PERPETRATOR	Unknown
4	5	FATALITIES	0
4	6	INJURED	1
4	7	TARGET TYPE	Government (General)
4	8	REGION	Sub-Saharan Africa
4	9	ATTACK TYPE	Assassination
4	10	WEAPON TYPE	Firearms

4	11		
5	1	DATE	1/23/1988
5	2	COUNTRY	Nigeria
5	3	CITY	Lagos
5	4	PERPETRATOR	Unknown
5	5	FATALITIES	1
5	6	INJURED	0
5	7	TARGET TYPE	Government (Diplomatic)
5	8	REGION	Sub-Saharan Africa
5	9	ATTACK TYPE	Assassination
5	10	WEAPON TYPE	Firearms
5	11		
6	1	DATE	3/13/1988
6	2	COUNTRY	Nigeria
6	3	CITY	Lagos
6	4	PERPETRATOR	Unknown
6	5	FATALITIES	3
6	6	INJURED	0
6	7	TARGET TYPE	Educational Institution
6	8	REGION	Sub-Saharan Africa
6	9	ATTACK TYPE	Assassination
6	10	WEAPON TYPE	Firearms
6	11		
7	1	DATE	3/28/1991
7	2	COUNTRY	Nigeria
7	3	CITY	Katsina state
7	4	PERPETRATOR	Katsina Muslim Society
7	5	FATALITIES	0
7	6	INJURED	0
7	7	TARGET TYPE	Journalists & Media
7	8	REGION	Sub-Saharan Africa
7	9	ATTACK TYPE	Facility/Infrastructure Attack
7	10	WEAPON TYPE	Incendiary
7	11		
8	1	DATE	8/30/1991
8	2	COUNTRY	Nigeria
8	3	CITY	Gusau City
8	4	PERPETRATOR	Unknown
8	5	FATALITIES	2
8	6	INJURED	0
8	7	TARGET TYPE	Government (General)
8	8	REGION	Sub-Saharan Africa
8	9	ATTACK TYPE	Facility/Infrastructure Attack
8	10	WEAPON TYPE	Incendiary
8	11		
9	1	DATE	10/14/1991

9	2	COUNTRY	Nigeria
9	3	CITY	Kano
9	4	PERPETRATOR	Muslim Militants
9	5	FATALITIES	8
9	6	INJURED	34
9	7	TARGET TYPE	Private Citizens & Property
9	8	REGION	Sub-Saharan Africa
9	9	ATTACK TYPE	Facility/Infrastructure Attack
9	10	WEAPON TYPE	Firearms,Incendiary
9	11		
10	1	DATE	1/5/1992
10	2	COUNTRY	Nigeria
10	3	CITY	Katsina
10	4	PERPETRATOR	Shiite Muslims
10	5	FATALITIES	0
10	6	INJURED	29
10	7	TARGET TYPE	Police
10	8	REGION	Sub-Saharan Africa
10	9	ATTACK TYPE	Armed Assault
10	10	WEAPON TYPE	Melee,Melee
10	11		
11	1	DATE	2/19/1992
11	2	COUNTRY	Nigeria
11	3	CITY	Utan Brama
11	4	PERPETRATOR	Effiat ethnic roup or Jbibio Peoples
11	5	FATALITIES	80
11	6	INJURED	0
11	7	TARGET TYPE	Private Citizens & Property
11	8	REGION	Sub-Saharan Africa
11	9	ATTACK TYPE	Armed Assault
11	10	WEAPON TYPE	Incendiary,Firearms
11	11		
12	1	DATE	2/22/1992
12	2	COUNTRY	Nigeria
12	3	CITY	Benin
12	4	PERPETRATOR	Unknown
12	5	FATALITIES	1
12	6	INJURED	0
12	7	TARGET TYPE	Government (General)
12	8	REGION	Sub-Saharan Africa
12	9	ATTACK TYPE	Assassination
12	10	WEAPON TYPE	Firearms
12	11		
13	1	DATE	3/13/1992
13	2	COUNTRY	Nigeria
13	3	CITY	Jalingo

13	4	PERPETRATOR	Muslims
13	5	FATALITIES	20
13	6	INJURED	0
13	7	TARGET TYPE	Religious Figures/Institutions
13	8	REGION	Sub-Saharan Africa
13	9	ATTACK TYPE	Bombing/Explosion
13	10	WEAPON TYPE	Firearms,Explosives/Bombs/Dynamite
13	11		
14	1	DATE	5/14/1992
14	2	COUNTRY	Nigeria
14	3	CITY	Lagos
14	4	PERPETRATOR	Anti-Government Group
14	5	FATALITIES	11
14	6	INJURED	0
14	7	TARGET TYPE	Business
14	8	REGION	Sub-Saharan Africa
14	9	ATTACK TYPE	Armed Assault
14	10	WEAPON TYPE	Incendiary,Firearms
14	11		
15	1	DATE	5/15/1992
15	2	COUNTRY	Nigeria
15	3	CITY	Akure
15	4	PERPETRATOR	Unknown
15	5	FATALITIES	0
15	6	INJURED	0
15	7	TARGET TYPE	Other
15	8	REGION	Sub-Saharan Africa
15	9	ATTACK TYPE	Facility/Infrastructure Attack
15	10	WEAPON TYPE	Incendiary
15	11		
16	1	DATE	5/17/1992
16	2	COUNTRY	Nigeria
16	3	CITY	Zango-Kataf
16	4	PERPETRATOR	Hauso Ethnic Group
16	5	FATALITIES	13
16	6	INJURED	100
16	7	TARGET TYPE	Private Citizens & Property
16	8	REGION	Sub-Saharan Africa
16	9	ATTACK TYPE	Armed Assault
16	10	WEAPON TYPE	Firearms,Melee
16	11		
17	1	DATE	5/17/1992
17	2	COUNTRY	Nigeria
17	3	CITY	Kaduna
17	4	PERPETRATOR	Katap Ethic Group
17	5	FATALITIES	10

17	6	INJURED	0
17	7	TARGET TYPE	Private Citizens & Property
17	8	REGION	Sub-Saharan Africa
17	9	ATTACK TYPE	Armed Assault
17	10	WEAPON TYPE	Firearms,Melee
17	11		
18	1	DATE	5/18/1992
18	2	COUNTRY	Nigeria
18	3	CITY	Kaduna
18	4	PERPETRATOR	rioters
18	5	FATALITIES	0
18	6	INJURED	0
18	7	TARGET TYPE	Private Citizens & Property
18	8	REGION	Sub-Saharan Africa
18	9	ATTACK TYPE	Facility/Infrastructure Attack
18	10	WEAPON TYPE	Incendiary
18	11		
19	1	DATE	5/21/1992
19	2	COUNTRY	Nigeria
19	3	CITY	Lagos
19	4	PERPETRATOR	Igbo tribal group
19	5	FATALITIES	0
19	6	INJURED	0
19	7	TARGET TYPE	Business
19	8	REGION	Sub-Saharan Africa
19	9	ATTACK TYPE	Armed Assault
19	10	WEAPON TYPE	Melee
19	11		
20	1	DATE	5/28/1992
20	2	COUNTRY	Nigeria
20	3	CITY	Lagos
20	4	PERPETRATOR	Unknown
20	5	FATALITIES	0
20	6	INJURED	0
20	7	TARGET TYPE	Business
20	8	REGION	Sub-Saharan Africa
20	9	ATTACK TYPE	Hostage Taking (Kidnapping)
20	10	WEAPON TYPE	Firearms
20	11		
21	1	DATE	10/7/1992
21	2	COUNTRY	Nigeria
21	3	CITY	Lagos
21	4	PERPETRATOR	Unknown
21	5	FATALITIES	0
21	6	INJURED	1
21	7	TARGET TYPE	Private Citizens & Property

21	8	REGION	Sub-Saharan Africa
21	9	ATTACK TYPE	Armed Assault
21	10	WEAPON TYPE	Firearms
21	11		
22	1	DATE	12/20/1992
22	2	COUNTRY	Nigeria
22	3	CITY	Lagos
22	4	PERPETRATOR	Unknown
22	5	FATALITIES	0
22	6	INJURED	1
22	7	TARGET TYPE	Government (Diplomatic)
22	8	REGION	Sub-Saharan Africa
22	9	ATTACK TYPE	Assassination
22	10	WEAPON TYPE	Firearms
22	11		
23	1	DATE	2/9/1994
23	2	COUNTRY	Nigeria
23	3	CITY	Brass area
23	4	PERPETRATOR	Unknown
23	5	FATALITIES	13
23	6	INJURED	0
23	7	TARGET TYPE	Maritime
23	8	REGION	Sub-Saharan Africa
23	9	ATTACK TYPE	Armed Assault
23	10	WEAPON TYPE	Firearms
23	11		
24	1	DATE	5/12/1994
24	2	COUNTRY	Nigeria
24	3	CITY	Bakassi Peninsula
24	4	PERPETRATOR	Unknown
24	5	FATALITIES	2
24	6	INJURED	0
24	7	TARGET TYPE	Military
24	8	REGION	Sub-Saharan Africa
24	9	ATTACK TYPE	Armed Assault
24	10	WEAPON TYPE	Firearms
24	11		
25	1	DATE	8/13/1994
25	2	COUNTRY	Nigeria
25	3	CITY	Lagos
25	4	PERPETRATOR	Council for Popular Justice
25	5	FATALITIES	0
25	6	INJURED	0
25	7	TARGET TYPE	Government (General)
25	8	REGION	Sub-Saharan Africa
25	9	ATTACK TYPE	Bombing/Explosion

25	10	WEAPON TYPE	Explosives/Bombs/Dynamite
25	11		
26	1	DATE	8/13/1994
26	2	COUNTRY	Nigeria
26	3	CITY	Lagos
26	4	PERPETRATOR	Council for Popular Justice
26	5	FATALITIES	0
26	6	INJURED	0
26	7	TARGET TYPE	Government (General)
26	8	REGION	Sub-Saharan Africa
26	9	ATTACK TYPE	Bombing/Explosion
26	10	WEAPON TYPE	Explosives/Bombs/Dynamite
26	11		
27	1	DATE	9/2/1994
27	2	COUNTRY	Nigeria
27	3	CITY	Abuja, Osun State
27	4	PERPETRATOR	Unknown
27	5	FATALITIES	0
27	6	INJURED	0
27	7	TARGET TYPE	Government (General)
27	8	REGION	Sub-Saharan Africa
27	9	ATTACK TYPE	Bombing/Explosion
27	10	WEAPON TYPE	Explosives/Bombs/Dynamite
27	11		
28	1	DATE	9/19/1994
28	2	COUNTRY	Nigeria
28	3	CITY	Lagos
28	4	PERPETRATOR	Unknown
28	5	FATALITIES	0
28	6	INJURED	0
28	7	TARGET TYPE	Government (General)
28	8	REGION	Sub-Saharan Africa
28	9	ATTACK TYPE	Facility/Infrastructure Attack
28	10	WEAPON TYPE	Incendiary
28	11		
29	1	DATE	9/28/1994
29	2	COUNTRY	Nigeria
29	3	CITY	Kaduna
29	4	PERPETRATOR	Unknown
29	5	FATALITIES	0
29	6	INJURED	0
29	7	TARGET TYPE	Government (General)
29	8	REGION	Sub-Saharan Africa
29	9	ATTACK TYPE	Bombing/Explosion
29	10	WEAPON TYPE	Explosives/Bombs/Dynamite
29	11		

30	1	DATE	9/30/1994
30	2	COUNTRY	Nigeria
30	3	CITY	Kaduna
30	4	PERPETRATOR	Unknown
30	5	FATALITIES	0
30	6	INJURED	0
30	7	TARGET TYPE	Government (General)
30	8	REGION	Sub-Saharan Africa
30	9	ATTACK TYPE	Bombing/Explosion
30	10	WEAPON TYPE	Explosives/Bombs/Dynamite
30	11		
31	1	DATE	10/6/1995
31	2	COUNTRY	Nigeria
31	3	CITY	Lagos
31	4	PERPETRATOR	Unknown
31	5	FATALITIES	1
31	6	INJURED	0
31	7	TARGET TYPE	Government (General)
31	8	REGION	Sub-Saharan Africa
31	9	ATTACK TYPE	Assassination
31	10	WEAPON TYPE	Firearms
31	11		
32	1	DATE	1/17/1996
32	2	COUNTRY	Nigeria
32	3	CITY	Kano
32	4	PERPETRATOR	United Front for Nigeria's Liberation (UFNL)
32	5	FATALITIES	14
32	6	INJURED	0
32	7	TARGET TYPE	Government (General)
32	8	REGION	Sub-Saharan Africa
32	9	ATTACK TYPE	Bombing/Explosion
32	10	WEAPON TYPE	Explosives/Bombs/Dynamite
32	11		
33	1	DATE	1/18/1996
33	2	COUNTRY	Nigeria
33	3	CITY	Kabuna
33	4	PERPETRATOR	Unknown
33	5	FATALITIES	1
33	6	INJURED	0
33	7	TARGET TYPE	Business
33	8	REGION	Sub-Saharan Africa
33	9	ATTACK TYPE	Bombing/Explosion
33	10	WEAPON TYPE	Explosives/Bombs/Dynamite
33	11		
34	1	DATE	2/2/1996
34	2	COUNTRY	Nigeria

34	3	CITY	Lagos
34	4	PERPETRATOR	Unknown
34	5	FATALITIES	0
34	6	INJURED	1
34	7	TARGET TYPE	Journalists & Media
34	8	REGION	Sub-Saharan Africa
34	9	ATTACK TYPE	Assassination
34	10	WEAPON TYPE	Firearms
34	11		
35	1	DATE	4/13/1996
35	2	COUNTRY	Nigeria
35	3	CITY	Lagos
35	4	PERPETRATOR	Unknown
35	5	FATALITIES	2
35	6	INJURED	0
35	7	TARGET TYPE	Military
35	8	REGION	Sub-Saharan Africa
35	9	ATTACK TYPE	Bombing/Explosion
35	10	WEAPON TYPE	Explosives/Bombs/Dynamite
35	11		
36	1	DATE	5/1/1996
36	2	COUNTRY	Nigeria
36	3	CITY	Lagos
36	4	PERPETRATOR	Unknown
36	5	FATALITIES	0
36	6	INJURED	0
36	7	TARGET TYPE	Military
36	8	REGION	Sub-Saharan Africa
36	9	ATTACK TYPE	Armed Assault
36	10	WEAPON TYPE	Incendiary
36	11		
37	1	DATE	5/23/1996
37	2	COUNTRY	Nigeria
37	3	CITY	Lagos
37	4	PERPETRATOR	Unknown
37	5	FATALITIES	1
37	6	INJURED	0
37	7	TARGET TYPE	Business
37	8	REGION	Sub-Saharan Africa
37	9	ATTACK TYPE	Assassination
37	10	WEAPON TYPE	Firearms
37	11		
38	1	DATE	5/31/1996
38	2	COUNTRY	Nigeria
38	3	CITY	Kabuna
38	4	PERPETRATOR	Unknown

38	5	FATALITIES	1
38	6	INJURED	0
38	7	TARGET TYPE	Business
38	8	REGION	Sub-Saharan Africa
38	9	ATTACK TYPE	Bombing/Explosion
38	10	WEAPON TYPE	Explosives/Bombs/Dynamite
38	11		
39	1	DATE	6/4/1996
39	2	COUNTRY	Nigeria
39	3	CITY	Lagos
39	4	PERPETRATOR	Unknown
39	5	FATALITIES	2
39	6	INJURED	0
39	7	TARGET TYPE	Private Citizens & Property
39	8	REGION	Sub-Saharan Africa
39	9	ATTACK TYPE	Assassination
39	10	WEAPON TYPE	Firearms
39	11		
40	1	DATE	11/14/1996
40	2	COUNTRY	Nigeria
40	3	CITY	Lagos
40	4	PERPETRATOR	Unknown
40	5	FATALITIES	3
40	6	INJURED	0
40	7	TARGET TYPE	Unknown
40	8	REGION	Sub-Saharan Africa
40	9	ATTACK TYPE	Bombing/Explosion
40	10	WEAPON TYPE	Explosives/Bombs/Dynamite
40	11		
41	1	DATE	12/16/1996
41	2	COUNTRY	Nigeria
41	3	CITY	Lagos
41	4	PERPETRATOR	Unknown
41	5	FATALITIES	0
41	6	INJURED	2
41	7	TARGET TYPE	Military
41	8	REGION	Sub-Saharan Africa
41	9	ATTACK TYPE	Assassination
41	10	WEAPON TYPE	Explosives/Bombs/Dynamite
41	11		
42	1	DATE	12/18/1996
42	2	COUNTRY	Nigeria
42	3	CITY	Lagos
42	4	PERPETRATOR	Unknown
42	5	FATALITIES	0
42	6	INJURED	12

42	7	TARGET TYPE	Transportation
42	8	REGION	Sub-Saharan Africa
42	9	ATTACK TYPE	Bombing/Explosion
42	10	WEAPON TYPE	Explosives/Bombs/Dynamite
42	11		
43	1	DATE	1/4/1997
43	2	COUNTRY	Nigeria
43	3	CITY	Lagoa
43	4	PERPETRATOR	Unknown
43	5	FATALITIES	0
43	6	INJURED	1
43	7	TARGET TYPE	Government (General)
43	8	REGION	Sub-Saharan Africa
43	9	ATTACK TYPE	Armed Assault
43	10	WEAPON TYPE	Firearms
43	11		
44	1	DATE	1/7/1997
44	2	COUNTRY	Nigeria
44	3	CITY	Lagos
44	4	PERPETRATOR	Unknown
44	5	FATALITIES	1
44	6	INJURED	15
44	7	TARGET TYPE	Military
44	8	REGION	Sub-Saharan Africa
44	9	ATTACK TYPE	Bombing/Explosion
44	10	WEAPON TYPE	Explosives/Bombs/Dynamite
44	11		
45	1	DATE	2/12/1997
45	2	COUNTRY	Nigeria
45	3	CITY	Lagos
45	4	PERPETRATOR	Unknown
45	5	FATALITIES	0
45	6	INJURED	8
45	7	TARGET TYPE	Military
45	8	REGION	Sub-Saharan Africa
45	9	ATTACK TYPE	Bombing/Explosion
45	10	WEAPON	Explosives/Bombs/Dynamite,Unknown,Unknown,Unknown TYPE
45	11		
46	1	DATE	3/11/1997
46	2	COUNTRY	Nigeria
46	3	CITY	off shore
46	4	PERPETRATOR	Unknown
46	5	FATALITIES	0
46	6	INJURED	0
46	7	TARGET TYPE	Business,Business,Business

46	8	REGION	Sub-Saharan Africa
46	9	ATTACK TYPE	Hostage Taking (Kidnapping)
46	10	WEAPON TYPE	Unknown
46	11		
47	1	DATE	5/7/1997
47	2	COUNTRY	Nigeria
47	3	CITY	Lagos
47	4	PERPETRATOR	Unknown
47	5	FATALITIES	0
47	6	INJURED	5
47	7	TARGET TYPE	Military
47	8	REGION	Sub-Saharan Africa
47	9	ATTACK TYPE	Bombing/Explosion
47	10	WEAPON TYPE	Explosives/Bombs/Dynamite
47	11		
48	1	DATE	5/12/1997
48	2	COUNTRY	Nigeria
48	3	CITY	Ibadan
48	4	PERPETRATOR	Unknown
48	5	FATALITIES	0
48	6	INJURED	0
48	7	TARGET TYPE	Military
48	8	REGION	Sub-Saharan Africa
48	9	ATTACK TYPE	Bombing/Explosion
48	10	WEAPON TYPE	Explosives/Bombs/Dynamite,Unknown,Unknown,Unknown
48	11		
49	1	DATE	5/16/1997
49	2	COUNTRY	Nigeria
49	3	CITY	Onitsha
49	4	PERPETRATOR	Unknown
49	5	FATALITIES	4
49	6	INJURED	3
49	7	TARGET TYPE	Religious Figures/Institutions
49	8	REGION	Sub-Saharan Africa
49	9	ATTACK TYPE	Bombing/Explosion
49	10	WEAPON TYPE	Explosives/Bombs/Dynamite
49	11		
50	1	DATE	5/16/1997
50	2	COUNTRY	Nigeria
50	3	CITY	Onitcha
50	4	PERPETRATOR	Unknown
50	5	FATALITIES	1
50	6	INJURED	0
50	7	TARGET TYPE	Unknown
50	8	REGION	Sub-Saharan Africa

50	9	ATTACK TYPE	Bombing/Explosion
50	10	WEAPON TYPE	Explosives/Bombs/Dynamite
50	11		
51	1	DATE	8/6/1997
51	2	COUNTRY	Nigeria
51	3	CITY	Port Harcourt
51	4	PERPETRATOR	Unknown
51	5	FATALITIES	1
51	6	INJURED	2
51	7	TARGET TYPE	Unknown
51	8	REGION	Sub-Saharan Africa
51	9	ATTACK TYPE	Bombing/Explosion
51	10	WEAPON TYPE	Explosives/Bombs/Dynamite
51	11		
52	1	DATE	8/15/1997
52	2	COUNTRY	Nigeria
52	3	CITY	Lagos
52	4	PERPETRATOR	Unknown
52	5	FATALITIES	0
52	6	INJURED	0
52	7	TARGET TYPE	Private Citizens & Property
52	8	REGION	Sub-Saharan Africa
52	9	ATTACK TYPE	Bombing/Explosion
52	10	WEAPON TYPE	Explosives/Bombs/Dynamite
52	11		
53	1	DATE	8/20/1997
53	2	COUNTRY	Nigeria
53	3	CITY	Ife
53	4	PERPETRATOR	Modakeke Ethnics
53	5	FATALITIES	16
53	6	INJURED	0
53	7	TARGET TYPE	Private Citizens & Property
53	8	REGION	Sub-Saharan Africa
53	9	ATTACK TYPE	Armed Assault
53	10	WEAPON TYPE	Firearms
53	11		
54	1	DATE	8/20/1997
54	2	COUNTRY	Nigeria
54	3	CITY	Ife
54	4	PERPETRATOR	Modakeke Ethnics
54	5	FATALITIES	16
54	6	INJURED	0
54	7	TARGET TYPE	Private Citizens & Property
54	8	REGION	Sub-Saharan Africa
54	9	ATTACK TYPE	Armed Assault
54	10	WEAPON TYPE	Firearms

54	11		
55	1	DATE	8/20/1997
55	2	COUNTRY	Nigeria
55	3	CITY	Ife
55	4	PERPETRATOR	Modakeke Ethnics
55	5	FATALITIES	16
55	6	INJURED	0
55	7	TARGET TYPE	Private Citizens & Property
55	8	REGION	Sub-Saharan Africa
55	9	ATTACK TYPE	Armed Assault
55	10	WEAPON TYPE	Firearms
55	11		
56	1	DATE	8/20/1997
56	2	COUNTRY	Nigeria
56	3	CITY	Ife
56	4	PERPETRATOR	Modakeke Ethnics
56	5	FATALITIES	16
56	6	INJURED	0
56	7	TARGET TYPE	Private Citizens & Property
56	8	REGION	Sub-Saharan Africa
56	9	ATTACK TYPE	Armed Assault
56	10	WEAPON TYPE	Firearms
56	11		
57	1	DATE	9/2/1997
57	2	COUNTRY	Nigeria
57	3	CITY	Ado-Ekiti
57	4	PERPETRATOR	Unknown
57	5	FATALITIES	0
57	6	INJURED	7
57	7	TARGET TYPE	Military
57	8	REGION	Sub-Saharan Africa
57	9	ATTACK TYPE	Bombing/Explosion
57	10	WEAPON TYPE	Explosives/Bombs/Dynamite
57	11		
58	1	DATE	9/17/1997
58	2	COUNTRY	Nigeria
58	3	CITY	Warri
58	4	PERPETRATOR	Unknown
58	5	FATALITIES	1
58	6	INJURED	0
58	7	TARGET TYPE	Military
58	8	REGION	Sub-Saharan Africa
58	9	ATTACK TYPE	Hostage Taking (Kidnapping)
58	10	WEAPON TYPE	Unknown
58	11		
59	1	DATE	9/19/1997

59	2	COUNTRY	Nigeria
59	3	CITY	Lagos
59	4	PERPETRATOR	Unknown
59	5	FATALITIES	0
59	6	INJURED	10
59	7	TARGET TYPE	Religious Figures/Institutions
59	8	REGION	Sub-Saharan Africa
59	9	ATTACK TYPE	Bombing/Explosion
59	10	WEAPON TYPE	Explosives/Bombs/Dynamite
59	11		
60	1	DATE	9/25/1997
60	2	COUNTRY	Nigeria
60	3	CITY	Ondo
60	4	PERPETRATOR	Unknown
60	5	FATALITIES	0
60	6	INJURED	0
60	7	TARGET TYPE	Government (General)
60	8	REGION	Sub-Saharan Africa
60	9	ATTACK TYPE	Bombing/Explosion
60	10	WEAPON	TYPE Explosives/Bombs/Dynamite,Unknown,Unknown,Unknown
60	11		
61	1	DATE	12/2/1997
61	2	COUNTRY	Nigeria
61	3	CITY	Ife
61	4	PERPETRATOR	Modakeke Ethnic Activists
61	5	FATALITIES	20
61	6	INJURED	0
61	7	TARGET TYPE	Private Citizens & Property
61	8	REGION	Sub-Saharan Africa
61	9	ATTACK TYPE	Armed Assault
61	10	WEAPON TYPE	Firearms
61	11		
62	1	DATE	12/6/1997
62	2	COUNTRY	Nigeria
62	3	CITY	Ife
62	4	PERPETRATOR	Modakeke Ethnic Activists
62	5	FATALITIES	15
62	6	INJURED	0
62	7	TARGET TYPE	Private Citizens & Property
62	8	REGION	Sub-Saharan Africa
62	9	ATTACK TYPE	Armed Assault
62	10	WEAPON TYPE	Firearms
62	11		
63	1	DATE	4/24/1998
63	2	COUNTRY	Nigeria

63	3	CITY	Lagos
63	4	PERPETRATOR	Unknown
63	5	FATALITIES	4
63	6	INJURED	Unknown
63	7	TARGET TYPE	Private Citizens & Property
63	8	REGION	Sub-Saharan Africa
63	9	ATTACK TYPE	Bombing/Explosion
63	10	WEAPON TYPE	Explosives/Bombs/Dynamite
63	11		
64	1	DATE	4/24/1998
64	2	COUNTRY	Nigeria
64	3	CITY	Ile-Ife
64	4	PERPETRATOR	Unknown
64	5	FATALITIES	5
64	6	INJURED	Unknown
64	7	TARGET TYPE	Private Citizens & Property
64	8	REGION	Sub-Saharan Africa
64	9	ATTACK TYPE	Bombing/Explosion
64	10	WEAPON TYPE	Explosives/Bombs/Dynamite
64	11		
65	1	DATE	2/9/1999
65	2	COUNTRY	Nigeria
65	3	CITY	Unknown
65	4	PERPETRATOR	Unknown
65	5	FATALITIES	0
65	6	INJURED	0
65	7	TARGET TYPE	Business,Private Citizens & Property
65	8	REGION	Sub-Saharan Africa
65	9	ATTACK TYPE	Hostage Taking (Kidnapping)
65	10	WEAPON TYPE	Unknown
65	11		
66	1	DATE	2/14/1999
66	2	COUNTRY	Nigeria
66	3	CITY	Unknown
66	4	PERPETRATOR	Unknown
66	5	FATALITIES	0
66	6	INJURED	0
66	7	TARGET TYPE	Business
66	8	REGION	Sub-Saharan Africa
66	9	ATTACK TYPE	Hostage Taking (Kidnapping)
66	10	WEAPON TYPE	Unknown
66	11		
67	1	DATE	4/5/1999
67	2	COUNTRY	Nigeria
67	3	CITY	Unknown

67	4	PERPETRATOR	Association of Mobil Spill Affected Communities (AMSAC)
67	5	FATALITIES	0
67	6	INJURED	0
67	7	TARGET TYPE	Business,Business
67	8	REGION	Sub-Saharan Africa
67	9	ATTACK TYPE	Armed Assault,Bombing/Explosion
67	10	WEAPON TYPE	Unknown
67	11		
68	1	DATE	6/19/1999
68	2	COUNTRY	Nigeria
68	3	CITY	Unknown
68	4	PERPETRATOR	Other (suspected)
68	5	FATALITIES	100
68	6	INJURED	200
68	7	TARGET TYPE	Private Citizens & Property
68	8	REGION	Sub-Saharan Africa
68	9	ATTACK TYPE	Armed Assault
68	10	WEAPON TYPE	Melee
68	11		
69	1	DATE	6/19/1999
69	2	COUNTRY	Nigeria
69	3	CITY	Kantu
69	4	PERPETRATOR	Other (suspected)
69	5	FATALITIES	5
69	6	INJURED	0
69	7	TARGET TYPE	Other
69	8	REGION	Sub-Saharan Africa
69	9	ATTACK TYPE	Armed Assault,Hostage Taking (Kidnapping),Facility/Infrastructure Attack
69	10	WEAPON TYPE	Incendiary,Unknown
69	11		
70	1	DATE	6/27/1999
70	2	COUNTRY	Nigeria
70	3	CITY	Unknown
70	4	PERPETRATOR	Unknown
70	5	FATALITIES	0
70	6	INJURED	0
70	7	TARGET TYPE	Business,Business,Business
70	8	REGION	Sub-Saharan Africa
70	9	ATTACK TYPE	Hostage Taking (Kidnapping)
70	10	WEAPON TYPE	Unknown
70	11		
71	1	DATE	7/8/1999
71	2	COUNTRY	Nigeria
71	3	CITY	Egwa

71	4	PERPETRATOR	Unknown
71	5	FATALITIES	0
71	6	INJURED	0
71	7	TARGET TYPE	Business,Business
71	8	REGION	Sub-Saharan Africa
71	9	ATTACK TYPE	Hostage Taking (Kidnapping)
71	10	WEAPON TYPE	Unknown
71	11		
72	1	DATE	7/20/1999
72	2	COUNTRY	Nigeria
72	3	CITY	Osoko
72	4	PERPETRATOR	Unknown
72	5	FATALITIES	0
72	6	INJURED	0
72	7	TARGET TYPE	Business,Business,Business
72	8	REGION	Sub-Saharan Africa
72	9	ATTACK TYPE	Facility/Infrastructure Attack,Hostage Taking (Kidnapping)
72	10	WEAPON TYPE	Unknown
72	11		
73	1	DATE	10/8/1999
73	2	COUNTRY	Nigeria
73	3	CITY	Unknown
73	4	PERPETRATOR	Unknown
73	5	FATALITIES	0
73	6	INJURED	8
73	7	TARGET TYPE	Business,Other,Other
73	8	REGION	Sub-Saharan Africa
73	9	ATTACK TYPE	Facility/Infrastructure Attack,Hostage Taking (Barricade Incident)
73	10	WEAPON TYPE	Firearms
73	11		
74	1	DATE	10/30/1999
74	2	COUNTRY	Nigeria
74	3	CITY	Warri
74	4	PERPETRATOR	Unknown
74	5	FATALITIES	0
74	6	INJURED	0
74	7	TARGET TYPE	Business,Business
74	8	REGION	Sub-Saharan Africa
74	9	ATTACK TYPE	Hostage Taking (Kidnapping)
74	10	WEAPON TYPE	Unknown
74	11		
75	1	DATE	11/1/1999
75	2	COUNTRY	Nigeria
75	3	CITY	Bonny Island

75	4	PERPETRATOR	Unknown
75	5	FATALITIES	0
75	6	INJURED	0
75	7	TARGET TYPE	Maritime,Private Citizens & Property,Private Citizens & Property
75	8	REGION	Sub-Saharan Africa
75	9	ATTACK TYPE	Facility/Infrastructure Attack,Hostage Taking (Kidnapping)
75	10	WEAPON TYPE	Firearms
75	11		
76	1	DATE	11/4/1999
76	2	COUNTRY	Nigeria
76	3	CITY	Unknown
76	4	PERPETRATOR	Ijaw militants
76	5	FATALITIES	7
76	6	INJURED	0
76	7	TARGET TYPE	Police
76	8	REGION	Sub-Saharan Africa
76	9	ATTACK TYPE	Hostage Taking (Kidnapping),Armed Assault
76	10	WEAPON TYPE	Unknown
76	11		
77	1	DATE	11/8/1999
77	2	COUNTRY	Nigeria
77	3	CITY	Escravos
77	4	PERPETRATOR	Unknown
77	5	FATALITIES	0
77	6	INJURED	0
77	7	TARGET TYPE	Maritime,Private Citizens & Property,Private Citizens & Property
77	8	REGION	Sub-Saharan Africa
77	9	ATTACK TYPE	Facility/Infrastructure Attack,Hostage Taking (Kidnapping)
77	10	WEAPON TYPE	Melee
77	11		
78	1	DATE	11/13/1999
78	2	COUNTRY	Nigeria
78	3	CITY	Unknown
78	4	PERPETRATOR	Egbesu Youths of the Bayelsa (suspected)
78	5	FATALITIES	10
78	6	INJURED	Unknown
78	7	TARGET TYPE	Police,Military
78	8	REGION	Sub-Saharan Africa
78	9	ATTACK TYPE	Armed Assault
78	10	WEAPON TYPE	Firearms,Melee
78	11		
79	1	DATE	11/13/1999

79	2	COUNTRY	Nigeria
79	3	CITY	Unknown
79	4	PERPETRATOR	Egbesu Youths of the Bayelsa
79	5	FATALITIES	12
79	6	INJURED	Unknown
79	7	TARGET TYPE	Police,Military
79	8	REGION	Sub-Saharan Africa
79	9	ATTACK TYPE	Armed Assault
79	10	WEAPON TYPE	Firearms,Melee
79	11		
80	1	DATE	11/13/1999
80	2	COUNTRY	Nigeria
80	3	CITY	Warri
80	4	PERPETRATOR	Ijaw militants
80	5	FATALITIES	0
80	6	INJURED	1
80	7	TARGET TYPE	Other
80	8	REGION	Sub-Saharan Africa
80	9	ATTACK TYPE	Armed Assault
80	10	WEAPON TYPE	Firearms,Melee
80	11		
81	1	DATE	11/13/1999
81	2	COUNTRY	Nigeria
81	3	CITY	Warri North
81	4	PERPETRATOR	Ijaw militants
81	5	FATALITIES	Unknown
81	6	INJURED	Unknown
81	7	TARGET TYPE	Private Citizens & Property
81	8	REGION	Sub-Saharan Africa
81	9	ATTACK TYPE	Hostage Taking (Kidnapping)
81	10	WEAPON TYPE	Firearms
81	11		
82	1	DATE	11/15/1999
82	2	COUNTRY	Nigeria
82	3	CITY	Ekakpamre
82	4	PERPETRATOR	Other
82	5	FATALITIES	0
82	6	INJURED	0
82	7	TARGET TYPE	Business
82	8	REGION	Sub-Saharan Africa
82	9	ATTACK TYPE	Unknown
82	10	WEAPON TYPE	Firearms,Unknown
82	11		
83	1	DATE	1/4/2000
83	2	COUNTRY	Nigeria
83	3	CITY	Lagos

83	4	PERPETRATOR	Odua Peoples' Congress (OPC)
83	5	FATALITIES	0
83	6	INJURED	2
83	7	TARGET TYPE	Police
83	8	REGION	Sub-Saharan Africa
83	9	ATTACK TYPE	Unarmed Assault
83	10	WEAPON TYPE	Chemical
83	11		
84	1	DATE	2/21/2000
84	2	COUNTRY	Nigeria
84	3	CITY	Kaduna
84	4	PERPETRATOR	Other
84	5	FATALITIES	20
84	6	INJURED	Unknown
84	7	TARGET TYPE	Private Citizens & Property
84	8	REGION	Sub-Saharan Africa
84	9	ATTACK TYPE	Facility/Infrastructure Attack,Armed Assault
84	10	WEAPON TYPE	Incendiary,Melee
84	11		
85	1	DATE	3/14/2000
85	2	COUNTRY	Nigeria
85	3	CITY	Lagos
85	4	PERPETRATOR	Unknown
85	5	FATALITIES	0
85	6	INJURED	0
85	7	TARGET TYPE	Business,Business,Police
85	8	REGION	Sub-Saharan Africa
85	9	ATTACK TYPE	Facility/Infrastructure Attack,Hostage Taking (Barricade Incident)
85	10	WEAPON TYPE	Firearms
85	11		
86	1	DATE	4/7/2000
86	2	COUNTRY	Nigeria
86	3	CITY	Port Harcourt
86	4	PERPETRATOR	Unknown
86	5	FATALITIES	0
86	6	INJURED	0
86	7	TARGET TYPE	Private Citizens & Property,Private Citizens & Property,Private Citizens & Property
86	8	REGION	Sub-Saharan Africa
86	9	ATTACK TYPE	Hostage Taking (Kidnapping)
86	10	WEAPON TYPE	Firearms
86	11		
87	1	DATE	4/14/2000
87	2	COUNTRY	Nigeria
87	3	CITY	Warri

87	4	PERPETRATOR	Unknown
87	5	FATALITIES	0
87	6	INJURED	0
87	7	TARGET TYPE	Business
87	8	REGION	Sub-Saharan Africa
87	9	ATTACK TYPE	Hostage Taking (Kidnapping)
87	10	WEAPON TYPE	Firearms
87	11		
88	1	DATE	6/18/2000
88	2	COUNTRY	Nigeria
88	3	CITY	Escravos
88	4	PERPETRATOR	Unknown
88	5	FATALITIES	0
88	6	INJURED	0
88	7	TARGET TYPE	Other,Other
88	8	REGION	Sub-Saharan Africa
88	9	ATTACK TYPE	Hostage Taking (Kidnapping)
88	10	WEAPON TYPE	Unknown
88	11		
89	1	DATE	7/31/2000
89	2	COUNTRY	Nigeria
89	3	CITY	Unknown
89	4	PERPETRATOR	Unknown
89	5	FATALITIES	0
89	6	INJURED	0
89	7	TARGET TYPE	Business,Business
89	8	REGION	Sub-Saharan Africa
89	9	ATTACK TYPE	Armed Assault,Hostage Taking (Kidnapping)
89	10	WEAPON TYPE	Unknown
89	11		
90	1	DATE	6/10/2001
90	2	COUNTRY	Nigeria
90	3	CITY	Unknown
90	4	PERPETRATOR	Unknown
90	5	FATALITIES	0
90	6	INJURED	2
90	7	TARGET TYPE	Government (General)
90	8	REGION	Sub-Saharan Africa
90	9	ATTACK TYPE	Bombing/Explosion
90	10	WEAPON TYPE	Explosives/Bombs/Dynamite
90	11		
91	1	DATE	6/27/2001
91	2	COUNTRY	Nigeria
91	3	CITY	Finima
91	4	PERPETRATOR	Militants (suspected)
91	5	FATALITIES	0

91	6	INJURED	0
91	7	TARGET TYPE	Business
91	8	REGION	Sub-Saharan Africa
91	9	ATTACK TYPE	Hostage Taking (Kidnapping)
91	10	WEAPON TYPE	Unknown
91	11		
92	1	DATE	8/19/2001
92	2	COUNTRY	Nigeria
92	3	CITY	Lagos
92	4	PERPETRATOR	Odua Peoples' Congress (OPC)
92	5	FATALITIES	0
92	6	INJURED	0
92	7	TARGET TYPE	Police
92	8	REGION	Sub-Saharan Africa
92	9	ATTACK TYPE	Facility/Infrastructure Attack,Hostage Taking (Kidnapping)
92	10	WEAPON TYPE	Firearms
92	11		
93	1	DATE	12/17/2001
93	2	COUNTRY	Nigeria
93	3	CITY	Abia
93	4	PERPETRATOR	Movement for the Actualization of the Sovereign State of Biafra (MASSOB)
93	5	FATALITIES	2
93	6	INJURED	1
93	7	TARGET TYPE	Police
93	8	REGION	Sub-Saharan Africa
93	9	ATTACK TYPE	Armed Assault
93	10	WEAPON TYPE	Firearms
93	11		
94	1	DATE	12/23/2001
94	2	COUNTRY	Nigeria
94	3	CITY	Ibadan
94	4	PERPETRATOR	People's Democratic Party (PDP) (suspected)
94	5	FATALITIES	1
94	6	INJURED	0
94	7	TARGET TYPE	Government (General)
94	8	REGION	Sub-Saharan Africa
94	9	ATTACK TYPE	Assassination
94	10	WEAPON TYPE	Firearms
94	11		
95	1	DATE	1/2/2002
95	2	COUNTRY	Nigeria
95	3	CITY	Donga
95	4	PERPETRATOR	Unknown
95	5	FATALITIES	8

95	6	INJURED	5
95	7	TARGET TYPE	Private Citizens & Property
95	8	REGION	Sub-Saharan Africa
95	9	ATTACK TYPE	Armed Assault
95	10	WEAPON TYPE	Firearms
95	11		
96	1	DATE	8/16/2002
96	2	COUNTRY	Nigeria
96	3	CITY	Ayetoro
96	4	PERPETRATOR	Unknown
96	5	FATALITIES	2
96	6	INJURED	1
96	7	TARGET TYPE	Government (General)
96	8	REGION	Sub-Saharan Africa
96	9	ATTACK TYPE	Assassination
96	10	WEAPON TYPE	Firearms
96	11		
97	1	DATE	9/22/2002
97	2	COUNTRY	Nigeria
97	3	CITY	Kano
97	4	PERPETRATOR	Gunmen (suspected)
97	5	FATALITIES	1
97	6	INJURED	0
97	7	TARGET TYPE	Government (General)
97	8	REGION	Sub-Saharan Africa
97	9	ATTACK TYPE	Assassination
97	10	WEAPON TYPE	Firearms
97	11		
98	1	DATE	11/2/2002
98	2	COUNTRY	Nigeria
98	3	CITY	Namaran
98	4	PERPETRATOR	Unknown
98	5	FATALITIES	3
98	6	INJURED	0
98	7	TARGET TYPE	Government (General)
98	8	REGION	Sub-Saharan Africa
98	9	ATTACK TYPE	Armed Assault
98	10	WEAPON TYPE	Melee
98	11		
99	1	DATE	11/15/2002
99	2	COUNTRY	Nigeria
99	3	CITY	Ilorin
99	4	PERPETRATOR	Unknown
99	5	FATALITIES	0
99	6	INJURED	5
99	7	TARGET TYPE	Journalists & Media,Private Citizens & Property

99	8	REGION	Sub-Saharan Africa
99	9	ATTACK TYPE	Bombing/Explosion
99	10	WEAPON TYPE	Explosives/Bombs/Dynamite
99	11		
100	1	DATE	12/13/2002
100	2	COUNTRY	Nigeria
100	3	CITY	Rim
100	4	PERPETRATOR	Other
100	5	FATALITIES	14
100	6	INJURED	0
100	7	TARGET TYPE	Private Citizens & Property
100	8	REGION	Sub-Saharan Africa
100	9	ATTACK TYPE	Armed Assault
100	10	WEAPON TYPE	Firearms
100	11		
101	1	DATE	2/2/2003
101	2	COUNTRY	Nigeria
101	3	CITY	Lagos
101	4	PERPETRATOR	Unknown
101	5	FATALITIES	20
101	6	INJURED	43
101	7	TARGET TYPE	Business,Private Citizens & Property
101	8	REGION	Sub-Saharan Africa
101	9	ATTACK TYPE	Bombing/Explosion
101	10	WEAPON TYPE	Explosives/Bombs/Dynamite
101	11		
102	1	DATE	2/8/2003
102	2	COUNTRY	Nigeria
102	3	CITY	Owerri
102	4	PERPETRATOR	Unknown
102	5	FATALITIES	1
102	6	INJURED	0
102	7	TARGET TYPE	Government (General)
102	8	REGION	Sub-Saharan Africa
102	9	ATTACK TYPE	Assassination
102	10	WEAPON TYPE	Firearms
102	11		
103	1	DATE	4/8/2003
103	2	COUNTRY	Nigeria
103	3	CITY	Warri
103	4	PERPETRATOR	Unknown
103	5	FATALITIES	0
103	6	INJURED	0
103	7	TARGET TYPE	Business
103	8	REGION	Sub-Saharan Africa
103	9	ATTACK TYPE	Bombing/Explosion

103	10	WEAPON TYPE	Explosives/Bombs/Dynamite
103	11		
104	1	DATE	4/14/2003
104	2	COUNTRY	Nigeria
104	3	CITY	Ugbuwangue
104	4	PERPETRATOR	Unknown
104	5	FATALITIES	6
104	6	INJURED	Unknown
104	7	TARGET TYPE	Private Citizens & Property
104	8	REGION	Sub-Saharan Africa
104	9	ATTACK TYPE	Armed Assault
104	10	WEAPON TYPE	Firearms
104	11		
105	1	DATE	4/19/2003
105	2	COUNTRY	Nigeria
105	3	CITY	Unknown
105	4	PERPETRATOR	Strikers
105	5	FATALITIES	0
105	6	INJURED	0
105	7	TARGET TYPE	Business,Private Citizens & Property
105	8	REGION	Sub-Saharan Africa
105	9	ATTACK TYPE	Hostage Taking (Barricade Incident)
105	10	WEAPON TYPE	Unknown
105	11		
106	1	DATE	5/24/2003
106	2	COUNTRY	Nigeria
106	3	CITY	Ajama
106	4	PERPETRATOR	Other (suspected)
106	5	FATALITIES	0
106	6	INJURED	0
106	7	TARGET TYPE	Utilities
106	8	REGION	Sub-Saharan Africa
106	9	ATTACK TYPE	Bombing/Explosion
106	10	WEAPON TYPE	Explosives/Bombs/Dynamite
106	11		
107	1	DATE	7/27/2003
107	2	COUNTRY	Nigeria
107	3	CITY	Warri
107	4	PERPETRATOR	Egbema National Front
107	5	FATALITIES	0
107	6	INJURED	0
107	7	TARGET TYPE	Business
107	8	REGION	Sub-Saharan Africa
107	9	ATTACK TYPE	Hostage Taking (Kidnapping)
107	10	WEAPON TYPE	Firearms
107	11		

108	1	DATE	11/19/2003
108	2	COUNTRY	Nigeria
108	3	CITY	Unknown
108	4	PERPETRATOR	Bini-Oru
108	5	FATALITIES	1
108	6	INJURED	1
108	7	TARGET TYPE	Business,Private Citizens & Property
108	8	REGION	Sub-Saharan Africa
108	9	ATTACK TYPE	Hostage Taking (Kidnapping),Armed Assault
108	10	WEAPON TYPE	Firearms
108	11		
109	1	DATE	11/27/2003
109	2	COUNTRY	Nigeria
109	3	CITY	Warri
109	4	PERPETRATOR	Ijaw militants
109	5	FATALITIES	0
109	6	INJURED	0
109	7	TARGET TYPE	Business,Business
109	8	REGION	Sub-Saharan Africa
109	9	ATTACK TYPE	Hostage Taking (Kidnapping),Armed Assault
109	10	WEAPON TYPE	Firearms
109	11		
110	1	DATE	1/7/2004
110	2	COUNTRY	Nigeria
110	3	CITY	Abuja
110	4	PERPETRATOR	Unknown
110	5	FATALITIES	1
110	6	INJURED	0
110	7	TARGET TYPE	Military
110	8	REGION	Sub-Saharan Africa
110	9	ATTACK TYPE	Assassination
110	10	WEAPON TYPE	Firearms
110	11		
111	1	DATE	1/8/2004
111	2	COUNTRY	Nigeria
111	3	CITY	Port Harcourt
111	4	PERPETRATOR	Unknown
111	5	FATALITIES	8
111	6	INJURED	2
111	7	TARGET TYPE	Police,Private Citizens & Property
111	8	REGION	Sub-Saharan Africa
111	9	ATTACK TYPE	Armed Assault,Bombing/Explosion
111	10	WEAPON TYPE	Firearms,Explosives/Bombs/Dynamite
111	11		
112	1	DATE	1/9/2004
112	2	COUNTRY	Nigeria

112	3	CITY	Warri
112	4	PERPETRATOR	Unknown
112	5	FATALITIES	18
112	6	INJURED	0
112	7	TARGET TYPE	Private Citizens & Property
112	8	REGION	Sub-Saharan Africa
112	9	ATTACK TYPE	Armed Assault
112	10	WEAPON TYPE	Firearms
112	11		
113	1	DATE	3/8/2004
113	2	COUNTRY	Nigeria
113	3	CITY	Lokoja
113	4	PERPETRATOR	Unknown
113	5	FATALITIES	1
113	6	INJURED	0
113	7	TARGET TYPE	Government (General)
113	8	REGION	Sub-Saharan Africa
113	9	ATTACK TYPE	Assassination
113	10	WEAPON TYPE	Firearms
113	11		
114	1	DATE	4/22/2004
114	2	COUNTRY	Nigeria
114	3	CITY	Warri
114	4	PERPETRATOR	Itsekiri (suspected)
114	5	FATALITIES	10
114	6	INJURED	4
114	7	TARGET TYPE	Private Citizens & Property
114	8	REGION	Sub-Saharan Africa
114	9	ATTACK TYPE	Armed Assault
114	10	WEAPON TYPE	Firearms
114	11		
115	1	DATE	10/9/2004
115	2	COUNTRY	Nigeria
115	3	CITY	Kala-Balge Bushes
115	4	PERPETRATOR	Al-Sunna wal Jamma (suspected)
115	5	FATALITIES	3
115	6	INJURED	Unknown
115	7	TARGET TYPE	Police
115	8	REGION	Sub-Saharan Africa
115	9	ATTACK TYPE	Armed Assault,Hostage Taking (Kidnapping)
115	10	WEAPON TYPE	Firearms
115	11		
116	1	DATE	1/3/2005
116	2	COUNTRY	Nigeria
116	3	CITY	Iyanomo
116	4	PERPETRATOR	Unknown

116	5	FATALITIES	0
116	6	INJURED	1
116	7	TARGET TYPE	Police,Military
116	8	REGION	Sub-Saharan Africa
116	9	ATTACK TYPE	Armed Assault
116	10	WEAPON TYPE	Firearms
116	11		
117	1	DATE	5/5/2005
117	2	COUNTRY	Nigeria
117	3	CITY	Nabordo
117	4	PERPETRATOR	Unknown
117	5	FATALITIES	1
117	6	INJURED	0
117	7	TARGET TYPE	Police,Utilities
117	8	REGION	Sub-Saharan Africa
117	9	ATTACK TYPE	Armed Assault,Facility/Infrastructure Attack
117	10	WEAPON TYPE	Firearms,Unknown
117	11		
118	1	DATE	5/13/2005
118	2	COUNTRY	Nigeria
118	3	CITY	Sokoto
118	4	PERPETRATOR	Other
118	5	FATALITIES	2
118	6	INJURED	35
118	7	TARGET TYPE	Religious Figures/Institutions
118	8	REGION	Sub-Saharan Africa
118	9	ATTACK TYPE	Armed Assault
118	10	WEAPON TYPE	Melee,Incendiary,Melee
118	11		
119	1	DATE	6/15/2005
119	2	COUNTRY	Nigeria
119	3	CITY	Warri
119	4	PERPETRATOR	Ijaw militants
119	5	FATALITIES	0
119	6	INJURED	0
119	7	TARGET TYPE	Business,Business
119	8	REGION	Sub-Saharan Africa
119	9	ATTACK TYPE	Hostage Taking (Barricade Incident)
119	10	WEAPON TYPE	Unknown
119	11		
120	1	DATE	6/16/2005
120	2	COUNTRY	Nigeria
120	3	CITY	Unknown
120	4	PERPETRATOR	Unknown
120	5	FATALITIES	0
120	6	INJURED	0

120	7	TARGET TYPE	Business,Private Citizens & Property
120	8	REGION	Sub-Saharan Africa
120	9	ATTACK TYPE	Hostage Taking (Barricade Incident)
120	10	WEAPON TYPE	Unknown
120	11		
121	1	DATE	9/22/2005
121	2	COUNTRY	Nigeria
121	3	CITY	Akututuru
121	4	PERPETRATOR	Niger Delta People's Volunteer Force (NDPVF) (suspected)
121	5	FATALITIES	0
121	6	INJURED	0
121	7	TARGET TYPE	Utilities
121	8	REGION	Sub-Saharan Africa
121	9	ATTACK TYPE	Facility/Infrastructure Attack
121	10	WEAPON TYPE	Firearms
121	11		
122	1	DATE	12/20/2005
122	2	COUNTRY	Nigeria
122	3	CITY	Agba Okwan Asarama
122	4	PERPETRATOR	Unknown
122	5	FATALITIES	11
122	6	INJURED	Unknown
122	7	TARGET TYPE	Business
122	8	REGION	Sub-Saharan Africa
122	9	ATTACK TYPE	Facility/Infrastructure Attack
122	10	WEAPON TYPE	Explosives/Bombs/Dynamite
122	11		
123	1	DATE	12/21/2005
123	2	COUNTRY	Nigeria
123	3	CITY	Ehor
123	4	PERPETRATOR	Unknown
123	5	FATALITIES	5
123	6	INJURED	Unknown
123	7	TARGET TYPE	Business
123	8	REGION	Sub-Saharan Africa
123	9	ATTACK TYPE	Facility/Infrastructure Attack
123	10	WEAPON TYPE	Explosives/Bombs/Dynamite
123	11		
124	1	DATE	12/26/2005
124	2	COUNTRY	Nigeria
124	3	CITY	Adeje
124	4	PERPETRATOR	Unknown
124	5	FATALITIES	Unknown
124	6	INJURED	Unknown
124	7	TARGET TYPE	Business

124	8	REGION	Sub-Saharan Africa
124	9	ATTACK TYPE	Bombing/Explosion,Facility/Infrastructure Attack
124	10	WEAPON TYPE	Explosives/Bombs/Dynamite
124	11		
125	1	DATE	1/11/2006
125	2	COUNTRY	Nigeria
125	3	CITY	Unknown
125	4	PERPETRATOR	Unknown
125	5	FATALITIES	0
125	6	INJURED	0
125	7	TARGET TYPE	Business
125	8	REGION	Sub-Saharan Africa
125	9	ATTACK TYPE	Hostage Taking (Kidnapping)
125	10	WEAPON TYPE	Firearms
125	11		
126	1	DATE	1/24/2006
126	2	COUNTRY	Nigeria
126	3	CITY	Port Harcourt
126	4	PERPETRATOR	Unknown
126	5	FATALITIES	9
126	6	INJURED	Unknown
126	7	TARGET TYPE	Business
126	8	REGION	Sub-Saharan Africa
126	9	ATTACK TYPE	Armed Assault
126	10	WEAPON TYPE	Firearms
126	11		
127	1	DATE	1/29/2006
127	2	COUNTRY	Nigeria
127	3	CITY	Port Harcourt
127	4	PERPETRATOR	Unknown
127	5	FATALITIES	0
127	6	INJURED	0
127	7	TARGET TYPE	Business
127	8	REGION	Sub-Saharan Africa
127	9	ATTACK TYPE	Armed Assault
127	10	WEAPON TYPE	Firearms
127	11		
128	1	DATE	1/29/2006
128	2	COUNTRY	Nigeria
128	3	CITY	Kano
128	4	PERPETRATOR	Unknown
128	5	FATALITIES	0
128	6	INJURED	0
128	7	TARGET TYPE	Government (General)
128	8	REGION	Sub-Saharan Africa
128	9	ATTACK TYPE	Facility/Infrastructure Attack

128	10	WEAPON TYPE	Incendiary
128	11		
129	1	DATE	3/3/2006
129	2	COUNTRY	Nigeria
129	3	CITY	0
129	4	PERPETRATOR	Unknown
129	5	FATALITIES	0
129	6	INJURED	0
129	7	TARGET TYPE	Business,Utilities
129	8	REGION	Sub-Saharan Africa
129	9	ATTACK TYPE	Facility/Infrastructure Attack
129	10	WEAPON TYPE	Sabotage Equipment
129	11		
130	1	DATE	4/19/2006
130	2	COUNTRY	Nigeria
130	3	CITY	Port Harcourt
130	4	PERPETRATOR	Movement for the Emancipation of the Niger Delta (MEND)
130	5	FATALITIES	2
130	6	INJURED	7
130	7	TARGET TYPE	Military
130	8	REGION	Sub-Saharan Africa
130	9	ATTACK TYPE	Facility/Infrastructure Attack
130	10	WEAPON TYPE	Explosives/Bombs/Dynamite
130	11		
131	1	DATE	5/10/2006
131	2	COUNTRY	Nigeria
131	3	CITY	0
131	4	PERPETRATOR	Unknown
131	5	FATALITIES	1
131	6	INJURED	0
131	7	TARGET TYPE	Business
131	8	REGION	Sub-Saharan Africa
131	9	ATTACK TYPE	Armed Assault
131	10	WEAPON TYPE	Firearms
131	11		
132	1	DATE	5/11/2006
132	2	COUNTRY	Nigeria
132	3	CITY	Port Harcourt
132	4	PERPETRATOR	Gugama Youth Federation
132	5	FATALITIES	0
132	6	INJURED	0
132	7	TARGET TYPE	Business
132	8	REGION	Sub-Saharan Africa
132	9	ATTACK TYPE	Hostage Taking (Kidnapping)
132	10	WEAPON TYPE	Unknown

132	11		
133	1	DATE	5/12/2006
133	2	COUNTRY	Nigeria
133	3	CITY	0
133	4	PERPETRATOR	Movement for the Emancipation of the Niger Delta (MEND)
133	5	FATALITIES	200
133	6	INJURED	Unknown
133	7	TARGET TYPE	Utilities
133	8	REGION	Sub-Saharan Africa
133	9	ATTACK TYPE	Bombing/Explosion
133	10	WEAPON TYPE	Explosives/Bombs/Dynamite
133	11		
134	1	DATE	5/14/2006
134	2	COUNTRY	Nigeria
134	3	CITY	Port Harcourt
134	4	PERPETRATOR	Unknown
134	5	FATALITIES	4
134	6	INJURED	2
134	7	TARGET TYPE	Police
134	8	REGION	Sub-Saharan Africa
134	9	ATTACK TYPE	Armed Assault
134	10	WEAPON TYPE	Firearms
134	11		
135	1	DATE	6/2/2006
135	2	COUNTRY	Nigeria
135	3	CITY	Warri
135	4	PERPETRATOR	Unknown
135	5	FATALITIES	0
135	6	INJURED	0
135	7	TARGET TYPE	Business
135	8	REGION	Sub-Saharan Africa
135	9	ATTACK TYPE	Hostage Taking (Kidnapping)
135	10	WEAPON TYPE	Firearms
135	11		
136	1	DATE	6/7/2006
136	2	COUNTRY	Nigeria
136	3	CITY	Port Harcourt
136	4	PERPETRATOR	Movement for the Emancipation of the Niger Delta (MEND)
136	5	FATALITIES	6
136	6	INJURED	0
136	7	TARGET TYPE	Business,Business,Military
136	8	REGION	Sub-Saharan Africa
136	9	ATTACK TYPE	Hostage Taking (Kidnapping),Armed Assault
136	10	WEAPON TYPE	Explosives/Bombs/Dynamite,Firearms

136	11		
137	1	DATE	6/28/2006
137	2	COUNTRY	Nigeria
137	3	CITY	Onitsha
137	4	PERPETRATOR	Movement for the Actualization of the Sovereign State of Biafra (MASSOB) (suspected)
137	5	FATALITIES	0
137	6	INJURED	1
137	7	TARGET TYPE	Private Citizens & Property
137	8	REGION	Sub-Saharan Africa
137	9	ATTACK TYPE	Armed Assault
137	10	WEAPON TYPE	Melee
137	11		
138	1	DATE	6/30/2006
138	2	COUNTRY	Nigeria
138	3	CITY	Jos
138	4	PERPETRATOR	People's Democratic Party (PDP) (suspected)
138	5	FATALITIES	1
138	6	INJURED	1
138	7	TARGET TYPE	Government (General)
138	8	REGION	Sub-Saharan Africa
138	9	ATTACK TYPE	Assassination
138	10	WEAPON TYPE	Unknown
138	11		
139	1	DATE	7/5/2006
139	2	COUNTRY	Nigeria
139	3	CITY	Off-shore Oil Rig
139	4	PERPETRATOR	Unknown
139	5	FATALITIES	Unknown
139	6	INJURED	Unknown
139	7	TARGET TYPE	Business
139	8	REGION	Sub-Saharan Africa
139	9	ATTACK TYPE	Hostage Taking (Kidnapping)
139	10	WEAPON TYPE	Firearms
139	11		
140	1	DATE	7/6/2006
140	2	COUNTRY	Nigeria
140	3	CITY	Sagana
140	4	PERPETRATOR	Unknown
140	5	FATALITIES	Unknown
140	6	INJURED	Unknown
140	7	TARGET TYPE	Business
140	8	REGION	Sub-Saharan Africa
140	9	ATTACK TYPE	Hostage Taking (Kidnapping)
140	10	WEAPON TYPE	Firearms
140	11		

141	1	DATE	7/6/2006
141	2	COUNTRY	Nigeria
141	3	CITY	Gbaran
141	4	PERPETRATOR	Unknown
141	5	FATALITIES	Unknown
141	6	INJURED	Unknown
141	7	TARGET TYPE	Business
141	8	REGION	Sub-Saharan Africa
141	9	ATTACK TYPE	Hostage Taking (Kidnapping)
141	10	WEAPON TYPE	Firearms
141	11		
142	1	DATE	7/27/2006
142	2	COUNTRY	Nigeria
142	3	CITY	Ikoyi
142	4	PERPETRATOR	Unknown
142	5	FATALITIES	1
142	6	INJURED	0
142	7	TARGET TYPE	Violent Political Party
142	8	REGION	Sub-Saharan Africa
142	9	ATTACK TYPE	Assassination
142	10	WEAPON TYPE	Melee,Melee
142	11		
143	1	DATE	8/3/2006
143	2	COUNTRY	Nigeria
143	3	CITY	Port Harcourt
143	4	PERPETRATOR	Movement for the Emancipation of the Niger Delta (MEND)
143	5	FATALITIES	0
143	6	INJURED	0
143	7	TARGET TYPE	Utilities
143	8	REGION	Sub-Saharan Africa
143	9	ATTACK TYPE	Hostage Taking (Kidnapping)
143	10	WEAPON TYPE	Firearms
143	11		
144	1	DATE	8/14/2006
144	2	COUNTRY	Nigeria
144	3	CITY	Ijan
144	4	PERPETRATOR	Unknown
144	5	FATALITIES	1
144	6	INJURED	0
144	7	TARGET TYPE	Violent Political Party
144	8	REGION	Sub-Saharan Africa
144	9	ATTACK TYPE	Assassination
144	10	WEAPON TYPE	Melee
144	11		
145	1	DATE	8/24/2006

145	2	COUNTRY	Nigeria
145	3	CITY	Port Harcourt
145	4	PERPETRATOR	Unknown
145	5	FATALITIES	1
145	6	INJURED	6
145	7	TARGET TYPE	Utilities
145	8	REGION	Sub-Saharan Africa
145	9	ATTACK TYPE	Facility/Infrastructure Attack
145	10	WEAPON TYPE	Firearms
145	11		
146	1	DATE	8/26/2006
146	2	COUNTRY	Nigeria
146	3	CITY	Port Harcourt
146	4	PERPETRATOR	Unknown
146	5	FATALITIES	1
146	6	INJURED	0
146	7	TARGET TYPE	Utilities
146	8	REGION	Sub-Saharan Africa
146	9	ATTACK TYPE	Hostage Taking (Kidnapping),Armed Assault
146	10	WEAPON TYPE	Firearms
146	11		
147	1	DATE	10/2/2006
147	2	COUNTRY	Nigeria
147	3	CITY	Niger Delta
147	4	PERPETRATOR	The Joint Revolutionary Council
147	5	FATALITIES	14
147	6	INJURED	Unknown
147	7	TARGET TYPE	Business
147	8	REGION	Sub-Saharan Africa
147	9	ATTACK TYPE	Armed Assault
147	10	WEAPON TYPE	Firearms
147	11		
148	1	DATE	10/4/2006
148	2	COUNTRY	Nigeria
148	3	CITY	Eket
148	4	PERPETRATOR	Unknown
148	5	FATALITIES	2
148	6	INJURED	Unknown
148	7	TARGET TYPE	Business
148	8	REGION	Sub-Saharan Africa
148	9	ATTACK TYPE	Armed Assault,Hostage Taking (Kidnapping)
148	10	WEAPON TYPE	Firearms
148	11		
149	1	DATE	10/10/2006
149	2	COUNTRY	Nigeria
149	3	CITY	0

149	4	PERPETRATOR	Unknown
149	5	FATALITIES	Unknown
149	6	INJURED	Unknown
149	7	TARGET TYPE	Military
149	8	REGION	Sub-Saharan Africa
149	9	ATTACK TYPE	Hostage Taking (Kidnapping),Armed Assault
149	10	WEAPON TYPE	Firearms
149	11		
150	1	DATE	11/6/2006
150	2	COUNTRY	Nigeria
150	3	CITY	Yenagoa
150	4	PERPETRATOR	Unknown
150	5	FATALITIES	0
150	6	INJURED	0
150	7	TARGET TYPE	Utilities
150	8	REGION	Sub-Saharan Africa
150	9	ATTACK TYPE	Hostage Taking (Kidnapping)
150	10	WEAPON TYPE	Firearms
150	11		
151	1	DATE	11/20/2006
151	2	COUNTRY	Nigeria
151	3	CITY	0
151	4	PERPETRATOR	Unknown
151	5	FATALITIES	2
151	6	INJURED	2
151	7	TARGET TYPE	Private Citizens & Property
151	8	REGION	Sub-Saharan Africa
151	9	ATTACK TYPE	Assassination
151	10	WEAPON TYPE	Firearms
151	11		
152	1	DATE	11/22/2006
152	2	COUNTRY	Nigeria
152	3	CITY	0
152	4	PERPETRATOR	Movement for the Emancipation of the Niger Delta (MEND) (suspected)
152	5	FATALITIES	4
152	6	INJURED	1
152	7	TARGET TYPE	Business
152	8	REGION	Sub-Saharan Africa
152	9	ATTACK TYPE	Hostage Taking (Barricade Incident)
152	10	WEAPON TYPE	Firearms
152	11		
153	1	DATE	12/3/2006
153	2	COUNTRY	Nigeria
153	3	CITY	Okono/Okpoho
153	4	PERPETRATOR	Niger Delta Vigilante (NDV)

153	5	FATALITIES	1
153	6	INJURED	Unknown
153	7	TARGET TYPE	Maritime
153	8	REGION	Sub-Saharan Africa
153	9	ATTACK TYPE	Hostage Taking (Barricade Incident),Facility/Infrastructure Attack
153	10	WEAPON TYPE	Unknown
153	11		
154	1	DATE	12/8/2006
154	2	COUNTRY	Nigeria
154	3	CITY	Brass
154	4	PERPETRATOR	Unknown
154	5	FATALITIES	1
154	6	INJURED	1
154	7	TARGET TYPE	Business
154	8	REGION	Sub-Saharan Africa
154	9	ATTACK TYPE	Facility/Infrastructure Attack,Hostage Taking (Kidnapping)
154	10	WEAPON TYPE	Firearms,Incendiary
154	11		
155	1	DATE	12/10/2006
155	2	COUNTRY	Nigeria
155	3	CITY	Port Harcourt
155	4	PERPETRATOR	Unknown
155	5	FATALITIES	0
155	6	INJURED	0
155	7	TARGET TYPE	Other
155	8	REGION	Sub-Saharan Africa
155	9	ATTACK TYPE	Bombing/Explosion
155	10	WEAPON TYPE	Explosives/Bombs/Dynamite
155	11		
156	1	DATE	12/13/2006
156	2	COUNTRY	Nigeria
156	3	CITY	Okono/Okpoho
156	4	PERPETRATOR	Movement for the Emancipation of the Niger Delta (MEND)
156	5	FATALITIES	0
156	6	INJURED	0
156	7	TARGET TYPE	Business
156	8	REGION	Sub-Saharan Africa
156	9	ATTACK TYPE	Facility/Infrastructure Attack,Hostage Taking (Kidnapping)
156	10	WEAPON TYPE	Unknown
156	11		
157	1	DATE	12/15/2006
157	2	COUNTRY	Nigeria

157	3	CITY	Okono/Okpoho
157	4	PERPETRATOR	Unknown
157	5	FATALITIES	0
157	6	INJURED	Unknown
157	7	TARGET TYPE	Business
157	8	REGION	Sub-Saharan Africa
157	9	ATTACK TYPE	Hostage Taking (Kidnapping)
157	10	WEAPON TYPE	Firearms
157	11		
158	1	DATE	12/18/2006
158	2	COUNTRY	Nigeria
158	3	CITY	Port Harcourt
158	4	PERPETRATOR	Movement for the Emancipation of the Niger Delta (MEND)
158	5	FATALITIES	0
158	6	INJURED	0
158	7	TARGET TYPE	Business,Business
158	8	REGION	Sub-Saharan Africa
158	9	ATTACK TYPE	Bombing/Explosion
158	10	WEAPON TYPE	Explosives/Bombs/Dynamite
158	11		
159	1	DATE	12/20/2006
159	2	COUNTRY	Nigeria
159	3	CITY	Obagi
159	4	PERPETRATOR	Unknown
159	5	FATALITIES	3
159	6	INJURED	0
159	7	TARGET TYPE	Business
159	8	REGION	Sub-Saharan Africa
159	9	ATTACK TYPE	Armed Assault
159	10	WEAPON TYPE	Firearms
159	11		
160	1	DATE	12/23/2006
160	2	COUNTRY	Nigeria
160	3	CITY	Port Harcourt and Warri
160	4	PERPETRATOR	Unknown
160	5	FATALITIES	0
160	6	INJURED	0
160	7	TARGET TYPE	Business
160	8	REGION	Sub-Saharan Africa
160	9	ATTACK TYPE	Bombing/Explosion
160	10	WEAPON TYPE	Explosives/Bombs/Dynamite
160	11		
161	1	DATE	12/24/2006
161	2	COUNTRY	Nigeria
161	3	CITY	Port Harcourt

161	4	PERPETRATOR	Movement for the Emancipation of the Niger Delta (MEND)
161	5	FATALITIES	0
161	6	INJURED	0
161	7	TARGET TYPE	Government (Diplomatic)
161	8	REGION	Sub-Saharan Africa
161	9	ATTACK TYPE	Bombing/Explosion
161	10	WEAPON TYPE	Explosives/Bombs/Dynamite
161	11		
162	1	DATE	1/5/2007
162	2	COUNTRY	Nigeria
162	3	CITY	Port Harcourt
162	4	PERPETRATOR	Unknown
162	5	FATALITIES	0
162	6	INJURED	0
162	7	TARGET TYPE	Business
162	8	REGION	Sub-Saharan Africa
162	9	ATTACK TYPE	Hostage Taking (Kidnapping)
162	10	WEAPON TYPE	Firearms
162	11		
163	1	DATE	1/10/2007
163	2	COUNTRY	Nigeria
163	3	CITY	Yenagoa
163	4	PERPETRATOR	Movement for the Emancipation of the Niger Delta (MEND)
163	5	FATALITIES	0
163	6	INJURED	0
163	7	TARGET TYPE	Business
163	8	REGION	Sub-Saharan Africa
163	9	ATTACK TYPE	Hostage Taking (Kidnapping)
163	10	WEAPON TYPE	Firearms
163	11		
164	1	DATE	1/13/2007
164	2	COUNTRY	Nigeria
164	3	CITY	Ekulama
164	4	PERPETRATOR	Unknown
164	5	FATALITIES	12
164	6	INJURED	0
164	7	TARGET TYPE	Government (Diplomatic),Private Citizens & Property
164	8	REGION	Sub-Saharan Africa
164	9	ATTACK TYPE	Armed Assault
164	10	WEAPON TYPE	Firearms
164	11		
165	1	DATE	1/20/2007
165	2	COUNTRY	Nigeria

165	3	CITY	0
165	4	PERPETRATOR	Movement for the Emancipation of the Niger Delta (MEND) (suspected)
165	5	FATALITIES	0
165	6	INJURED	0
165	7	TARGET TYPE	Private Citizens & Property
165	8	REGION	Sub-Saharan Africa
165	9	ATTACK TYPE	Hostage Taking (Kidnapping)
165	10	WEAPON TYPE	Firearms
165	11		
166	1	DATE	1/23/2007
166	2	COUNTRY	Nigeria
166	3	CITY	Port Harcourt
166	4	PERPETRATOR	Unknown
166	5	FATALITIES	0
166	6	INJURED	0
166	7	TARGET TYPE	Business
166	8	REGION	Sub-Saharan Africa
166	9	ATTACK TYPE	Hostage Taking (Kidnapping)
166	10	WEAPON TYPE	Firearms
166	11		
167	1	DATE	1/25/2007
167	2	COUNTRY	Nigeria
167	3	CITY	Sagbama
167	4	PERPETRATOR	Unknown
167	5	FATALITIES	1
167	6	INJURED	0
167	7	TARGET TYPE	Business
167	8	REGION	Sub-Saharan Africa
167	9	ATTACK TYPE	Hostage Taking (Kidnapping)
167	10	WEAPON TYPE	Firearms
167	11		
168	1	DATE	2/6/2007
168	2	COUNTRY	Nigeria
168	3	CITY	0
168	4	PERPETRATOR	Unknown
168	5	FATALITIES	0
168	6	INJURED	0
168	7	TARGET TYPE	Business
168	8	REGION	Sub-Saharan Africa
168	9	ATTACK TYPE	Hostage Taking (Kidnapping)
168	10	WEAPON TYPE	Firearms
168	11		
169	1	DATE	2/9/2007
169	2	COUNTRY	Nigeria
169	3	CITY	Port Hartcourt

169	4	PERPETRATOR	Unknown
169	5	FATALITIES	Unknown
169	6	INJURED	Unknown
169	7	TARGET TYPE	Private Citizens & Property
169	8	REGION	Sub-Saharan Africa
169	9	ATTACK TYPE	Hostage Taking (Kidnapping)
169	10	WEAPON TYPE	Melee
169	11		
170	1	DATE	2/9/2007
170	2	COUNTRY	Nigeria
170	3	CITY	Port Hartcourt
170	4	PERPETRATOR	Unknown
170	5	FATALITIES	2
170	6	INJURED	0
170	7	TARGET TYPE	Military
170	8	REGION	Sub-Saharan Africa
170	9	ATTACK TYPE	Armed Assault
170	10	WEAPON TYPE	Firearms
170	11		
171	1	DATE	2/9/2007
171	2	COUNTRY	Nigeria
171	3	CITY	Port Hartcourt
171	4	PERPETRATOR	Unknown
171	5	FATALITIES	0
171	6	INJURED	1
171	7	TARGET TYPE	Business
171	8	REGION	Sub-Saharan Africa
171	9	ATTACK TYPE	Hostage Taking (Kidnapping)
171	10	WEAPON TYPE	Firearms
171	11		
172	1	DATE	2/19/2007
172	2	COUNTRY	Nigeria
172	3	CITY	Port Harcourt
172	4	PERPETRATOR	Unknown
172	5	FATALITIES	0
172	6	INJURED	0
172	7	TARGET TYPE	Private Citizens & Property
172	8	REGION	Sub-Saharan Africa
172	9	ATTACK TYPE	Hostage Taking (Kidnapping)
172	10	WEAPON TYPE	Firearms
172	11		
173	1	DATE	2/23/2007
173	2	COUNTRY	Nigeria
173	3	CITY	Port Harcourt
173	4	PERPETRATOR	Unknown
173	5	FATALITIES	0

173	6	INJURED	Unknown
173	7	TARGET TYPE	Business
173	8	REGION	Sub-Saharan Africa
173	9	ATTACK TYPE	Hostage Taking (Kidnapping)
173	10	WEAPON TYPE	Firearms
173	11		
174	1	DATE	2/23/2007
174	2	COUNTRY	Nigeria
174	3	CITY	0
174	4	PERPETRATOR	Unknown
174	5	FATALITIES	1
174	6	INJURED	1
174	7	TARGET TYPE	Private Citizens & Property
174	8	REGION	Sub-Saharan Africa
174	9	ATTACK TYPE	Armed Assault
174	10	WEAPON TYPE	Firearms
174	11		
175	1	DATE	2/28/2007
175	2	COUNTRY	Nigeria
175	3	CITY	0
175	4	PERPETRATOR	Unknown
175	5	FATALITIES	Unknown
175	6	INJURED	Unknown
175	7	TARGET TYPE	Private Citizens & Property
175	8	REGION	Sub-Saharan Africa
175	9	ATTACK TYPE	Hostage Taking (Kidnapping)
175	10	WEAPON TYPE	Firearms
175	11		
176	1	DATE	3/23/2007
176	2	COUNTRY	Nigeria
176	3	CITY	Port Harcourt
176	4	PERPETRATOR	Unknown
176	5	FATALITIES	0
176	6	INJURED	0
176	7	TARGET TYPE	Utilities
176	8	REGION	Sub-Saharan Africa
176	9	ATTACK TYPE	Hostage Taking (Kidnapping)
176	10	WEAPON TYPE	Firearms
176	11		
177	1	DATE	3/25/2007
177	2	COUNTRY	Nigeria
177	3	CITY	Ilorin
177	4	PERPETRATOR	Unknown
177	5	FATALITIES	0
177	6	INJURED	0
177	7	TARGET TYPE	Government (General)

177	8	REGION	Sub-Saharan Africa
177	9	ATTACK TYPE	Armed Assault
177	10	WEAPON TYPE	Unknown
177	11		
178	1	DATE	3/31/2007
178	2	COUNTRY	Nigeria
178	3	CITY	Offshore oil rig
178	4	PERPETRATOR	Unknown
178	5	FATALITIES	Unknown
178	6	INJURED	Unknown
178	7	TARGET TYPE	Business
178	8	REGION	Sub-Saharan Africa
178	9	ATTACK TYPE	Armed Assault
178	10	WEAPON TYPE	Unknown
178	11		
179	1	DATE	4/2/2007
179	2	COUNTRY	Nigeria
179	3	CITY	Kano
179	4	PERPETRATOR	Unknown
179	5	FATALITIES	0
179	6	INJURED	0
179	7	TARGET TYPE	Journalists & Media
179	8	REGION	Sub-Saharan Africa
179	9	ATTACK TYPE	Facility/Infrastructure Attack
179	10	WEAPON TYPE	Melee,Melee
179	11		
180	1	DATE	4/2/2007
180	2	COUNTRY	Nigeria
180	3	CITY	Unknown
180	4	PERPETRATOR	Unknown
180	5	FATALITIES	0
180	6	INJURED	0
180	7	TARGET TYPE	Utilities
180	8	REGION	Sub-Saharan Africa
180	9	ATTACK TYPE	Hostage Taking (Kidnapping)
180	10	WEAPON TYPE	Firearms
180	11		
181	1	DATE	4/6/2007
181	2	COUNTRY	Nigeria
181	3	CITY	Unknown
181	4	PERPETRATOR	Unknown
181	5	FATALITIES	0
181	6	INJURED	0
181	7	TARGET TYPE	Utilities
181	8	REGION	Sub-Saharan Africa
181	9	ATTACK TYPE	Hostage Taking (Kidnapping)

181	10	WEAPON TYPE	Firearms
181	11		
182	1	DATE	4/13/2007
182	2	COUNTRY	Nigeria
182	3	CITY	Kano
182	4	PERPETRATOR	Unknown
182	5	FATALITIES	2
182	6	INJURED	0
182	7	TARGET TYPE	Religious Figures/Institutions
182	8	REGION	Sub-Saharan Africa
182	9	ATTACK TYPE	Armed Assault,Assassination
182	10	WEAPON TYPE	Firearms
182	11		
183	1	DATE	4/14/2007
183	2	COUNTRY	Nigeria
183	3	CITY	Elelenwo and Okoro
183	4	PERPETRATOR	Unknown
183	5	FATALITIES	7
183	6	INJURED	0
183	7	TARGET TYPE	Police,Police
183	8	REGION	Sub-Saharan Africa
183	9	ATTACK TYPE	Armed Assault
183	10	WEAPON TYPE	Firearms
183	11		
184	1	DATE	4/17/2007
184	2	COUNTRY	Nigeria
184	3	CITY	Kano
184	4	PERPETRATOR	Unknown
184	5	FATALITIES	12
184	6	INJURED	0
184	7	TARGET TYPE	Police,Private Citizens & Property
184	8	REGION	Sub-Saharan Africa
184	9	ATTACK TYPE	Armed Assault
184	10	WEAPON TYPE	Firearms
184	11		
185	1	DATE	4/20/2007
185	2	COUNTRY	Nigeria
185	3	CITY	0
185	4	PERPETRATOR	Unknown
185	5	FATALITIES	0
185	6	INJURED	6
185	7	TARGET TYPE	Utilities
185	8	REGION	Sub-Saharan Africa
185	9	ATTACK TYPE	Armed Assault,Hostage Taking (Kidnapping)
185	10	WEAPON TYPE	Firearms
185	11		

186	1	DATE	4/27/2007
186	2	COUNTRY	Nigeria
186	3	CITY	Port Harcourt
186	4	PERPETRATOR	Unknown
186	5	FATALITIES	7
186	6	INJURED	0
186	7	TARGET TYPE	Police,Utilities
186	8	REGION	Sub-Saharan Africa
186	9	ATTACK TYPE	Armed Assault,Hostage Taking (Kidnapping)
186	10	WEAPON TYPE	Firearms
186	11		
187	1	DATE	5/2/2007
187	2	COUNTRY	Nigeria
187	3	CITY	0
187	4	PERPETRATOR	Movement for the Emancipation of the Niger Delta (MEND)
187	5	FATALITIES	1
187	6	INJURED	0
187	7	TARGET TYPE	Business,Private Citizens & Property
187	8	REGION	Sub-Saharan Africa
187	9	ATTACK TYPE	Armed Assault,Bombing/Explosion,Hostage Taking (Kidnapping)
187	10	WEAPON TYPE	Firearms,Explosives/Bombs/Dynamite
187	11		
188	1	DATE	5/3/2007
188	2	COUNTRY	Nigeria
188	3	CITY	Rivers State
188	4	PERPETRATOR	Unknown
188	5	FATALITIES	Unknown
188	6	INJURED	Unknown
188	7	TARGET TYPE	Government (General),Private Citizens & Property
188	8	REGION	Sub-Saharan Africa
188	9	ATTACK TYPE	Armed Assault,Hostage Taking (Kidnapping)
188	10	WEAPON TYPE	Firearms
188	11		
189	1	DATE	5/6/2007
189	2	COUNTRY	Nigeria
189	3	CITY	Bayelsa
189	4	PERPETRATOR	Movement for the Emancipation of the Niger Delta (MEND)
189	5	FATALITIES	0
189	6	INJURED	0
189	7	TARGET TYPE	Government (General)
189	8	REGION	Sub-Saharan Africa
189	9	ATTACK TYPE	Bombing/Explosion
189	10	WEAPON TYPE	Explosives/Bombs/Dynamite

189	11		
190	1	DATE	5/8/2007
190	2	COUNTRY	Nigeria
190	3	CITY	Delta
190	4	PERPETRATOR	Movement for the Emancipation of the Niger Delta (MEND)
190	5	FATALITIES	0
190	6	INJURED	0
190	7	TARGET TYPE	Utilities
190	8	REGION	Sub-Saharan Africa
190	9	ATTACK TYPE	Bombing/Explosion,Facility/Infrastructure Attack
190	10	WEAPON TYPE	Explosives/Bombs/Dynamite
190	11		
191	1	DATE	5/9/2007
191	2	COUNTRY	Nigeria
191	3	CITY	Escravos
191	4	PERPETRATOR	Unknown
191	5	FATALITIES	0
191	6	INJURED	4
191	7	TARGET TYPE	Business,Private Citizens & Property
191	8	REGION	Sub-Saharan Africa
191	9	ATTACK TYPE	Hostage Taking (Kidnapping)
191	10	WEAPON TYPE	Firearms
191	11		
192	1	DATE	5/16/2007
192	2	COUNTRY	Nigeria
192	3	CITY	Otu-Eke village
192	4	PERPETRATOR	Unknown
192	5	FATALITIES	0
192	6	INJURED	Unknown
192	7	TARGET TYPE	Government (Diplomatic)
192	8	REGION	Sub-Saharan Africa
192	9	ATTACK TYPE	Bombing/Explosion
192	10	WEAPON TYPE	Explosives/Bombs/Dynamite
192	11		
193	1	DATE	5/19/2007
193	2	COUNTRY	Nigeria
193	3	CITY	Eleme
193	4	PERPETRATOR	Unknown
193	5	FATALITIES	1
193	6	INJURED	1
193	7	TARGET TYPE	Business,Police,Utilities
193	8	REGION	Sub-Saharan Africa
193	9	ATTACK TYPE	Hostage Taking (Kidnapping)
193	10	WEAPON TYPE	Explosives/Bombs/Dynamite,Firearms
193	11		

194	1	DATE	5/22/2007
194	2	COUNTRY	Nigeria
194	3	CITY	Warri
194	4	PERPETRATOR	Unknown
194	5	FATALITIES	0
194	6	INJURED	0
194	7	TARGET TYPE	Private Citizens & Property
194	8	REGION	Sub-Saharan Africa
194	9	ATTACK TYPE	Hostage Taking (Kidnapping)
194	10	WEAPON TYPE	Firearms
194	11		
195	1	DATE	5/25/2007
195	2	COUNTRY	Nigeria
195	3	CITY	0
195	4	PERPETRATOR	Unknown
195	5	FATALITIES	0
195	6	INJURED	0
195	7	TARGET TYPE	Private Citizens & Property
195	8	REGION	Sub-Saharan Africa
195	9	ATTACK TYPE	Hostage Taking (Kidnapping)
195	10	WEAPON TYPE	Firearms
195	11		
196	1	DATE	6/1/2007
196	2	COUNTRY	Nigeria
196	3	CITY	Port Harcourt
196	4	PERPETRATOR	Movement for the Emancipation of the Niger Delta (MEND) (suspected)
196	5	FATALITIES	2
196	6	INJURED	0
196	7	TARGET TYPE	Business,Police
196	8	REGION	Sub-Saharan Africa
196	9	ATTACK TYPE	Hostage Taking (Kidnapping)
196	10	WEAPON TYPE	Firearms
196	11		
197	1	DATE	6/2/2007
197	2	COUNTRY	Nigeria
197	3	CITY	Port Harcourt
197	4	PERPETRATOR	Niger Delta People's Volunteer Force (NDPVF)
197	5	FATALITIES	0
197	6	INJURED	0
197	7	TARGET TYPE	Private Citizens & Property
197	8	REGION	Sub-Saharan Africa
197	9	ATTACK TYPE	Hostage Taking (Kidnapping)
197	10	WEAPON TYPE	Firearms
197	11		
198	1	DATE	6/3/2007

198	2	COUNTRY	Nigeria
198	3	CITY	Ikot Abasi
198	4	PERPETRATOR	Unknown
198	5	FATALITIES	1
198	6	INJURED	0
198	7	TARGET TYPE	Private Citizens & Property,Private Citizens & Property
198	8	REGION	Sub-Saharan Africa
198	9	ATTACK TYPE	Hostage Taking (Kidnapping),Bombing/Explosion
198	10	WEAPON TYPE	Explosives/Bombs/Dynamite
198	11		
199	1	DATE	6/10/2007
199	2	COUNTRY	Nigeria
199	3	CITY	Nembe Oil Field
199	4	PERPETRATOR	Movement for the Emancipation of the Niger Delta (MEND),Niger Delta People's Volunteer Force (NDPVF)
199	5	FATALITIES	0
199	6	INJURED	0
199	7	TARGET TYPE	Business
199	8	REGION	Sub-Saharan Africa
199	9	ATTACK TYPE	Bombing/Explosion
199	10	WEAPON TYPE	Explosives/Bombs/Dynamite
199	11		
200	1	DATE	6/13/2007
200	2	COUNTRY	Nigeria
200	3	CITY	Unknown
200	4	PERPETRATOR	Unknown
200	5	FATALITIES	0
200	6	INJURED	0
200	7	TARGET TYPE	Private Citizens & Property
200	8	REGION	Sub-Saharan Africa
200	9	ATTACK TYPE	Hostage Taking (Kidnapping)
200	10	WEAPON TYPE	Unknown
200	11		
201	1	DATE	6/14/2007
201	2	COUNTRY	Nigeria
201	3	CITY	Unknown
201	4	PERPETRATOR	Unknown
201	5	FATALITIES	0
201	6	INJURED	0
201	7	TARGET TYPE	Private Citizens & Property
201	8	REGION	Sub-Saharan Africa
201	9	ATTACK TYPE	Hostage Taking (Kidnapping)
201	10	WEAPON TYPE	Unknown
201	11		
202	1	DATE	6/15/2007

202	2	COUNTRY	Nigeria
202	3	CITY	Unknown
202	4	PERPETRATOR	Unknown
202	5	FATALITIES	0
202	6	INJURED	0
202	7	TARGET TYPE	Private Citizens & Property
202	8	REGION	Sub-Saharan Africa
202	9	ATTACK TYPE	Hostage Taking (Kidnapping)
202	10	WEAPON TYPE	Unknown
202	11		
203	1	DATE	6/17/2007
203	2	COUNTRY	Nigeria
203	3	CITY	Bayelsa
203	4	PERPETRATOR	Unknown
203	5	FATALITIES	10
203	6	INJURED	Unknown
203	7	TARGET TYPE	Business
203	8	REGION	Sub-Saharan Africa
203	9	ATTACK TYPE	Hostage Taking (Barricade Incident)
203	10	WEAPON TYPE	Firearms
203	11		
204	1	DATE	7/4/2007
204	2	COUNTRY	Nigeria
204	3	CITY	Ibadan
204	4	PERPETRATOR	Unknown
204	5	FATALITIES	Unknown
204	6	INJURED	Unknown
204	7	TARGET TYPE	Government (General)
204	8	REGION	Sub-Saharan Africa
204	9	ATTACK TYPE	Assassination
204	10	WEAPON TYPE	Firearms
204	11		
205	1	DATE	7/4/2007
205	2	COUNTRY	Nigeria
205	3	CITY	0
205	4	PERPETRATOR	Movement for the Emancipation of the Niger Delta (MEND) (suspected)
205	5	FATALITIES	0
205	6	INJURED	0
205	7	TARGET TYPE	Business,Business
205	8	REGION	Sub-Saharan Africa
205	9	ATTACK TYPE	Hostage Taking (Kidnapping)
205	10	WEAPON TYPE	Firearms
205	11		
206	1	DATE	7/6/2007
206	2	COUNTRY	Nigeria

206	3	CITY	Port Harcourt
206	4	PERPETRATOR	Movement for the Emancipation of the Niger Delta (MEND)
206	5	FATALITIES	0
206	6	INJURED	0
206	7	TARGET TYPE	Private Citizens & Property
206	8	REGION	Sub-Saharan Africa
206	9	ATTACK TYPE	Hostage Taking (Kidnapping)
206	10	WEAPON TYPE	Firearms
206	11		
207	1	DATE	7/9/2007
207	2	COUNTRY	Nigeria
207	3	CITY	0
207	4	PERPETRATOR	Unknown
207	5	FATALITIES	0
207	6	INJURED	0
207	7	TARGET TYPE	Business,Business
207	8	REGION	Sub-Saharan Africa
207	9	ATTACK TYPE	Hostage Taking (Kidnapping)
207	10	WEAPON TYPE	Firearms
207	11		
208	1	DATE	7/12/2007
208	2	COUNTRY	Nigeria
208	3	CITY	Unknown
208	4	PERPETRATOR	Unknown
208	5	FATALITIES	0
208	6	INJURED	0
208	7	TARGET TYPE	Private Citizens & Property
208	8	REGION	Sub-Saharan Africa
208	9	ATTACK TYPE	Hostage Taking (Kidnapping)
208	10	WEAPON TYPE	Firearms
208	11		
209	1	DATE	8/1/2007
209	2	COUNTRY	Nigeria
209	3	CITY	Lekki
209	4	PERPETRATOR	Unknown
209	5	FATALITIES	0
209	6	INJURED	Unknown
209	7	TARGET TYPE	Government (Diplomatic)
209	8	REGION	Sub-Saharan Africa
209	9	ATTACK TYPE	Assassination
209	10	WEAPON TYPE	Firearms
209	11		
210	1	DATE	8/10/2007
210	2	COUNTRY	Nigeria
210	3	CITY	Port Harcourt

210	4	PERPETRATOR	Unknown
210	5	FATALITIES	Unknown
210	6	INJURED	Unknown
210	7	TARGET TYPE	Business
210	8	REGION	Sub-Saharan Africa
210	9	ATTACK TYPE	Hostage Taking (Kidnapping)
210	10	WEAPON TYPE	Unknown
210	11		
211	1	DATE	8/14/2007
211	2	COUNTRY	Nigeria
211	3	CITY	Port Harcourt
211	4	PERPETRATOR	Movement for the Actualization of the Sovereign State of Biafra (MASSOB) (suspected)
211	5	FATALITIES	14
211	6	INJURED	0
211	7	TARGET TYPE	Journalists & Media,Private Citizens & Property
211	8	REGION	Sub-Saharan Africa
211	9	ATTACK TYPE	Armed Assault,Facility/Infrastructure Attack
211	10	WEAPON TYPE	Firearms
211	11		
212	1	DATE	8/20/2007
212	2	COUNTRY	Nigeria
212	3	CITY	Agadez
212	4	PERPETRATOR	Tuaregs (suspected)
212	5	FATALITIES	4
212	6	INJURED	3
212	7	TARGET TYPE	Police
212	8	REGION	Sub-Saharan Africa
212	9	ATTACK TYPE	Bombing/Explosion
212	10	WEAPON TYPE	Explosives/Bombs/Dynamite
212	11		
213	1	DATE	8/31/2007
213	2	COUNTRY	Nigeria
213	3	CITY	Sokoto
213	4	PERPETRATOR	Unknown
213	5	FATALITIES	1
213	6	INJURED	0
213	7	TARGET TYPE	Private Citizens & Property
213	8	REGION	Sub-Saharan Africa
213	9	ATTACK TYPE	Armed Assault
213	10	WEAPON TYPE	Melee
213	11		
214	1	DATE	9/27/2007
214	2	COUNTRY	Nigeria
214	3	CITY	0
214	4	PERPETRATOR	Unknown

214	5	FATALITIES	1
214	6	INJURED	0
214	7	TARGET TYPE	Business
214	8	REGION	Sub-Saharan Africa
214	9	ATTACK TYPE	Armed Assault
214	10	WEAPON TYPE	Firearms
214	11		
215	1	DATE	10/31/2007
215	2	COUNTRY	Nigeria
215	3	CITY	Penington (Estuary)
215	4	PERPETRATOR	Movement for the Emancipation of the Niger Delta (MEND)
215	5	FATALITIES	1
215	6	INJURED	Unknown
215	7	TARGET TYPE	Military
215	8	REGION	Sub-Saharan Africa
215	9	ATTACK TYPE	Armed Assault
215	10	WEAPON TYPE	Firearms
215	11		
216	1	DATE	11/5/2007
216	2	COUNTRY	Nigeria
216	3	CITY	Riverine Area
216	4	PERPETRATOR	Movement for the Emancipation of the Niger Delta (MEND)
216	5	FATALITIES	0
216	6	INJURED	0
216	7	TARGET TYPE	Government (General)
216	8	REGION	Sub-Saharan Africa
216	9	ATTACK TYPE	Hostage Taking (Kidnapping)
216	10	WEAPON TYPE	Unknown
216	11		
217	1	DATE	11/8/2007
217	2	COUNTRY	Nigeria
217	3	CITY	0
217	4	PERPETRATOR	Unknown
217	5	FATALITIES	0
217	6	INJURED	Unknown
217	7	TARGET TYPE	Government (General)
217	8	REGION	Sub-Saharan Africa
217	9	ATTACK TYPE	Facility/Infrastructure Attack,Hostage Taking (Barricade Incident)
217	10	WEAPON TYPE	Incendiary,Firearms
217	11		
218	1	DATE	11/8/2007
218	2	COUNTRY	Nigeria
218	3	CITY	Owerri

218	4	PERPETRATOR	Unknown
218	5	FATALITIES	0
218	6	INJURED	0
218	7	TARGET TYPE	Other
218	8	REGION	Sub-Saharan Africa
218	9	ATTACK TYPE	Armed Assault
218	10	WEAPON TYPE	Firearms
218	11		
219	1	DATE	11/12/2007
219	2	COUNTRY	Nigeria
219	3	CITY	Ibeno
219	4	PERPETRATOR	Unknown
219	5	FATALITIES	1
219	6	INJURED	25
219	7	TARGET TYPE	Business
219	8	REGION	Sub-Saharan Africa
219	9	ATTACK TYPE	Facility/Infrastructure Attack
219	10	WEAPON TYPE	Firearms
219	11		
220	1	DATE	11/14/2007
220	2	COUNTRY	Nigeria
220	3	CITY	Bomadi
220	4	PERPETRATOR	Unknown
220	5	FATALITIES	1
220	6	INJURED	Unknown
220	7	TARGET TYPE	Police
220	8	REGION	Sub-Saharan Africa
220	9	ATTACK TYPE	Facility/Infrastructure Attack
220	10	WEAPON TYPE	Firearms
220	11		
221	1	DATE	11/15/2007
221	2	COUNTRY	Nigeria
221	3	CITY	0
221	4	PERPETRATOR	Movement for the Emancipation of the Niger Delta (MEND)
221	5	FATALITIES	0
221	6	INJURED	0
221	7	TARGET TYPE	Utilities
221	8	REGION	Sub-Saharan Africa
221	9	ATTACK TYPE	Facility/Infrastructure Attack
221	10	WEAPON TYPE	Sabotage Equipment
221	11		
222	1	DATE	11/27/2007
222	2	COUNTRY	Nigeria
222	3	CITY	Bonny
222	4	PERPETRATOR	Unknown

222	5	FATALITIES	3
222	6	INJURED	0
222	7	TARGET TYPE	Police,Private Citizens & Property
222	8	REGION	Sub-Saharan Africa
222	9	ATTACK TYPE	Armed Assault
222	10	WEAPON TYPE	Firearms
222	11		
223	1	DATE	12/4/2007
223	2	COUNTRY	Nigeria
223	3	CITY	Unknown
223	4	PERPETRATOR	Unknown
223	5	FATALITIES	1
223	6	INJURED	1
223	7	TARGET TYPE	Maritime
223	8	REGION	Sub-Saharan Africa
223	9	ATTACK TYPE	Armed Assault
223	10	WEAPON TYPE	Firearms
223	11		
224	1	DATE	1/1/2008
224	2	COUNTRY	Nigeria
224	3	CITY	Port Harcourt
224	4	PERPETRATOR	Niger Delta Vigilante (NDV)
224	5	FATALITIES	18
224	6	INJURED	Unknown
224	7	TARGET TYPE	Business,Police
224	8	REGION	Sub-Saharan Africa
224	9	ATTACK TYPE	Armed Assault
224	10	WEAPON TYPE	Firearms
224	11		
225	1	DATE	1/4/2008
225	2	COUNTRY	Nigeria
225	3	CITY	Ogbogu
225	4	PERPETRATOR	Unknown
225	5	FATALITIES	0
225	6	INJURED	0
225	7	TARGET TYPE	Private Citizens & Property
225	8	REGION	Sub-Saharan Africa
225	9	ATTACK TYPE	Hostage Taking (Kidnapping)
225	10	WEAPON TYPE	Firearms
225	11		
226	1	DATE	1/6/2008
226	2	COUNTRY	Nigeria
226	3	CITY	Buruto
226	4	PERPETRATOR	Movement for the Emancipation of the Niger Delta (MEND) (suspected)
226	5	FATALITIES	0

226	6	INJURED	0
226	7	TARGET TYPE	Utilities
226	8	REGION	Sub-Saharan Africa
226	9	ATTACK TYPE	Bombing/Explosion
226	10	WEAPON TYPE	Explosives/Bombs/Dynamite
226	11		
227	1	DATE	1/6/2008
227	2	COUNTRY	Nigeria
227	3	CITY	Beniboye
227	4	PERPETRATOR	Movement for the Emancipation of the Niger Delta (MEND) (suspected)
227	5	FATALITIES	0
227	6	INJURED	0
227	7	TARGET TYPE	Utilities
227	8	REGION	Sub-Saharan Africa
227	9	ATTACK TYPE	Bombing/Explosion
227	10	WEAPON TYPE	Explosives/Bombs/Dynamite
227	11		
228	1	DATE	1/10/2008
228	2	COUNTRY	Nigeria
228	3	CITY	Bonny Channel
228	4	PERPETRATOR	Movement for the Emancipation of the Niger Delta (MEND)
228	5	FATALITIES	0
228	6	INJURED	Unknown
228	7	TARGET TYPE	Business
228	8	REGION	Sub-Saharan Africa
228	9	ATTACK TYPE	Facility/Infrastructure Attack
228	10	WEAPON TYPE	Firearms
228	11		
229	1	DATE	1/16/2008
229	2	COUNTRY	Nigeria
229	3	CITY	Aker base
229	4	PERPETRATOR	Unknown
229	5	FATALITIES	0
229	6	INJURED	Unknown
229	7	TARGET TYPE	Maritime
229	8	REGION	Sub-Saharan Africa
229	9	ATTACK TYPE	Armed Assault
229	10	WEAPON TYPE	Firearms
229	11		
230	1	DATE	1/16/2008
230	2	COUNTRY	Nigeria
230	3	CITY	Sand fill
230	4	PERPETRATOR	Movement for the Emancipation of the Niger Delta (MEND)

230	5	FATALITIES	1
230	6	INJURED	2
230	7	TARGET TYPE	Government (General)
230	8	REGION	Sub-Saharan Africa
230	9	ATTACK TYPE	Bombing/Explosion
230	10	WEAPON TYPE	Explosives/Bombs/Dynamite
230	11		
231	1	DATE	1/23/2008
231	2	COUNTRY	Nigeria
231	3	CITY	Port Harcourt
231	4	PERPETRATOR	Unknown
231	5	FATALITIES	Unknown
231	6	INJURED	Unknown
231	7	TARGET TYPE	Private Citizens & Property
231	8	REGION	Sub-Saharan Africa
231	9	ATTACK TYPE	Hostage Taking (Kidnapping)
231	10	WEAPON TYPE	Firearms
231	11		
232	1	DATE	1/28/2008
232	2	COUNTRY	Nigeria
232	3	CITY	Unknown
232	4	PERPETRATOR	Unknown
232	5	FATALITIES	Unknown
232	6	INJURED	Unknown
232	7	TARGET TYPE	Private Citizens & Property
232	8	REGION	Sub-Saharan Africa
232	9	ATTACK TYPE	Hostage Taking (Kidnapping)
232	10	WEAPON TYPE	Unknown
232	11		
233	1	DATE	2/24/2008
233	2	COUNTRY	Nigeria
233	3	CITY	Port Harcourt
233	4	PERPETRATOR	Unknown
233	5	FATALITIES	0
233	6	INJURED	0
233	7	TARGET TYPE	Private Citizens & Property
233	8	REGION	Sub-Saharan Africa
233	9	ATTACK TYPE	Hostage Taking (Kidnapping)
233	10	WEAPON TYPE	Firearms
233	11		
234	1	DATE	3/22/2008
234	2	COUNTRY	Nigeria
234	3	CITY	Port Harcourt
234	4	PERPETRATOR	Movement for the Emancipation of the Niger Delta (MEND)
234	5	FATALITIES	4

234	6	INJURED	Unknown
234	7	TARGET TYPE	Military
234	8	REGION	Sub-Saharan Africa
234	9	ATTACK TYPE	Bombing/Explosion
234	10	WEAPON TYPE	Explosives/Bombs/Dynamite
234	11		
235	1	DATE	4/8/2008
235	2	COUNTRY	Nigeria
235	3	CITY	Asaba
235	4	PERPETRATOR	Unknown
235	5	FATALITIES	0
235	6	INJURED	1
235	7	TARGET TYPE	Government (General)
235	8	REGION	Sub-Saharan Africa
235	9	ATTACK TYPE	Armed Assault
235	10	WEAPON TYPE	Melee
235	11		
236	1	DATE	4/16/2008
236	2	COUNTRY	Nigeria
236	3	CITY	Unknown
236	4	PERPETRATOR	Unknown
236	5	FATALITIES	Unknown
236	6	INJURED	Unknown
236	7	TARGET TYPE	Business
236	8	REGION	Sub-Saharan Africa
236	9	ATTACK TYPE	Armed Assault
236	10	WEAPON TYPE	Firearms
236	11		
237	1	DATE	4/20/2008
237	2	COUNTRY	Nigeria
237	3	CITY	Unknown
237	4	PERPETRATOR	Movement for the Emancipation of the Niger Delta (MEND) (suspected)
237	5	FATALITIES	0
237	6	INJURED	0
237	7	TARGET TYPE	Utilities
237	8	REGION	Sub-Saharan Africa
237	9	ATTACK TYPE	Facility/Infrastructure Attack
237	10	WEAPON TYPE	Explosives/Bombs/Dynamite
237	11		
238	1	DATE	5/4/2008
238	2	COUNTRY	Nigeria
238	3	CITY	Unknown
238	4	PERPETRATOR	Movement for the Emancipation of the Niger Delta (MEND)
238	5	FATALITIES	0

238	6	INJURED	0
238	7	TARGET TYPE	Utilities
238	8	REGION	Sub-Saharan Africa
238	9	ATTACK TYPE	Bombing/Explosion
238	10	WEAPON TYPE	Explosives/Bombs/Dynamite
238	11		
239	1	DATE	5/7/2008
239	2	COUNTRY	Nigeria
239	3	CITY	Owerri
239	4	PERPETRATOR	Unknown
239	5	FATALITIES	0
239	6	INJURED	0
239	7	TARGET TYPE	Government (General)
239	8	REGION	Sub-Saharan Africa
239	9	ATTACK TYPE	Hostage Taking (Kidnapping)
239	10	WEAPON TYPE	Unknown
239	11		
240	1	DATE	5/9/2008
240	2	COUNTRY	Nigeria
240	3	CITY	Port Harcourt
240	4	PERPETRATOR	Unknown
240	5	FATALITIES	0
240	6	INJURED	0
240	7	TARGET TYPE	Educational Institution
240	8	REGION	Sub-Saharan Africa
240	9	ATTACK TYPE	Hostage Taking (Kidnapping),Armed Assault
240	10	WEAPON TYPE	Firearms
240	11		
241	1	DATE	5/13/2008
241	2	COUNTRY	Nigeria
241	3	CITY	Unknown
241	4	PERPETRATOR	Unknown
241	5	FATALITIES	0
241	6	INJURED	0
241	7	TARGET TYPE	Maritime
241	8	REGION	Sub-Saharan Africa
241	9	ATTACK TYPE	Hijacking,Hostage Taking (Kidnapping)
241	10	WEAPON TYPE	Firearms
241	11		
242	1	DATE	5/16/2008
242	2	COUNTRY	Nigeria
242	3	CITY	Port Harcourt
242	4	PERPETRATOR	Unknown
242	5	FATALITIES	0
242	6	INJURED	0
242	7	TARGET TYPE	Utilities

242	8	REGION	Sub-Saharan Africa
242	9	ATTACK TYPE	Hostage Taking (Kidnapping)
242	10	WEAPON TYPE	Firearms
242	11		
243	1	DATE	5/18/2008
243	2	COUNTRY	Nigeria
243	3	CITY	Port Harcourt
243	4	PERPETRATOR	Unknown
243	5	FATALITIES	0
243	6	INJURED	0
243	7	TARGET TYPE	Business,Business
243	8	REGION	Sub-Saharan Africa
243	9	ATTACK TYPE	Hostage Taking (Kidnapping)
243	10	WEAPON TYPE	Firearms,Explosives/Bombs/Dynamite
243	11		
244	1	DATE	5/22/2008
244	2	COUNTRY	Nigeria
244	3	CITY	Okrika
244	4	PERPETRATOR	Movement for the Emancipation of the Niger Delta (MEND) (suspected)
244	5	FATALITIES	0
244	6	INJURED	0
244	7	TARGET TYPE	Private Citizens & Property
244	8	REGION	Sub-Saharan Africa
244	9	ATTACK TYPE	Armed Assault
244	10	WEAPON TYPE	Firearms
244	11		
245	1	DATE	5/22/2008
245	2	COUNTRY	Nigeria
245	3	CITY	Port Harcourt
245	4	PERPETRATOR	Unknown
245	5	FATALITIES	2
245	6	INJURED	0
245	7	TARGET TYPE	Utilities
245	8	REGION	Sub-Saharan Africa
245	9	ATTACK TYPE	Armed Assault
245	10	WEAPON TYPE	Firearms
245	11		
246	1	DATE	5/26/2008
246	2	COUNTRY	Nigeria
246	3	CITY	Awoba
246	4	PERPETRATOR	Movement for the Emancipation of the Niger Delta (MEND)
246	5	FATALITIES	11
246	6	INJURED	0
246	7	TARGET TYPE	Business

246	8	REGION	Sub-Saharan Africa
246	9	ATTACK TYPE	Bombing/Explosion,Armed Assault
246	10	WEAPON TYPE	Explosives/Bombs/Dynamite,Firearms
246	11		
247	1	DATE	5/31/2008
247	2	COUNTRY	Nigeria
247	3	CITY	Warri
247	4	PERPETRATOR	Unknown
247	5	FATALITIES	0
247	6	INJURED	1
247	7	TARGET TYPE	Private Citizens & Property
247	8	REGION	Sub-Saharan Africa
247	9	ATTACK TYPE	Armed Assault
247	10	WEAPON TYPE	Unknown
247	11		
248	1	DATE	6/4/2008
248	2	COUNTRY	Nigeria
248	3	CITY	Aba
248	4	PERPETRATOR	Unknown
248	5	FATALITIES	0
248	6	INJURED	0
248	7	TARGET TYPE	Government (General)
248	8	REGION	Sub-Saharan Africa
248	9	ATTACK TYPE	Hostage Taking (Kidnapping)
248	10	WEAPON TYPE	Firearms
248	11		
249	1	DATE	6/9/2008
249	2	COUNTRY	Nigeria
249	3	CITY	Unknown
249	4	PERPETRATOR	Unknown
249	5	FATALITIES	1
249	6	INJURED	4
249	7	TARGET TYPE	Maritime
249	8	REGION	Sub-Saharan Africa
249	9	ATTACK TYPE	Armed Assault
249	10	WEAPON TYPE	Firearms
249	11		
250	1	DATE	6/10/2008
250	2	COUNTRY	Nigeria
250	3	CITY	Unknown
250	4	PERPETRATOR	Unknown
250	5	FATALITIES	9
250	6	INJURED	4
250	7	TARGET TYPE	Maritime
250	8	REGION	Sub-Saharan Africa
250	9	ATTACK TYPE	Armed Assault

250	10	WEAPON TYPE	Firearms
250	11		
251	1	DATE	6/12/2008
251	2	COUNTRY	Nigeria
251	3	CITY	Opobo
251	4	PERPETRATOR	Unknown
251	5	FATALITIES	1
251	6	INJURED	0
251	7	TARGET TYPE	Private Citizens & Property
251	8	REGION	Sub-Saharan Africa
251	9	ATTACK TYPE	Hostage Taking (Kidnapping),Armed Assault
251	10	WEAPON TYPE	Firearms,Explosives/Bombs/Dynamite
251	11		
252	1	DATE	6/14/2008
252	2	COUNTRY	Nigeria
252	3	CITY	Bonny
252	4	PERPETRATOR	Unknown
252	5	FATALITIES	0
252	6	INJURED	0
252	7	TARGET TYPE	Government (General)
252	8	REGION	Sub-Saharan Africa
252	9	ATTACK TYPE	Bombing/Explosion,Armed Assault
252	10	WEAPON TYPE	Explosives/Bombs/Dynamite
252	11		
253	1	DATE	6/14/2008
253	2	COUNTRY	Nigeria
253	3	CITY	Bonny
253	4	PERPETRATOR	Unknown
253	5	FATALITIES	0
253	6	INJURED	0
253	7	TARGET TYPE	Business,Private Citizens & Property
253	8	REGION	Sub-Saharan Africa
253	9	ATTACK TYPE	Facility/Infrastructure Attack
253	10	WEAPON TYPE	Firearms
253	11		
254	1	DATE	6/16/2008
254	2	COUNTRY	Nigeria
254	3	CITY	Unknown
254	4	PERPETRATOR	Niger Delta Freedom Fighters (NDDF)
254	5	FATALITIES	0
254	6	INJURED	0
254	7	TARGET TYPE	Utilities
254	8	REGION	Sub-Saharan Africa
254	9	ATTACK TYPE	Bombing/Explosion
254	10	WEAPON TYPE	Explosives/Bombs/Dynamite
254	11		

255	1	DATE	6/19/2008
255	2	COUNTRY	Nigeria
255	3	CITY	0
255	4	PERPETRATOR	Unknown
255	5	FATALITIES	0
255	6	INJURED	0
255	7	TARGET TYPE	Business
255	8	REGION	Sub-Saharan Africa
255	9	ATTACK TYPE	Bombing/Explosion
255	10	WEAPON TYPE	Explosives/Bombs/Dynamite
255	11		
256	1	DATE	6/19/2008
256	2	COUNTRY	Nigeria
256	3	CITY	Unknown
256	4	PERPETRATOR	Movement for the Emancipation of the Niger Delta (MEND)
256	5	FATALITIES	0
256	6	INJURED	0
256	7	TARGET TYPE	Maritime
256	8	REGION	Sub-Saharan Africa
256	9	ATTACK TYPE	Hostage Taking (Kidnapping)
256	10	WEAPON TYPE	Unknown
256	11		
257	1	DATE	6/19/2008
257	2	COUNTRY	Nigeria
257	3	CITY	Unknown
257	4	PERPETRATOR	Movement for the Emancipation of the Niger Delta (MEND)
257	5	FATALITIES	0
257	6	INJURED	0
257	7	TARGET TYPE	Maritime
257	8	REGION	Sub-Saharan Africa
257	9	ATTACK TYPE	Armed Assault
257	10	WEAPON TYPE	Unknown
257	11		
258	1	DATE	6/19/2008
258	2	COUNTRY	Nigeria
258	3	CITY	Unknown
258	4	PERPETRATOR	Movement for the Emancipation of the Niger Delta (MEND)
258	5	FATALITIES	0
258	6	INJURED	0
258	7	TARGET TYPE	Utilities
258	8	REGION	Sub-Saharan Africa
258	9	ATTACK TYPE	Armed Assault
258	10	WEAPON TYPE	Unknown

258	11		
259	1	DATE	6/20/2008
259	2	COUNTRY	Nigeria
259	3	CITY	Unknown
259	4	PERPETRATOR	Movement for the Emancipation of the Niger Delta (MEND)
259	5	FATALITIES	0
259	6	INJURED	0
259	7	TARGET TYPE	Utilities
259	8	REGION	Sub-Saharan Africa
259	9	ATTACK TYPE	Bombing/Explosion
259	10	WEAPON TYPE	Explosives/Bombs/Dynamite
259	11		
260	1	DATE	6/21/2008
260	2	COUNTRY	Nigeria
260	3	CITY	Escravos
260	4	PERPETRATOR	Movement for the Emancipation of the Niger Delta (MEND)
260	5	FATALITIES	0
260	6	INJURED	0
260	7	TARGET TYPE	Business
260	8	REGION	Sub-Saharan Africa
260	9	ATTACK TYPE	Bombing/Explosion
260	10	WEAPON TYPE	Explosives/Bombs/Dynamite
260	11		
261	1	DATE	6/28/2008
261	2	COUNTRY	Nigeria
261	3	CITY	Lagos
261	4	PERPETRATOR	Unknown
261	5	FATALITIES	4
261	6	INJURED	2
261	7	TARGET TYPE	Military
261	8	REGION	Sub-Saharan Africa
261	9	ATTACK TYPE	Armed Assault
261	10	WEAPON TYPE	Melee,Firearms
261	11		
262	1	DATE	7/1/2008
262	2	COUNTRY	Nigeria
262	3	CITY	Makurdi
262	4	PERPETRATOR	Unknown
262	5	FATALITIES	1
262	6	INJURED	1
262	7	TARGET TYPE	Private Citizens & Property
262	8	REGION	Sub-Saharan Africa
262	9	ATTACK TYPE	Armed Assault
262	10	WEAPON TYPE	Firearms

262	11		
263	1	DATE	7/8/2008
263	2	COUNTRY	Nigeria
263	3	CITY	Igbokoda
263	4	PERPETRATOR	Unknown
263	5	FATALITIES	0
263	6	INJURED	1
263	7	TARGET TYPE	Government (General)
263	8	REGION	Sub-Saharan Africa
263	9	ATTACK TYPE	Armed Assault
263	10	WEAPON TYPE	Firearms
263	11		
264	1	DATE	7/15/2008
264	2	COUNTRY	Nigeria
264	3	CITY	Abakaliki
264	4	PERPETRATOR	Unknown
264	5	FATALITIES	0
264	6	INJURED	3
264	7	TARGET TYPE	Journalists & Media
264	8	REGION	Sub-Saharan Africa
264	9	ATTACK TYPE	Armed Assault
264	10	WEAPON TYPE	Firearms
264	11		
265	1	DATE	7/17/2008
265	2	COUNTRY	Nigeria
265	3	CITY	Tebidaba
265	4	PERPETRATOR	Unknown
265	5	FATALITIES	Unknown
265	6	INJURED	Unknown
265	7	TARGET TYPE	Business
265	8	REGION	Sub-Saharan Africa
265	9	ATTACK TYPE	Bombing/Explosion
265	10	WEAPON TYPE	Explosives/Bombs/Dynamite
265	11		
266	1	DATE	7/20/2008
266	2	COUNTRY	Nigeria
266	3	CITY	Boji Boji
266	4	PERPETRATOR	Unknown
266	5	FATALITIES	0
266	6	INJURED	0
266	7	TARGET TYPE	Private Citizens & Property
266	8	REGION	Sub-Saharan Africa
266	9	ATTACK TYPE	Hostage Taking (Kidnapping),Armed Assault
266	10	WEAPON TYPE	Firearms
266	11		
267	1	DATE	7/25/2008

267	2	COUNTRY	Nigeria
267	3	CITY	Port Harcourt
267	4	PERPETRATOR	Unknown
267	5	FATALITIES	0
267	6	INJURED	0
267	7	TARGET TYPE	Utilities,Utilities
267	8	REGION	Sub-Saharan Africa
267	9	ATTACK TYPE	Hostage Taking (Kidnapping),Armed Assault
267	10	WEAPON TYPE	Firearms
267	11		
268	1	DATE	7/26/2008
268	2	COUNTRY	Nigeria
268	3	CITY	Unknown
268	4	PERPETRATOR	Unknown
268	5	FATALITIES	0
268	6	INJURED	0
268	7	TARGET TYPE	Maritime,Other,Other
268	8	REGION	Sub-Saharan Africa
268	9	ATTACK TYPE	Hostage Taking (Kidnapping),Armed Assault
268	10	WEAPON TYPE	Unknown
268	11		
269	1	DATE	7/28/2008
269	2	COUNTRY	Nigeria
269	3	CITY	Kula
269	4	PERPETRATOR	Movement for the Emancipation of the Niger Delta (MEND)
269	5	FATALITIES	0
269	6	INJURED	0
269	7	TARGET TYPE	Utilities
269	8	REGION	Sub-Saharan Africa
269	9	ATTACK TYPE	Bombing/Explosion
269	10	WEAPON TYPE	Explosives/Bombs/Dynamite
269	11		
270	1	DATE	7/30/2008
270	2	COUNTRY	Nigeria
270	3	CITY	Rumuolumeni
270	4	PERPETRATOR	Unknown
270	5	FATALITIES	0
270	6	INJURED	0
270	7	TARGET TYPE	Government (General)
270	8	REGION	Sub-Saharan Africa
270	9	ATTACK TYPE	Hostage Taking (Kidnapping)
270	10	WEAPON TYPE	Firearms
270	11		
271	1	DATE	8/2/2008
271	2	COUNTRY	Nigeria

271	3	CITY	Port Harcourt
271	4	PERPETRATOR	Unknown
271	5	FATALITIES	0
271	6	INJURED	0
271	7	TARGET TYPE	Private Citizens & Property
271	8	REGION	Sub-Saharan Africa
271	9	ATTACK TYPE	Hostage Taking (Kidnapping)
271	10	WEAPON TYPE	Firearms
271	11		
272	1	DATE	8/3/2008
272	2	COUNTRY	Nigeria
272	3	CITY	Unknown
272	4	PERPETRATOR	Movement for the Emancipation of the Niger Delta (MEND)
272	5	FATALITIES	0
272	6	INJURED	0
272	7	TARGET TYPE	Violent Political Party
272	8	REGION	Sub-Saharan Africa
272	9	ATTACK TYPE	Hostage Taking (Kidnapping)
272	10	WEAPON TYPE	Unknown
272	11		
273	1	DATE	8/12/2008
273	2	COUNTRY	Nigeria
273	3	CITY	Port Harcourt
273	4	PERPETRATOR	Niger Delta Patriotic Force,Niger Delta Vigilante (NDV)
273	5	FATALITIES	0
273	6	INJURED	0
273	7	TARGET TYPE	Utilities
273	8	REGION	Sub-Saharan Africa
273	9	ATTACK TYPE	Bombing/Explosion
273	10	WEAPON TYPE	Explosives/Bombs/Dynamite
273	11		
274	1	DATE	8/21/2008
274	2	COUNTRY	Nigeria
274	3	CITY	Kalaa
274	4	PERPETRATOR	Unknown
274	5	FATALITIES	0
274	6	INJURED	1
274	7	TARGET TYPE	Government (General),Private Citizens & Property
274	8	REGION	Sub-Saharan Africa
274	9	ATTACK TYPE	Armed Assault
274	10	WEAPON TYPE	Firearms
274	11		
275	1	DATE	8/24/2008
275	2	COUNTRY	Nigeria

275	3	CITY	Bonny
275	4	PERPETRATOR	Unknown
275	5	FATALITIES	0
275	6	INJURED	0
275	7	TARGET TYPE	Maritime
275	8	REGION	Sub-Saharan Africa
275	9	ATTACK TYPE	Hijacking
275	10	WEAPON TYPE	Firearms
275	11		
276	1	DATE	8/27/2008
276	2	COUNTRY	Nigeria
276	3	CITY	Port Harcourt
276	4	PERPETRATOR	Unknown
276	5	FATALITIES	0
276	6	INJURED	0
276	7	TARGET TYPE	Private Citizens & Property
276	8	REGION	Sub-Saharan Africa
276	9	ATTACK TYPE	Hostage Taking (Kidnapping)
276	10	WEAPON TYPE	Firearms
276	11		
277	1	DATE	9/15/2008
277	2	COUNTRY	Nigeria
277	3	CITY	Port Harcourt
277	4	PERPETRATOR	Movement for the Emancipation of the Niger Delta (MEND) (suspected)
277	5	FATALITIES	1
277	6	INJURED	4
277	7	TARGET TYPE	Business
277	8	REGION	Sub-Saharan Africa
277	9	ATTACK TYPE	Bombing/Explosion
277	10	WEAPON TYPE	Explosives/Bombs/Dynamite
277	11		
278	1	DATE	9/17/2008
278	2	COUNTRY	Nigeria
278	3	CITY	Port Harcourt
278	4	PERPETRATOR	Movement for the Emancipation of the Niger Delta (MEND) (suspected)
278	5	FATALITIES	0
278	6	INJURED	0
278	7	TARGET TYPE	Business
278	8	REGION	Sub-Saharan Africa
278	9	ATTACK TYPE	Bombing/Explosion
278	10	WEAPON TYPE	Explosives/Bombs/Dynamite
278	11		
279	1	DATE	9/19/2008
279	2	COUNTRY	Nigeria

279	3	CITY	Owerri
279	4	PERPETRATOR	Unknown
279	5	FATALITIES	0
279	6	INJURED	0
279	7	TARGET TYPE	Government (General)
279	8	REGION	Sub-Saharan Africa
279	9	ATTACK TYPE	Armed Assault
279	10	WEAPON TYPE	Firearms
279	11		
280	1	DATE	9/19/2008
280	2	COUNTRY	Nigeria
280	3	CITY	Bugama
280	4	PERPETRATOR	Movement for the Emancipation of the Niger Delta (MEND) (suspected)
280	5	FATALITIES	0
280	6	INJURED	0
280	7	TARGET TYPE	Business
280	8	REGION	Sub-Saharan Africa
280	9	ATTACK TYPE	Bombing/Explosion
280	10	WEAPON TYPE	Explosives/Bombs/Dynamite
280	11		
281	1	DATE	10/16/2008
281	2	COUNTRY	Nigeria
281	3	CITY	Uyo
281	4	PERPETRATOR	Unknown
281	5	FATALITIES	0
281	6	INJURED	1
281	7	TARGET TYPE	Private Citizens & Property
281	8	REGION	Sub-Saharan Africa
281	9	ATTACK TYPE	Hostage Taking (Kidnapping)
281	10	WEAPON TYPE	Firearms
281	11		
282	1	DATE	10/16/2008
282	2	COUNTRY	Nigeria
282	3	CITY	Port Harcourt
282	4	PERPETRATOR	Unknown
282	5	FATALITIES	0
282	6	INJURED	0
282	7	TARGET TYPE	Business
282	8	REGION	Sub-Saharan Africa
282	9	ATTACK TYPE	Hostage Taking (Kidnapping)
282	10	WEAPON TYPE	Firearms
282	11		
283	1	DATE	11/3/2008
283	2	COUNTRY	Nigeria
283	3	CITY	Port Harcourt

283	4	PERPETRATOR	Unknown
283	5	FATALITIES	1
283	6	INJURED	1
283	7	TARGET TYPE	Business
283	8	REGION	Sub-Saharan Africa
283	9	ATTACK TYPE	Hostage Taking (Kidnapping),Armed Assault
283	10	WEAPON TYPE	Firearms
283	11		
284	1	DATE	11/3/2008
284	2	COUNTRY	Nigeria
284	3	CITY	Enugu Ukwa
284	4	PERPETRATOR	Unknown
284	5	FATALITIES	Unknown
284	6	INJURED	Unknown
284	7	TARGET TYPE	Private Citizens & Property
284	8	REGION	Sub-Saharan Africa
284	9	ATTACK TYPE	Hostage Taking (Kidnapping)
284	10	WEAPON TYPE	Firearms
284	11		
285	1	DATE	11/3/2008
285	2	COUNTRY	Nigeria
285	3	CITY	Port Harcourt
285	4	PERPETRATOR	Unknown
285	5	FATALITIES	Unknown
285	6	INJURED	Unknown
285	7	TARGET TYPE	Private Citizens & Property
285	8	REGION	Sub-Saharan Africa
285	9	ATTACK TYPE	Hostage Taking (Kidnapping)
285	10	WEAPON TYPE	Firearms
285	11		
286	1	DATE	11/10/2008
286	2	COUNTRY	Nigeria
286	3	CITY	Soku
286	4	PERPETRATOR	Unknown
286	5	FATALITIES	8
286	6	INJURED	Unknown
286	7	TARGET TYPE	Business
286	8	REGION	Sub-Saharan Africa
286	9	ATTACK TYPE	Facility/Infrastructure Attack
286	10	WEAPON TYPE	Firearms
286	11		
287	1	DATE	11/13/2008
287	2	COUNTRY	Nigeria
287	3	CITY	Yenagoa
287	4	PERPETRATOR	Unknown
287	5	FATALITIES	0

287	6	INJURED	0
287	7	TARGET TYPE	Business
287	8	REGION	Sub-Saharan Africa
287	9	ATTACK TYPE	Facility/Infrastructure Attack
287	10	WEAPON TYPE	Sabotage Equipment
287	11		
288	1	DATE	11/19/2008
288	2	COUNTRY	Nigeria
288	3	CITY	Ibadan
288	4	PERPETRATOR	Unknown
288	5	FATALITIES	1
288	6	INJURED	1
288	7	TARGET TYPE	Government (General),Government (General)
288	8	REGION	Sub-Saharan Africa
288	9	ATTACK TYPE	Armed Assault
288	10	WEAPON TYPE	Firearms
288	11		
289	1	DATE	11/20/2008
289	2	COUNTRY	Nigeria
289	3	CITY	Escravos
289	4	PERPETRATOR	Unknown
289	5	FATALITIES	Unknown
289	6	INJURED	Unknown
289	7	TARGET TYPE	Business
289	8	REGION	Sub-Saharan Africa
289	9	ATTACK TYPE	Armed Assault
289	10	WEAPON TYPE	Firearms
289	11		
290	1	DATE	11/21/2008
290	2	COUNTRY	Nigeria
290	3	CITY	Opobo
290	4	PERPETRATOR	Unknown
290	5	FATALITIES	2
290	6	INJURED	0
290	7	TARGET TYPE	Government (General)
290	8	REGION	Sub-Saharan Africa
290	9	ATTACK TYPE	Hostage Taking (Kidnapping),Armed Assault
290	10	WEAPON TYPE	Firearms
290	11		
291	1	DATE	11/28/2008
291	2	COUNTRY	Nigeria
291	3	CITY	Port Harcourt
291	4	PERPETRATOR	Unknown
291	5	FATALITIES	Unknown
291	6	INJURED	Unknown
291	7	TARGET TYPE	Private Citizens & Property

291	8	REGION	Sub-Saharan Africa
291	9	ATTACK TYPE	Hostage Taking (Kidnapping)
291	10	WEAPON TYPE	Firearms
291	11		
292	1	DATE	11/30/2008
292	2	COUNTRY	Nigeria
292	3	CITY	Enugu
292	4	PERPETRATOR	Unknown
292	5	FATALITIES	1
292	6	INJURED	0
292	7	TARGET TYPE	Other
292	8	REGION	Sub-Saharan Africa
292	9	ATTACK TYPE	Assassination,Hostage Taking (Kidnapping)
292	10	WEAPON TYPE	Unknown
292	11		
293	1	DATE	12/1/2008
293	2	COUNTRY	Nigeria
293	3	CITY	Unknown
293	4	PERPETRATOR	Unknown
293	5	FATALITIES	1
293	6	INJURED	0
293	7	TARGET TYPE	Government (General)
293	8	REGION	Sub-Saharan Africa
293	9	ATTACK TYPE	Armed Assault
293	10	WEAPON TYPE	Unknown
293	11		
294	1	DATE	12/3/2008
294	2	COUNTRY	Nigeria
294	3	CITY	Eket
294	4	PERPETRATOR	Unknown
294	5	FATALITIES	1
294	6	INJURED	0
294	7	TARGET TYPE	Business
294	8	REGION	Sub-Saharan Africa
294	9	ATTACK TYPE	Armed Assault
294	10	WEAPON TYPE	Firearms
294	11		
295	1	DATE	12/6/2008
295	2	COUNTRY	Nigeria
295	3	CITY	Unknown
295	4	PERPETRATOR	Unknown
295	5	FATALITIES	2
295	6	INJURED	0
295	7	TARGET TYPE	Military
295	8	REGION	Sub-Saharan Africa
295	9	ATTACK TYPE	Armed Assault

295	10	WEAPON TYPE	Firearms
295	11		
296	1	DATE	12/8/2008
296	2	COUNTRY	Nigeria
296	3	CITY	Makurdi
296	4	PERPETRATOR	Unknown
296	5	FATALITIES	2
296	6	INJURED	1
296	7	TARGET TYPE	Police
296	8	REGION	Sub-Saharan Africa
296	9	ATTACK TYPE	Armed Assault
296	10	WEAPON TYPE	Firearms
296	11		
297	1	DATE	12/16/2008
297	2	COUNTRY	Nigeria
297	3	CITY	Ughelli
297	4	PERPETRATOR	Unknown
297	5	FATALITIES	0
297	6	INJURED	0
297	7	TARGET TYPE	Educational Institution
297	8	REGION	Sub-Saharan Africa
297	9	ATTACK TYPE	Hostage Taking (Kidnapping)
297	10	WEAPON TYPE	Unknown
297	11		
298	1	DATE	12/16/2008
298	2	COUNTRY	Nigeria
298	3	CITY	Port Harcourt
298	4	PERPETRATOR	Unknown
298	5	FATALITIES	0
298	6	INJURED	0
298	7	TARGET TYPE	Private Citizens & Property
298	8	REGION	Sub-Saharan Africa
298	9	ATTACK TYPE	Hostage Taking (Kidnapping)
298	10	WEAPON TYPE	Unknown
298	11		
299	1	DATE	12/20/2008
299	2	COUNTRY	Nigeria
299	3	CITY	Ikot Abasi
299	4	PERPETRATOR	Unknown
299	5	FATALITIES	0
299	6	INJURED	0
299	7	TARGET TYPE	Business
299	8	REGION	Sub-Saharan Africa
299	9	ATTACK TYPE	Hostage Taking (Kidnapping)
299	10	WEAPON TYPE	Firearms
299	11		

300	1	DATE	1/6/2009
300	2	COUNTRY	Nigeria
300	3	CITY	Zaria
300	4	PERPETRATOR	Unknown
300	5	FATALITIES	0
300	6	INJURED	0
300	7	TARGET TYPE	Private Citizens & Property
300	8	REGION	Sub-Saharan Africa
300	9	ATTACK TYPE	Facility/Infrastructure Attack
300	10	WEAPON TYPE	Incendiary
300	11		
301	1	DATE	1/18/2009
301	2	COUNTRY	Nigeria
301	3	CITY	Bonny
301	4	PERPETRATOR	Unknown
301	5	FATALITIES	1
301	6	INJURED	1
301	7	TARGET TYPE	Business
301	8	REGION	Sub-Saharan Africa
301	9	ATTACK TYPE	Hostage Taking (Kidnapping),Armed Assault
301	10	WEAPON TYPE	Unknown
301	11		
302	1	DATE	1/21/2009
302	2	COUNTRY	Nigeria
302	3	CITY	Unknown
302	4	PERPETRATOR	Movement for the Emancipation of the Niger Delta (MEND)
302	5	FATALITIES	0
302	6	INJURED	0
302	7	TARGET TYPE	Military,Maritime
302	8	REGION	Sub-Saharan Africa
302	9	ATTACK TYPE	Bombing/Explosion,Hostage Taking (Kidnapping)
302	10	WEAPON TYPE	Explosives/Bombs/Dynamite
302	11		
303	1	DATE	1/27/2009
303	2	COUNTRY	Nigeria
303	3	CITY	Warri
303	4	PERPETRATOR	Unknown
303	5	FATALITIES	0
303	6	INJURED	0
303	7	TARGET TYPE	Business
303	8	REGION	Sub-Saharan Africa
303	9	ATTACK TYPE	Hostage Taking (Kidnapping)
303	10	WEAPON TYPE	Firearms
303	11		
304	1	DATE	1/29/2009

304	2	COUNTRY	Nigeria
304	3	CITY	Port Harcourt
304	4	PERPETRATOR	Unknown
304	5	FATALITIES	1
304	6	INJURED	0
304	7	TARGET TYPE	Private Citizens & Property
304	8	REGION	Sub-Saharan Africa
304	9	ATTACK TYPE	Hostage Taking (Kidnapping),Armed Assault
304	10	WEAPON TYPE	Unknown
304	11		
305	1	DATE	2/4/2009
305	2	COUNTRY	Nigeria
305	3	CITY	Uyo
305	4	PERPETRATOR	Unknown
305	5	FATALITIES	0
305	6	INJURED	0
305	7	TARGET TYPE	Government (General),Private Citizens & Property
305	8	REGION	Sub-Saharan Africa
305	9	ATTACK TYPE	Hostage Taking (Kidnapping),Armed Assault
305	10	WEAPON TYPE	Unknown
305	11		
306	1	DATE	2/7/2009
306	2	COUNTRY	Nigeria
306	3	CITY	Utorogu
306	4	PERPETRATOR	Movement for the Emancipation of the Niger Delta (MEND)
306	5	FATALITIES	3
306	6	INJURED	5
306	7	TARGET TYPE	Business
306	8	REGION	Sub-Saharan Africa
306	9	ATTACK TYPE	Armed Assault
306	10	WEAPON TYPE	Firearms
306	11		
307	1	DATE	2/17/2009
307	2	COUNTRY	Nigeria
307	3	CITY	Nembe Creek
307	4	PERPETRATOR	Unknown
307	5	FATALITIES	0
307	6	INJURED	0
307	7	TARGET TYPE	Business,Police
307	8	REGION	Sub-Saharan Africa
307	9	ATTACK TYPE	Facility/Infrastructure Attack,Armed Assault
307	10	WEAPON TYPE	Unknown
307	11		
308	1	DATE	2/17/2009
308	2	COUNTRY	Nigeria

308	3	CITY	Eket
308	4	PERPETRATOR	Unknown
308	5	FATALITIES	0
308	6	INJURED	0
308	7	TARGET TYPE	Business
308	8	REGION	Sub-Saharan Africa
308	9	ATTACK TYPE	Facility/Infrastructure Attack
308	10	WEAPON TYPE	Firearms
308	11		
309	1	DATE	2/26/2009
309	2	COUNTRY	Nigeria
309	3	CITY	Tebidaba
309	4	PERPETRATOR	Movement for the Emancipation of the Niger Delta (MEND)
309	5	FATALITIES	0
309	6	INJURED	1
309	7	TARGET TYPE	Business
309	8	REGION	Sub-Saharan Africa
309	9	ATTACK TYPE	Armed Assault
309	10	WEAPON TYPE	Firearms
309	11		
310	1	DATE	3/4/2009
310	2	COUNTRY	Nigeria
310	3	CITY	Escravos
310	4	PERPETRATOR	Unknown
310	5	FATALITIES	0
310	6	INJURED	0
310	7	TARGET TYPE	Utilities
310	8	REGION	Sub-Saharan Africa
310	9	ATTACK TYPE	Bombing/Explosion
310	10	WEAPON TYPE	Explosives/Bombs/Dynamite
310	11		
311	1	DATE	3/16/2009
311	2	COUNTRY	Nigeria
311	3	CITY	Nembe Creek
311	4	PERPETRATOR	Unknown
311	5	FATALITIES	0
311	6	INJURED	0
311	7	TARGET TYPE	Business
311	8	REGION	Sub-Saharan Africa
311	9	ATTACK TYPE	Armed Assault
311	10	WEAPON TYPE	Firearms
311	11		
312	1	DATE	4/5/2009
312	2	COUNTRY	Nigeria
312	3	CITY	Yenagoa

312	4	PERPETRATOR	Unknown
312	5	FATALITIES	0
312	6	INJURED	0
312	7	TARGET TYPE	Business
312	8	REGION	Sub-Saharan Africa
312	9	ATTACK TYPE	Armed Assault
312	10	WEAPON TYPE	Unknown
312	11		
313	1	DATE	5/13/2009
313	2	COUNTRY	Nigeria
313	3	CITY	Escravos
313	4	PERPETRATOR	Movement for the Emancipation of the Niger Delta (MEND) (suspected)
313	5	FATALITIES	0
313	6	INJURED	0
313	7	TARGET TYPE	Business
313	8	REGION	Sub-Saharan Africa
313	9	ATTACK TYPE	Bombing/Explosion
313	10	WEAPON TYPE	Explosives/Bombs/Dynamite
313	11		
314	1	DATE	5/13/2009
314	2	COUNTRY	Nigeria
314	3	CITY	Unknown
314	4	PERPETRATOR	Movement for the Emancipation of the Niger Delta (MEND) (suspected)
314	5	FATALITIES	0
314	6	INJURED	6
314	7	TARGET TYPE	Maritime,Maritime
314	8	REGION	Sub-Saharan Africa
314	9	ATTACK TYPE	Armed Assault,Hijacking,Hostage Taking (Kidnapping)
314	10	WEAPON TYPE	Firearms
314	11		
315	1	DATE	5/25/2009
315	2	COUNTRY	Nigeria
315	3	CITY	Warri
315	4	PERPETRATOR	Movement for the Emancipation of the Niger Delta (MEND) (suspected)
315	5	FATALITIES	0
315	6	INJURED	0
315	7	TARGET TYPE	Business
315	8	REGION	Sub-Saharan Africa
315	9	ATTACK TYPE	Bombing/Explosion
315	10	WEAPON TYPE	Explosives/Bombs/Dynamite
315	11		
316	1	DATE	6/5/2009

316	2	COUNTRY	Nigeria
316	3	CITY	Benin
316	4	PERPETRATOR	Unknown
316	5	FATALITIES	0
316	6	INJURED	1
316	7	TARGET TYPE	Government (General)
316	8	REGION	Sub-Saharan Africa
316	9	ATTACK TYPE	Hostage Taking (Kidnapping),Armed Assault
316	10	WEAPON TYPE	Firearms
316	11		
317	1	DATE	6/7/2009
317	2	COUNTRY	Nigeria
317	3	CITY	Ibandan
317	4	PERPETRATOR	Unknown
317	5	FATALITIES	2
317	6	INJURED	2
317	7	TARGET TYPE	Other
317	8	REGION	Sub-Saharan Africa
317	9	ATTACK TYPE	Armed Assault
317	10	WEAPON TYPE	Firearms
317	11		
318	1	DATE	6/17/2009
318	2	COUNTRY	Nigeria
318	3	CITY	Agoro
318	4	PERPETRATOR	Movement for the Emancipation of the Niger Delta (MEND) (suspected)
318	5	FATALITIES	0
318	6	INJURED	0
318	7	TARGET TYPE	Business
318	8	REGION	Sub-Saharan Africa
318	9	ATTACK TYPE	Bombing/Explosion
318	10	WEAPON TYPE	Explosives/Bombs/Dynamite
318	11		
319	1	DATE	6/19/2009
319	2	COUNTRY	Nigeria
319	3	CITY	Nembe Creek
319	4	PERPETRATOR	Movement for the Emancipation of the Niger Delta (MEND) (suspected)
319	5	FATALITIES	0
319	6	INJURED	0
319	7	TARGET TYPE	Business
319	8	REGION	Sub-Saharan Africa
319	9	ATTACK TYPE	Bombing/Explosion
319	10	WEAPON TYPE	Explosives/Bombs/Dynamite
319	11		
320	1	DATE	6/21/2009

320	2	COUNTRY	Nigeria
320	3	CITY	Unknown
320	4	PERPETRATOR	Movement for the Emancipation of the Niger Delta (MEND) (suspected)
320	5	FATALITIES	0
320	6	INJURED	0
320	7	TARGET TYPE	Business,Business
320	8	REGION	Sub-Saharan Africa
320	9	ATTACK TYPE	Bombing/Explosion
320	10	WEAPON TYPE	Explosives/Bombs/Dynamite
320	11		
321	1	DATE	6/25/2009
321	2	COUNTRY	Nigeria
321	3	CITY	Unknown
321	4	PERPETRATOR	Movement for the Emancipation of the Niger Delta (MEND) (suspected)
321	5	FATALITIES	0
321	6	INJURED	0
321	7	TARGET TYPE	Business
321	8	REGION	Sub-Saharan Africa
321	9	ATTACK TYPE	Bombing/Explosion
321	10	WEAPON TYPE	Explosives/Bombs/Dynamite
321	11		
322	1	DATE	6/29/2009
322	2	COUNTRY	Nigeria
322	3	CITY	Forcados
322	4	PERPETRATOR	Movement for the Emancipation of the Niger Delta (MEND) (suspected)
322	5	FATALITIES	0
322	6	INJURED	0
322	7	TARGET TYPE	Business
322	8	REGION	Sub-Saharan Africa
322	9	ATTACK TYPE	Bombing/Explosion
322	10	WEAPON TYPE	Explosives/Bombs/Dynamite
322	11		
323	1	DATE	7/5/2009
323	2	COUNTRY	Nigeria
323	3	CITY	Bonny
323	4	PERPETRATOR	Movement for the Emancipation of the Niger Delta (MEND)
323	5	FATALITIES	0
323	6	INJURED	0
323	7	TARGET TYPE	Utilities
323	8	REGION	Sub-Saharan Africa
323	9	ATTACK TYPE	Armed Assault
323	10	WEAPON TYPE	Unknown

323	11		
324	1	DATE	7/5/2009
324	2	COUNTRY	Nigeria
324	3	CITY	Unknown
324	4	PERPETRATOR	Movement for the Emancipation of the Niger Delta (MEND)
324	5	FATALITIES	0
324	6	INJURED	0
324	7	TARGET TYPE	Utilities
324	8	REGION	Sub-Saharan Africa
324	9	ATTACK TYPE	Bombing/Explosion
324	10	WEAPON TYPE	Explosives/Bombs/Dynamite
324	11		
325	1	DATE	7/5/2009
325	2	COUNTRY	Nigeria
325	3	CITY	Escravos
325	4	PERPETRATOR	Movement for the Emancipation of the Niger Delta (MEND)
325	5	FATALITIES	0
325	6	INJURED	0
325	7	TARGET TYPE	Maritime
325	8	REGION	Sub-Saharan Africa
325	9	ATTACK TYPE	Armed Assault,Hostage Taking (Kidnapping)
325	10	WEAPON TYPE	Firearms
325	11		
326	1	DATE	7/8/2009
326	2	COUNTRY	Nigeria
326	3	CITY	Nembe Creek
326	4	PERPETRATOR	Movement for the Emancipation of the Niger Delta (MEND)
326	5	FATALITIES	0
326	6	INJURED	0
326	7	TARGET TYPE	Utilities
326	8	REGION	Sub-Saharan Africa
326	9	ATTACK TYPE	Bombing/Explosion
326	10	WEAPON TYPE	Explosives/Bombs/Dynamite
326	11		
327	1	DATE	7/8/2009
327	2	COUNTRY	Nigeria
327	3	CITY	Nembe Creek
327	4	PERPETRATOR	Movement for the Emancipation of the Niger Delta (MEND)
327	5	FATALITIES	0
327	6	INJURED	0
327	7	TARGET TYPE	Utilities
327	8	REGION	Sub-Saharan Africa

327	9	ATTACK TYPE	Bombing/Explosion
327	10	WEAPON TYPE	Explosives/Bombs/Dynamite
327	11		
328	1	DATE	7/12/2009
328	2	COUNTRY	Nigeria
328	3	CITY	Tarkwa
328	4	PERPETRATOR	Movement for the Emancipation of the Niger Delta (MEND) (suspected)
328	5	FATALITIES	5
328	6	INJURED	0
328	7	TARGET TYPE	Maritime
328	8	REGION	Sub-Saharan Africa
328	9	ATTACK TYPE	Bombing/Explosion,Armed Assault
328	10	WEAPON TYPE	Explosives/Bombs/Dynamite,Firearms
328	11		
329	1	DATE	7/14/2009
329	2	COUNTRY	Nigeria
329	3	CITY	Unknown
329	4	PERPETRATOR	Movement for the Emancipation of the Niger Delta (MEND)
329	5	FATALITIES	0
329	6	INJURED	0
329	7	TARGET TYPE	Utilities
329	8	REGION	Sub-Saharan Africa
329	9	ATTACK TYPE	Bombing/Explosion
329	10	WEAPON TYPE	Explosives/Bombs/Dynamite
329	11		
330	1	DATE	7/27/2009
330	2	COUNTRY	Nigeria
330	3	CITY	Gambaru
330	4	PERPETRATOR	Boko Haram (suspected)
330	5	FATALITIES	Unknown
330	6	INJURED	0
330	7	TARGET TYPE	Government (General),Private Citizens & Property
330	8	REGION	Sub-Saharan Africa
330	9	ATTACK TYPE	Armed Assault,Facility/Infrastructure Attack
330	10	WEAPON TYPE	Incendiary,Unknown
330	11		
331	1	DATE	7/27/2009
331	2	COUNTRY	Nigeria
331	3	CITY	Gambaru
331	4	PERPETRATOR	Boko Haram (suspected)
331	5	FATALITIES	Unknown
331	6	INJURED	0
331	7	TARGET TYPE	Private Citizens & Property,Religious Figures/Institutions

331	8	REGION	Sub-Saharan Africa
331	9	ATTACK TYPE	Armed Assault,Facility/Infrastructure Attack
331	10	WEAPON TYPE	Incendiary,Unknown
331	11		
332	1	DATE	7/27/2009
332	2	COUNTRY	Nigeria
332	3	CITY	Maiduguri
332	4	PERPETRATOR	Boko Haram (suspected)
332	5	FATALITIES	75
332	6	INJURED	Unknown
332	7	TARGET TYPE	Educational Institution,Private Citizens & Property
332	8	REGION	Sub-Saharan Africa
332	9	ATTACK TYPE	Armed Assault
332	10	WEAPON TYPE	Unknown
332	11		
333	1	DATE	7/27/2009
333	2	COUNTRY	Nigeria
333	3	CITY	Maiduguri
333	4	PERPETRATOR	Boko Haram (suspected)
333	5	FATALITIES	76
333	6	INJURED	Unknown
333	7	TARGET TYPE	Private Citizens & Property,Religious Figures/Institutions
333	8	REGION	Sub-Saharan Africa
333	9	ATTACK TYPE	Armed Assault
333	10	WEAPON TYPE	Unknown
333	11		
334	1	DATE	7/27/2009
334	2	COUNTRY	Nigeria
334	3	CITY	Maiduguri
334	4	PERPETRATOR	Boko Haram (suspected)
334	5	FATALITIES	76
334	6	INJURED	Unknown
334	7	TARGET TYPE	Police,Private Citizens & Property
334	8	REGION	Sub-Saharan Africa
334	9	ATTACK TYPE	Armed Assault
334	10	WEAPON TYPE	Unknown
334	11		
335	1	DATE	7/27/2009
335	2	COUNTRY	Nigeria
335	3	CITY	Maiduguri
335	4	PERPETRATOR	Boko Haram (suspected)
335	5	FATALITIES	0
335	6	INJURED	0
335	7	TARGET TYPE	Government (General),Private Citizens & Property
335	8	REGION	Sub-Saharan Africa

335	9	ATTACK TYPE	Facility/Infrastructure Attack
335	10	WEAPON TYPE	Incendiary
335	11		
336	1	DATE	7/27/2009
336	2	COUNTRY	Nigeria
336	3	CITY	Maiduguri
336	4	PERPETRATOR	Boko Haram (suspected)
336	5	FATALITIES	0
336	6	INJURED	0
336	7	TARGET TYPE	Police,Private Citizens & Property
336	8	REGION	Sub-Saharan Africa
336	9	ATTACK TYPE	Facility/Infrastructure Attack
336	10	WEAPON TYPE	Incendiary
336	11		
337	1	DATE	7/27/2009
337	2	COUNTRY	Nigeria
337	3	CITY	Maiduguri
337	4	PERPETRATOR	Boko Haram (suspected)
337	5	FATALITIES	0
337	6	INJURED	0
337	7	TARGET TYPE	Private Citizens & Property
337	8	REGION	Sub-Saharan Africa
337	9	ATTACK TYPE	Facility/Infrastructure Attack
337	10	WEAPON TYPE	Incendiary
337	11		
338	1	DATE	7/27/2009
338	2	COUNTRY	Nigeria
338	3	CITY	Maiduguri
338	4	PERPETRATOR	Boko Haram (suspected)
338	5	FATALITIES	77
338	6	INJURED	Unknown
338	7	TARGET TYPE	Police,Private Citizens & Property
338	8	REGION	Sub-Saharan Africa
338	9	ATTACK TYPE	Armed Assault
338	10	WEAPON TYPE	Unknown
338	11		
339	1	DATE	7/27/2009
339	2	COUNTRY	Nigeria
339	3	CITY	Gambaru
339	4	PERPETRATOR	Boko Haram (suspected)
339	5	FATALITIES	Unknown
339	6	INJURED	0
339	7	TARGET TYPE	Police,Private Citizens & Property
339	8	REGION	Sub-Saharan Africa
339	9	ATTACK TYPE	Armed Assault,Facility/Infrastructure Attack
339	10	WEAPON TYPE	Incendiary,Unknown

339	11		
340	1	DATE	8/8/2009
340	2	COUNTRY	Nigeria
340	3	CITY	Utorogu
340	4	PERPETRATOR	Niger Delta People's Volunteer Force (NDPVF)
340	5	FATALITIES	0
340	6	INJURED	0
340	7	TARGET TYPE	Utilities
340	8	REGION	Sub-Saharan Africa
340	9	ATTACK TYPE	Bombing/Explosion
340	10	WEAPON TYPE	Explosives/Bombs/Dynamite
340	11		
341	1	DATE	8/13/2009
341	2	COUNTRY	Nigeria
341	3	CITY	Ughelli
341	4	PERPETRATOR	Urhobo Revolutionary Army (suspected)
341	5	FATALITIES	0
341	6	INJURED	0
341	7	TARGET TYPE	Utilities
341	8	REGION	Sub-Saharan Africa
341	9	ATTACK TYPE	Bombing/Explosion
341	10	WEAPON TYPE	Explosives/Bombs/Dynamite
341	11		
342	1	DATE	1/25/2010
342	2	COUNTRY	Nigeria
342	3	CITY	Unknown
342	4	PERPETRATOR	Unknown
342	5	FATALITIES	1
342	6	INJURED	0
342	7	TARGET TYPE	Government (General)
342	8	REGION	Sub-Saharan Africa
342	9	ATTACK TYPE	Assassination
342	10	WEAPON TYPE	Firearms
342	11		
343	1	DATE	2/10/2010
343	2	COUNTRY	Nigeria
343	3	CITY	Abonema
343	4	PERPETRATOR	The Joint Revolutionary Council
343	5	FATALITIES	0
343	6	INJURED	0
343	7	TARGET TYPE	Utilities
343	8	REGION	Sub-Saharan Africa
343	9	ATTACK TYPE	Armed Assault
343	10	WEAPON TYPE	Unknown
343	11		
344	1	DATE	2/10/2010

344	2	COUNTRY	Nigeria
344	3	CITY	Abonema
344	4	PERPETRATOR	The Joint Revolutionary Council
344	5	FATALITIES	0
344	6	INJURED	0
344	7	TARGET TYPE	Utilities
344	8	REGION	Sub-Saharan Africa
344	9	ATTACK TYPE	Armed Assault
344	10	WEAPON TYPE	Unknown
344	11		
345	1	DATE	2/11/2010
345	2	COUNTRY	Nigeria
345	3	CITY	Lagos
345	4	PERPETRATOR	The Joint Revolutionary Council
345	5	FATALITIES	0
345	6	INJURED	0
345	7	TARGET TYPE	Utilities,Utilities
345	8	REGION	Sub-Saharan Africa
345	9	ATTACK TYPE	Armed Assault,Bombing/Explosion
345	10	WEAPON TYPE	Explosives/Bombs/Dynamite
345	11		
346	1	DATE	3/2/2010
346	2	COUNTRY	Nigeria
346	3	CITY	Warri
346	4	PERPETRATOR	The Joint Revolutionary Council (suspected)
346	5	FATALITIES	0
346	6	INJURED	0
346	7	TARGET TYPE	Utilities
346	8	REGION	Sub-Saharan Africa
346	9	ATTACK TYPE	Bombing/Explosion
346	10	WEAPON TYPE	Explosives/Bombs/Dynamite
346	11		
347	1	DATE	3/3/2010
347	2	COUNTRY	Nigeria
347	3	CITY	Abonema
347	4	PERPETRATOR	The Joint Revolutionary Council
347	5	FATALITIES	0
347	6	INJURED	0
347	7	TARGET TYPE	Utilities
347	8	REGION	Sub-Saharan Africa
347	9	ATTACK TYPE	Bombing/Explosion
347	10	WEAPON TYPE	Explosives/Bombs/Dynamite
347	11		
348	1	DATE	3/15/2010
348	2	COUNTRY	Nigeria
348	3	CITY	Warri

348	4	PERPETRATOR	Movement for the Emancipation of the Niger Delta (MEND)
348	5	FATALITIES	3
348	6	INJURED	2
348	7	TARGET TYPE	Government (General)
348	8	REGION	Sub-Saharan Africa
348	9	ATTACK TYPE	Bombing/Explosion
348	10	WEAPON TYPE	Explosives/Bombs/Dynamite
348	11		
349	1	DATE	3/19/2010
349	2	COUNTRY	Nigeria
349	3	CITY	Bugama
349	4	PERPETRATOR	The Joint Revolutionary Council
349	5	FATALITIES	0
349	6	INJURED	0
349	7	TARGET TYPE	Utilities
349	8	REGION	Sub-Saharan Africa
349	9	ATTACK TYPE	Bombing/Explosion
349	10	WEAPON TYPE	Explosives/Bombs/Dynamite
349	11		
350	1	DATE	3/23/2010
350	2	COUNTRY	Nigeria
350	3	CITY	Asaba
350	4	PERPETRATOR	Unknown
350	5	FATALITIES	0
350	6	INJURED	0
350	7	TARGET TYPE	Private Citizens & Property
350	8	REGION	Sub-Saharan Africa
350	9	ATTACK TYPE	Hostage Taking (Kidnapping)
350	10	WEAPON TYPE	Unknown
350	11		
351	1	DATE	4/5/2010
351	2	COUNTRY	Nigeria
351	3	CITY	Benin
351	4	PERPETRATOR	Unknown
351	5	FATALITIES	0
351	6	INJURED	0
351	7	TARGET TYPE	Educational Institution
351	8	REGION	Sub-Saharan Africa
351	9	ATTACK TYPE	Hostage Taking (Kidnapping)
351	10	WEAPON TYPE	Firearms
351	11		
352	1	DATE	4/9/2010
352	2	COUNTRY	Nigeria
352	3	CITY	Port Harcourt
352	4	PERPETRATOR	Unknown

352	5	FATALITIES	0
352	6	INJURED	0
352	7	TARGET TYPE	Business,Private Citizens & Property
352	8	REGION	Sub-Saharan Africa
352	9	ATTACK TYPE	Hostage Taking (Kidnapping)
352	10	WEAPON TYPE	Firearms
352	11		
353	1	DATE	4/11/2010
353	2	COUNTRY	Nigeria
353	3	CITY	Jos
353	4	PERPETRATOR	Unknown
353	5	FATALITIES	0
353	6	INJURED	0
353	7	TARGET TYPE	Private Citizens & Property
353	8	REGION	Sub-Saharan Africa
353	9	ATTACK TYPE	Bombing/Explosion
353	10	WEAPON TYPE	Explosives/Bombs/Dynamite
353	11		
354	1	DATE	4/11/2010
354	2	COUNTRY	Nigeria
354	3	CITY	Jos
354	4	PERPETRATOR	Fulani Militants (suspected)
354	5	FATALITIES	0
354	6	INJURED	0
354	7	TARGET TYPE	Private Citizens & Property,Private Citizens & Property
354	8	REGION	Sub-Saharan Africa
354	9	ATTACK TYPE	Facility/Infrastructure Attack
354	10	WEAPON TYPE	Incendiary
354	11		
355	1	DATE	4/18/2010
355	2	COUNTRY	Nigeria
355	3	CITY	Unknown
355	4	PERPETRATOR	Unknown
355	5	FATALITIES	0
355	6	INJURED	0
355	7	TARGET TYPE	Private Citizens & Property
355	8	REGION	Sub-Saharan Africa
355	9	ATTACK TYPE	Hostage Taking (Kidnapping)
355	10	WEAPON TYPE	Firearms
355	11		
356	1	DATE	4/19/2010
356	2	COUNTRY	Nigeria
356	3	CITY	Benin
356	4	PERPETRATOR	Unknown
356	5	FATALITIES	0

356	6	INJURED	0
356	7	TARGET TYPE	Other
356	8	REGION	Sub-Saharan Africa
356	9	ATTACK TYPE	Hostage Taking (Kidnapping)
356	10	WEAPON TYPE	Firearms
356	11		
357	1	DATE	5/2/2010
357	2	COUNTRY	Nigeria
357	3	CITY	Yenagoa
357	4	PERPETRATOR	Unknown
357	5	FATALITIES	0
357	6	INJURED	0
357	7	TARGET TYPE	Business
357	8	REGION	Sub-Saharan Africa
357	9	ATTACK TYPE	Bombing/Explosion
357	10	WEAPON TYPE	Explosives/Bombs/Dynamite
357	11		
358	1	DATE	5/10/2010
358	2	COUNTRY	Nigeria
358	3	CITY	Warri
358	4	PERPETRATOR	Movement for the Emancipation of the Niger Delta (MEND) (suspected)
358	5	FATALITIES	0
358	6	INJURED	0
358	7	TARGET TYPE	Government (General)
358	8	REGION	Sub-Saharan Africa
358	9	ATTACK TYPE	Bombing/Explosion
358	10	WEAPON TYPE	Explosives/Bombs/Dynamite
358	11		
359	1	DATE	5/29/2010
359	2	COUNTRY	Nigeria
359	3	CITY	Port Harcourt
359	4	PERPETRATOR	Unknown
359	5	FATALITIES	2
359	6	INJURED	0
359	7	TARGET TYPE	Government (General)
359	8	REGION	Sub-Saharan Africa
359	9	ATTACK TYPE	Hostage Taking (Kidnapping)
359	10	WEAPON TYPE	Firearms
359	11		
360	1	DATE	6/2/2010
360	2	COUNTRY	Nigeria
360	3	CITY	Yenagoa
360	4	PERPETRATOR	Unknown
360	5	FATALITIES	0
360	6	INJURED	0

360	7	TARGET TYPE	Business
360	8	REGION	Sub-Saharan Africa
360	9	ATTACK TYPE	Bombing/Explosion
360	10	WEAPON TYPE	Explosives/Bombs/Dynamite
360	11		
361	1	DATE	6/2/2010
361	2	COUNTRY	Nigeria
361	3	CITY	Yenagoa
361	4	PERPETRATOR	Unknown
361	5	FATALITIES	0
361	6	INJURED	0
361	7	TARGET TYPE	Government (General)
361	8	REGION	Sub-Saharan Africa
361	9	ATTACK TYPE	Bombing/Explosion
361	10	WEAPON TYPE	Explosives/Bombs/Dynamite
361	11		
362	1	DATE	6/13/2010
362	2	COUNTRY	Nigeria
362	3	CITY	Port Harcourt
362	4	PERPETRATOR	Unknown
362	5	FATALITIES	2
362	6	INJURED	5
362	7	TARGET TYPE	Other,Private Citizens & Property
362	8	REGION	Sub-Saharan Africa
362	9	ATTACK TYPE	Armed Assault,Hostage Taking (Kidnapping)
362	10	WEAPON TYPE	Firearms
362	11		
363	1	DATE	7/3/2010
363	2	COUNTRY	Nigeria
363	3	CITY	Unknown
363	4	PERPETRATOR	Fulani Militants (suspected)
363	5	FATALITIES	7
363	6	INJURED	5
363	7	TARGET TYPE	Private Citizens & Property
363	8	REGION	Sub-Saharan Africa
363	9	ATTACK TYPE	Armed Assault
363	10	WEAPON TYPE	Firearms,Incendiary
363	11		
364	1	DATE	7/27/2010
364	2	COUNTRY	Nigeria
364	3	CITY	Yenagoa
364	4	PERPETRATOR	Unknown
364	5	FATALITIES	1
364	6	INJURED	1
364	7	TARGET TYPE	Government (General)
364	8	REGION	Sub-Saharan Africa

364	9	ATTACK TYPE	Assassination
364	10	WEAPON TYPE	Firearms
364	11		
365	1	DATE	8/2/2010
365	2	COUNTRY	Nigeria
365	3	CITY	Aba
365	4	PERPETRATOR	Unknown
365	5	FATALITIES	1
365	6	INJURED	3
365	7	TARGET TYPE	Private Citizens & Property
365	8	REGION	Sub-Saharan Africa
365	9	ATTACK TYPE	Armed Assault,Hostage Taking (Kidnapping)
365	10	WEAPON TYPE	Firearms
365	11		
366	1	DATE	8/29/2010
366	2	COUNTRY	Nigeria
366	3	CITY	Benin
366	4	PERPETRATOR	Unknown
366	5	FATALITIES	0
366	6	INJURED	0
366	7	TARGET TYPE	Government (General)
366	8	REGION	Sub-Saharan Africa
366	9	ATTACK TYPE	Hostage Taking (Kidnapping)
366	10	WEAPON TYPE	Firearms
366	11		
367	1	DATE	9/5/2010
367	2	COUNTRY	Nigeria
367	3	CITY	Maiduguri
367	4	PERPETRATOR	Boko Haram
367	5	FATALITIES	0
367	6	INJURED	2
367	7	TARGET TYPE	Private Citizens & Property
367	8	REGION	Sub-Saharan Africa
367	9	ATTACK TYPE	Armed Assault
367	10	WEAPON TYPE	Firearms
367	11		
368	1	DATE	9/5/2010
368	2	COUNTRY	Nigeria
368	3	CITY	Maiduguri
368	4	PERPETRATOR	Boko Haram (suspected)
368	5	FATALITIES	1
368	6	INJURED	2
368	7	TARGET TYPE	Government (General)
368	8	REGION	Sub-Saharan Africa
368	9	ATTACK TYPE	Assassination
368	10	WEAPON TYPE	Firearms

368	11		
369	1	DATE	9/5/2010
369	2	COUNTRY	Nigeria
369	3	CITY	Bama
369	4	PERPETRATOR	Boko Haram
369	5	FATALITIES	1
369	6	INJURED	0
369	7	TARGET TYPE	Private Citizens & Property
369	8	REGION	Sub-Saharan Africa
369	9	ATTACK TYPE	Armed Assault
369	10	WEAPON TYPE	Firearms
369	11		
370	1	DATE	9/16/2010
370	2	COUNTRY	Nigeria
370	3	CITY	Omuma
370	4	PERPETRATOR	Unknown
370	5	FATALITIES	0
370	6	INJURED	0
370	7	TARGET TYPE	Government (General)
370	8	REGION	Sub-Saharan Africa
370	9	ATTACK TYPE	Hostage Taking (Kidnapping)
370	10	WEAPON TYPE	Unknown
370	11		
371	1	DATE	9/21/2010
371	2	COUNTRY	Nigeria
371	3	CITY	Maiduguri
371	4	PERPETRATOR	Boko Haram
371	5	FATALITIES	2
371	6	INJURED	0
371	7	TARGET TYPE	Government (General),Private Citizens & Property
371	8	REGION	Sub-Saharan Africa
371	9	ATTACK TYPE	Armed Assault
371	10	WEAPON TYPE	Firearms
371	11		
372	1	DATE	10/1/2010
372	2	COUNTRY	Nigeria
372	3	CITY	Abuja
372	4	PERPETRATOR	Movement for the Emancipation of the Niger Delta (MEND)
372	5	FATALITIES	4
372	6	INJURED	13
372	7	TARGET TYPE	Private Citizens & Property
372	8	REGION	Sub-Saharan Africa
372	9	ATTACK TYPE	Bombing/Explosion
372	10	WEAPON TYPE	Explosives/Bombs/Dynamite
372	11		

373	1	DATE	10/1/2010
373	2	COUNTRY	Nigeria
373	3	CITY	Abuja
373	4	PERPETRATOR	Movement for the Emancipation of the Niger Delta (MEND)
373	5	FATALITIES	7
373	6	INJURED	27
373	7	TARGET TYPE	Police,Private Citizens & Property
373	8	REGION	Sub-Saharan Africa
373	9	ATTACK TYPE	Bombing/Explosion
373	10	WEAPON TYPE	Explosives/Bombs/Dynamite
373	11		
374	1	DATE	10/6/2010
374	2	COUNTRY	Nigeria
374	3	CITY	Maiduguri
374	4	PERPETRATOR	Boko Haram (suspected)
374	5	FATALITIES	1
374	6	INJURED	0
374	7	TARGET TYPE	Government (General)
374	8	REGION	Sub-Saharan Africa
374	9	ATTACK TYPE	Assassination
374	10	WEAPON TYPE	Firearms
374	11		
375	1	DATE	10/6/2010
375	2	COUNTRY	Nigeria
375	3	CITY	Maiduguri
375	4	PERPETRATOR	Boko Haram (suspected)
375	5	FATALITIES	1
375	6	INJURED	0
375	7	TARGET TYPE	NGO
375	8	REGION	Sub-Saharan Africa
375	9	ATTACK TYPE	Assassination
375	10	WEAPON TYPE	Firearms
375	11		
376	1	DATE	10/9/2010
376	2	COUNTRY	Nigeria
376	3	CITY	Maiduguri
376	4	PERPETRATOR	Boko Haram (suspected)
376	5	FATALITIES	2
376	6	INJURED	0
376	7	TARGET TYPE	Religious Figures/Institutions
376	8	REGION	Sub-Saharan Africa
376	9	ATTACK TYPE	Armed Assault
376	10	WEAPON TYPE	Firearms
376	11		
377	1	DATE	10/13/2010

377	2	COUNTRY	Nigeria
377	3	CITY	Eket
377	4	PERPETRATOR	Unknown
377	5	FATALITIES	2
377	6	INJURED	0
377	7	TARGET TYPE	Business,Police,Private Citizens & Property
377	8	REGION	Sub-Saharan Africa
377	9	ATTACK TYPE	Armed Assault,Hostage Taking (Kidnapping)
377	10	WEAPON TYPE	Firearms
377	11		
378	1	DATE	10/19/2010
378	2	COUNTRY	Nigeria
378	3	CITY	Maiduguri
378	4	PERPETRATOR	Boko Haram (suspected)
378	5	FATALITIES	1
378	6	INJURED	0
378	7	TARGET TYPE	Police
378	8	REGION	Sub-Saharan Africa
378	9	ATTACK TYPE	Armed Assault
378	10	WEAPON TYPE	Firearms
378	11		
379	1	DATE	10/22/2010
379	2	COUNTRY	Nigeria
379	3	CITY	Ganuwa
379	4	PERPETRATOR	Boko Haram (suspected)
379	5	FATALITIES	1
379	6	INJURED	0
379	7	TARGET TYPE	Private Citizens & Property
379	8	REGION	Sub-Saharan Africa
379	9	ATTACK TYPE	Armed Assault
379	10	WEAPON TYPE	Unknown
379	11		
380	1	DATE	10/26/2010
380	2	COUNTRY	Nigeria
380	3	CITY	Jos
380	4	PERPETRATOR	Fulani Militants (suspected)
380	5	FATALITIES	6
380	6	INJURED	3
380	7	TARGET TYPE	Private Citizens & Property
380	8	REGION	Sub-Saharan Africa
380	9	ATTACK TYPE	Armed Assault
380	10	WEAPON TYPE	Unknown
380	11		
381	1	DATE	10/28/2010
381	2	COUNTRY	Nigeria
381	3	CITY	Ilorin

381	4	PERPETRATOR	Unknown
381	5	FATALITIES	0
381	6	INJURED	0
381	7	TARGET TYPE	Private Citizens & Property
381	8	REGION	Sub-Saharan Africa
381	9	ATTACK TYPE	Hostage Taking (Kidnapping)
381	10	WEAPON TYPE	Unknown
381	11		
382	1	DATE	10/28/2010
382	2	COUNTRY	Nigeria
382	3	CITY	Unknown
382	4	PERPETRATOR	Unknown
382	5	FATALITIES	0
382	6	INJURED	0
382	7	TARGET TYPE	Utilities
382	8	REGION	Sub-Saharan Africa
382	9	ATTACK TYPE	Bombing/Explosion
382	10	WEAPON TYPE	Explosives/Bombs/Dynamite
382	11		
383	1	DATE	11/3/2010
383	2	COUNTRY	Nigeria
383	3	CITY	Lagos
383	4	PERPETRATOR	Movement for the Emancipation of the Niger Delta (MEND) (suspected)
383	5	FATALITIES	0
383	6	INJURED	0
383	7	TARGET TYPE	Business
383	8	REGION	Sub-Saharan Africa
383	9	ATTACK TYPE	Armed Assault
383	10	WEAPON TYPE	Unknown
383	11		
384	1	DATE	11/7/2010
384	2	COUNTRY	Nigeria
384	3	CITY	Unknown
384	4	PERPETRATOR	Movement for the Emancipation of the Niger Delta (MEND)
384	5	FATALITIES	0
384	6	INJURED	0
384	7	TARGET TYPE	Business,Private Citizens & Property
384	8	REGION	Sub-Saharan Africa
384	9	ATTACK TYPE	Hostage Taking (Kidnapping),Armed Assault
384	10	WEAPON TYPE	Firearms
384	11		
385	1	DATE	11/11/2010
385	2	COUNTRY	Nigeria
385	3	CITY	Kolokuma/Opokuma

385	4	PERPETRATOR	Unknown
385	5	FATALITIES	0
385	6	INJURED	0
385	7	TARGET TYPE	Government (General)
385	8	REGION	Sub-Saharan Africa
385	9	ATTACK TYPE	Assassination
385	10	WEAPON TYPE	Explosives/Bombs/Dynamite
385	11		
386	1	DATE	11/14/2010
386	2	COUNTRY	Nigeria
386	3	CITY	Unknown
386	4	PERPETRATOR	Movement for the Emancipation of the Niger Delta (MEND)
386	5	FATALITIES	0
386	6	INJURED	0
386	7	TARGET TYPE	Business,Private Citizens & Property
386	8	REGION	Sub-Saharan Africa
386	9	ATTACK TYPE	Hostage Taking (Kidnapping),Armed Assault,Bombing/Explosion
386	10	WEAPON TYPE	Explosives/Bombs/Dynamite
386	11		
387	1	DATE	11/19/2010
387	2	COUNTRY	Nigeria
387	3	CITY	Maiduguri
387	4	PERPETRATOR	Boko Haram (suspected)
387	5	FATALITIES	3
387	6	INJURED	1
387	7	TARGET TYPE	Private Citizens & Property
387	8	REGION	Sub-Saharan Africa
387	9	ATTACK TYPE	Armed Assault
387	10	WEAPON TYPE	Firearms
387	11		
388	1	DATE	11/21/2010
388	2	COUNTRY	Nigeria
388	3	CITY	Warri
388	4	PERPETRATOR	Movement for the Emancipation of the Niger Delta (MEND)
388	5	FATALITIES	0
388	6	INJURED	0
388	7	TARGET TYPE	Utilities
388	8	REGION	Sub-Saharan Africa
388	9	ATTACK TYPE	Armed Assault
388	10	WEAPON TYPE	Unknown
388	11		
389	1	DATE	11/22/2010
389	2	COUNTRY	Nigeria

389	3	CITY	Brass
389	4	PERPETRATOR	Unknown
389	5	FATALITIES	1
389	6	INJURED	0
389	7	TARGET TYPE	Private Citizens & Property
389	8	REGION	Sub-Saharan Africa
389	9	ATTACK TYPE	Armed Assault
389	10	WEAPON TYPE	Melee
389	11		
390	1	DATE	11/29/2010
390	2	COUNTRY	Nigeria
390	3	CITY	Unknown
390	4	PERPETRATOR	Boko Haram (suspected)
390	5	FATALITIES	1
390	6	INJURED	0
390	7	TARGET TYPE	Private Citizens & Property
390	8	REGION	Sub-Saharan Africa
390	9	ATTACK TYPE	Armed Assault
390	10	WEAPON TYPE	Firearms,Melee
390	11		
391	1	DATE	12/1/2010
391	2	COUNTRY	Nigeria
391	3	CITY	Unknown
391	4	PERPETRATOR	Unknown
391	5	FATALITIES	1
391	6	INJURED	0
391	7	TARGET TYPE	Business,Private Citizens & Property
391	8	REGION	Sub-Saharan Africa
391	9	ATTACK TYPE	Armed Assault,Hostage Taking (Kidnapping)
391	10	WEAPON TYPE	Firearms
391	11		
392	1	DATE	12/3/2010
392	2	COUNTRY	Nigeria
392	3	CITY	Jos
392	4	PERPETRATOR	Unknown
392	5	FATALITIES	7
392	6	INJURED	0
392	7	TARGET TYPE	Private Citizens & Property
392	8	REGION	Sub-Saharan Africa
392	9	ATTACK TYPE	Armed Assault
392	10	WEAPON TYPE	Firearms,Melee
392	11		
393	1	DATE	12/17/2010
393	2	COUNTRY	Nigeria
393	3	CITY	Unknown
393	4	PERPETRATOR	Niger Delta Liberation Force (NDLF)-Nigeria

393	5	FATALITIES	0
393	6	INJURED	0
393	7	TARGET TYPE	Utilities
393	8	REGION	Sub-Saharan Africa
393	9	ATTACK TYPE	Bombing/Explosion
393	10	WEAPON TYPE	Explosives/Bombs/Dynamite
393	11		
394	1	DATE	12/17/2010
394	2	COUNTRY	Nigeria
394	3	CITY	Unknown
394	4	PERPETRATOR	Niger Delta Liberation Force (NDLF)-Nigeria
394	5	FATALITIES	0
394	6	INJURED	0
394	7	TARGET TYPE	Utilities
394	8	REGION	Sub-Saharan Africa
394	9	ATTACK TYPE	Bombing/Explosion
394	10	WEAPON TYPE	Explosives/Bombs/Dynamite
394	11		
395	1	DATE	12/17/2010
395	2	COUNTRY	Nigeria
395	3	CITY	Unknown
395	4	PERPETRATOR	Niger Delta Liberation Force (NDLF)-Nigeria
395	5	FATALITIES	0
395	6	INJURED	0
395	7	TARGET TYPE	Utilities
395	8	REGION	Sub-Saharan Africa
395	9	ATTACK TYPE	Bombing/Explosion
395	10	WEAPON TYPE	Explosives/Bombs/Dynamite
395	11		
396	1	DATE	12/24/2010
396	2	COUNTRY	Nigeria
396	3	CITY	Jos
396	4	PERPETRATOR	Boko Haram
396	5	FATALITIES	0
396	6	INJURED	0
396	7	TARGET TYPE	Private Citizens & Property
396	8	REGION	Sub-Saharan Africa
396	9	ATTACK TYPE	Bombing/Explosion
396	10	WEAPON TYPE	Explosives/Bombs/Dynamite
396	11		
397	1	DATE	12/24/2010
397	2	COUNTRY	Nigeria
397	3	CITY	Jos
397	4	PERPETRATOR	Boko Haram
397	5	FATALITIES	38
397	6	INJURED	74

397	7	TARGET TYPE	Private Citizens & Property
397	8	REGION	Sub-Saharan Africa
397	9	ATTACK TYPE	Bombing/Explosion
397	10	WEAPON TYPE	Explosives/Bombs/Dynamite
397	11		
398	1	DATE	12/24/2010
398	2	COUNTRY	Nigeria
398	3	CITY	Maiduguri
398	4	PERPETRATOR	Unknown
398	5	FATALITIES	0
398	6	INJURED	0
398	7	TARGET TYPE	Religious Figures/Institutions
398	8	REGION	Sub-Saharan Africa
398	9	ATTACK TYPE	Bombing/Explosion
398	10	WEAPON TYPE	Explosives/Bombs/Dynamite
398	11		
399	1	DATE	12/24/2010
399	2	COUNTRY	Nigeria
399	3	CITY	Maiduguri
399	4	PERPETRATOR	Boko Haram
399	5	FATALITIES	1
399	6	INJURED	0
399	7	TARGET TYPE	Religious Figures/Institutions
399	8	REGION	Sub-Saharan Africa
399	9	ATTACK TYPE	Armed Assault,Bombing/Explosion
399	10	WEAPON TYPE	Firearms,Explosives/Bombs/Dynamite
399	11		
400	1	DATE	12/24/2010
400	2	COUNTRY	Nigeria
400	3	CITY	Maiduguri
400	4	PERPETRATOR	Boko Haram
400	5	FATALITIES	5
400	6	INJURED	25
400	7	TARGET TYPE	Religious Figures/Institutions
400	8	REGION	Sub-Saharan Africa
400	9	ATTACK TYPE	Armed Assault,Bombing/Explosion
400	10	WEAPON TYPE	Explosives/Bombs/Dynamite,Firearms
400	11		
401	1	DATE	12/28/2010
401	2	COUNTRY	Nigeria
401	3	CITY	Maiduguri
401	4	PERPETRATOR	Boko Haram (suspected)
401	5	FATALITIES	3
401	6	INJURED	0
401	7	TARGET TYPE	Business,Police,Private Citizens & Property
401	8	REGION	Sub-Saharan Africa

401	9	ATTACK TYPE	Armed Assault
401	10	WEAPON TYPE	Firearms
401	11		
402	1	DATE	12/29/2010
402	2	COUNTRY	Nigeria
402	3	CITY	Yenagoa
402	4	PERPETRATOR	Unknown
402	5	FATALITIES	0
402	6	INJURED	2
402	7	TARGET TYPE	Government (General),Private Citizens & Property
402	8	REGION	Sub-Saharan Africa
402	9	ATTACK TYPE	Bombing/Explosion
402	10	WEAPON TYPE	Explosives/Bombs/Dynamite
402	11		
403	1	DATE	12/31/2010
403	2	COUNTRY	Nigeria
403	3	CITY	Abuja
403	4	PERPETRATOR	Unknown
403	5	FATALITIES	0
403	6	INJURED	0
403	7	TARGET TYPE	Religious Figures/Institutions
403	8	REGION	Sub-Saharan Africa
403	9	ATTACK TYPE	Bombing/Explosion
403	10	WEAPON TYPE	Explosives/Bombs/Dynamite
403	11		
404	1	DATE	12/31/2010
404	2	COUNTRY	Nigeria
404	3	CITY	Abuja
404	4	PERPETRATOR	Boko Haram (suspected)
404	5	FATALITIES	11
404	6	INJURED	26
404	7	TARGET TYPE	Private Citizens & Property
404	8	REGION	Sub-Saharan Africa
404	9	ATTACK TYPE	Bombing/Explosion
404	10	WEAPON TYPE	Explosives/Bombs/Dynamite
404	11		
405	1	DATE	1/1/2011
405	2	COUNTRY	Nigeria
405	3	CITY	Maiduguri
405	4	PERPETRATOR	Boko Haram (suspected)
405	5	FATALITIES	0
405	6	INJURED	0
405	7	TARGET TYPE	Religious Figures/Institutions
405	8	REGION	Sub-Saharan Africa
405	9	ATTACK TYPE	Facility/Infrastructure Attack
405	10	WEAPON TYPE	Incendiary

405	11		
406	1	DATE	1/3/2011
406	2	COUNTRY	Nigeria
406	3	CITY	Ughelli
406	4	PERPETRATOR	Delta Democratic Militia
406	5	FATALITIES	0
406	6	INJURED	3
406	7	TARGET TYPE	Government (General)
406	8	REGION	Sub-Saharan Africa
406	9	ATTACK TYPE	Bombing/Explosion
406	10	WEAPON TYPE	Explosives/Bombs/Dynamite
406	11		
407	1	DATE	1/3/2011
407	2	COUNTRY	Nigeria
407	3	CITY	Maiduguri
407	4	PERPETRATOR	Boko Haram (suspected)
407	5	FATALITIES	1
407	6	INJURED	0
407	7	TARGET TYPE	Police
407	8	REGION	Sub-Saharan Africa
407	9	ATTACK TYPE	Armed Assault
407	10	WEAPON TYPE	Firearms
407	11		
408	1	DATE	1/7/2011
408	2	COUNTRY	Nigeria
408	3	CITY	Jos
408	4	PERPETRATOR	Unknown
408	5	FATALITIES	9
408	6	INJURED	0
408	7	TARGET TYPE	Private Citizens & Property
408	8	REGION	Sub-Saharan Africa
408	9	ATTACK TYPE	Armed Assault
408	10	WEAPON TYPE	Melee
408	11		
409	1	DATE	1/7/2011
409	2	COUNTRY	Nigeria
409	3	CITY	Gombe
409	4	PERPETRATOR	Boko Haram (suspected)
409	5	FATALITIES	8
409	6	INJURED	2
409	7	TARGET TYPE	Private Citizens & Property
409	8	REGION	Sub-Saharan Africa
409	9	ATTACK TYPE	Armed Assault
409	10	WEAPON TYPE	Firearms
409	11		
410	1	DATE	1/7/2011

410	2	COUNTRY	Nigeria
410	3	CITY	Kolokuma/Opokuma
410	4	PERPETRATOR	Unknown
410	5	FATALITIES	2
410	6	INJURED	6
410	7	TARGET TYPE	Private Citizens & Property
410	8	REGION	Sub-Saharan Africa
410	9	ATTACK TYPE	Armed Assault
410	10	WEAPON TYPE	Firearms,Melee
410	11		
411	1	DATE	1/10/2011
411	2	COUNTRY	Nigeria
411	3	CITY	Jos
411	4	PERPETRATOR	Unknown
411	5	FATALITIES	0
411	6	INJURED	0
411	7	TARGET TYPE	Private Citizens & Property,Religious Figures/Institutions
411	8	REGION	Sub-Saharan Africa
411	9	ATTACK TYPE	Facility/Infrastructure Attack
411	10	WEAPON TYPE	Incendiary
411	11		
412	1	DATE	1/10/2011
412	2	COUNTRY	Nigeria
412	3	CITY	Jos
412	4	PERPETRATOR	Unknown
412	5	FATALITIES	13
412	6	INJURED	0
412	7	TARGET TYPE	Private Citizens & Property
412	8	REGION	Sub-Saharan Africa
412	9	ATTACK TYPE	Armed Assault
412	10	WEAPON TYPE	Melee,Firearms
412	11		
413	1	DATE	1/10/2011
413	2	COUNTRY	Nigeria
413	3	CITY	Jos
413	4	PERPETRATOR	Unknown
413	5	FATALITIES	2
413	6	INJURED	3
413	7	TARGET TYPE	Private Citizens & Property
413	8	REGION	Sub-Saharan Africa
413	9	ATTACK TYPE	Armed Assault,Facility/Infrastructure Attack
413	10	WEAPON TYPE	Melee,Firearms,Incendiary
413	11		
414	1	DATE	1/10/2011
414	2	COUNTRY	Nigeria

414	3	CITY	Jos
414	4	PERPETRATOR	Unknown
414	5	FATALITIES	3
414	6	INJURED	0
414	7	TARGET TYPE	Private Citizens & Property
414	8	REGION	Sub-Saharan Africa
414	9	ATTACK TYPE	Armed Assault,Facility/Infrastructure Attack
414	10	WEAPON TYPE	Melee,Firearms,Incendiary
414	11		
415	1	DATE	1/10/2011
415	2	COUNTRY	Nigeria
415	3	CITY	Jos
415	4	PERPETRATOR	Unknown
415	5	FATALITIES	18
415	6	INJURED	0
415	7	TARGET TYPE	Private Citizens & Property
415	8	REGION	Sub-Saharan Africa
415	9	ATTACK TYPE	Armed Assault
415	10	WEAPON TYPE	Melee,Firearms
415	11		
416	1	DATE	1/13/2011
416	2	COUNTRY	Nigeria
416	3	CITY	Yenagoa
416	4	PERPETRATOR	Unknown
416	5	FATALITIES	0
416	6	INJURED	0
416	7	TARGET TYPE	Government (General)
416	8	REGION	Sub-Saharan Africa
416	9	ATTACK TYPE	Bombing/Explosion
416	10	WEAPON TYPE	Explosives/Bombs/Dynamite
416	11		
417	1	DATE	1/17/2011
417	2	COUNTRY	Nigeria
417	3	CITY	Enugu
417	4	PERPETRATOR	Unknown
417	5	FATALITIES	0
417	6	INJURED	0
417	7	TARGET TYPE	Transportation
417	8	REGION	Sub-Saharan Africa
417	9	ATTACK TYPE	Bombing/Explosion
417	10	WEAPON TYPE	Explosives/Bombs/Dynamite
417	11		
418	1	DATE	1/23/2011
418	2	COUNTRY	Nigeria
418	3	CITY	Jos
418	4	PERPETRATOR	Unknown

418	5	FATALITIES	0
418	6	INJURED	0
418	7	TARGET TYPE	Private Citizens & Property
418	8	REGION	Sub-Saharan Africa
418	9	ATTACK TYPE	Facility/Infrastructure Attack
418	10	WEAPON TYPE	Incendiary,Firearms
418	11		
419	1	DATE	1/23/2011
419	2	COUNTRY	Nigeria
419	3	CITY	Jos
419	4	PERPETRATOR	Unknown
419	5	FATALITIES	4
419	6	INJURED	2
419	7	TARGET TYPE	Private Citizens & Property
419	8	REGION	Sub-Saharan Africa
419	9	ATTACK TYPE	Armed Assault
419	10	WEAPON TYPE	Melee,Firearms
419	11		
420	1	DATE	1/23/2011
420	2	COUNTRY	Nigeria
420	3	CITY	Jos
420	4	PERPETRATOR	Unknown
420	5	FATALITIES	4
420	6	INJURED	Unknown
420	7	TARGET TYPE	Private Citizens & Property
420	8	REGION	Sub-Saharan Africa
420	9	ATTACK TYPE	Armed Assault
420	10	WEAPON TYPE	Melee,Firearms
420	11		
421	1	DATE	1/24/2011
421	2	COUNTRY	Nigeria
421	3	CITY	Sokoto
421	4	PERPETRATOR	Unknown
421	5	FATALITIES	1
421	6	INJURED	0
421	7	TARGET TYPE	Government (General)
421	8	REGION	Sub-Saharan Africa
421	9	ATTACK TYPE	Armed Assault
421	10	WEAPON TYPE	Firearms
421	11		
422	1	DATE	1/26/2011
422	2	COUNTRY	Nigeria
422	3	CITY	Maiduguri
422	4	PERPETRATOR	Unknown
422	5	FATALITIES	1
422	6	INJURED	0

422	7	TARGET TYPE	Police
422	8	REGION	Sub-Saharan Africa
422	9	ATTACK TYPE	Armed Assault
422	10	WEAPON TYPE	Firearms
422	11		
423	1	DATE	1/28/2011
423	2	COUNTRY	Nigeria
423	3	CITY	Maiduguri
423	4	PERPETRATOR	Boko Haram
423	5	FATALITIES	7
423	6	INJURED	5
423	7	TARGET TYPE	Government (General)
423	8	REGION	Sub-Saharan Africa
423	9	ATTACK TYPE	Armed Assault
423	10	WEAPON TYPE	Firearms
423	11		
424	1	DATE	1/30/2011
424	2	COUNTRY	Nigeria
424	3	CITY	Bauchi
424	4	PERPETRATOR	Unknown
424	5	FATALITIES	0
424	6	INJURED	0
424	7	TARGET TYPE	Religious Figures/Institutions
424	8	REGION	Sub-Saharan Africa
424	9	ATTACK TYPE	Bombing/Explosion
424	10	WEAPON TYPE	Explosives/Bombs/Dynamite
424	11		
425	1	DATE	2/1/2011
425	2	COUNTRY	Nigeria
425	3	CITY	Maiduguri
425	4	PERPETRATOR	Boko Haram (suspected)
425	5	FATALITIES	1
425	6	INJURED	1
425	7	TARGET TYPE	Police
425	8	REGION	Sub-Saharan Africa
425	9	ATTACK TYPE	Assassination
425	10	WEAPON TYPE	Firearms
425	11		
426	1	DATE	2/2/2011
426	2	COUNTRY	Nigeria
426	3	CITY	Biu
426	4	PERPETRATOR	Boko Haram (suspected)
426	5	FATALITIES	1
426	6	INJURED	1
426	7	TARGET TYPE	Police
426	8	REGION	Sub-Saharan Africa

426	9	ATTACK TYPE	Armed Assault
426	10	WEAPON TYPE	Firearms
426	11		
427	1	DATE	2/15/2011
427	2	COUNTRY	Nigeria
427	3	CITY	Maiduguri
427	4	PERPETRATOR	Boko Haram (suspected)
427	5	FATALITIES	0
427	6	INJURED	0
427	7	TARGET TYPE	Religious Figures/Institutions
427	8	REGION	Sub-Saharan Africa
427	9	ATTACK TYPE	Armed Assault
427	10	WEAPON TYPE	Firearms
427	11		
428	1	DATE	2/15/2011
428	2	COUNTRY	Nigeria
428	3	CITY	Maiduguri
428	4	PERPETRATOR	Boko Haram (suspected)
428	5	FATALITIES	2
428	6	INJURED	0
428	7	TARGET TYPE	Military,Religious Figures/Institutions
428	8	REGION	Sub-Saharan Africa
428	9	ATTACK TYPE	Armed Assault
428	10	WEAPON TYPE	Firearms
428	11		
429	1	DATE	2/17/2011
429	2	COUNTRY	Nigeria
429	3	CITY	Darazo
429	4	PERPETRATOR	Boko Haram (suspected)
429	5	FATALITIES	1
429	6	INJURED	0
429	7	TARGET TYPE	Business,Private Citizens & Property
429	8	REGION	Sub-Saharan Africa
429	9	ATTACK TYPE	Armed Assault
429	10	WEAPON TYPE	Firearms
429	11		
430	1	DATE	2/17/2011
430	2	COUNTRY	Nigeria
430	3	CITY	Darazo
430	4	PERPETRATOR	Boko Haram (suspected)
430	5	FATALITIES	1
430	6	INJURED	3
430	7	TARGET TYPE	Police
430	8	REGION	Sub-Saharan Africa
430	9	ATTACK TYPE	Armed Assault,Bombing/Explosion
430	10	WEAPON TYPE	Firearms,Explosives/Bombs/Dynamite

430	11		
431	1	DATE	2/18/2011
431	2	COUNTRY	Nigeria
431	3	CITY	Enugu
431	4	PERPETRATOR	Unknown
431	5	FATALITIES	0
431	6	INJURED	0
431	7	TARGET TYPE	Government (General),Government (General)
431	8	REGION	Sub-Saharan Africa
431	9	ATTACK TYPE	Assassination
431	10	WEAPON TYPE	Explosives/Bombs/Dynamite
431	11		
432	1	DATE	2/21/2011
432	2	COUNTRY	Nigeria
432	3	CITY	Yenagoa
432	4	PERPETRATOR	Unknown
432	5	FATALITIES	0
432	6	INJURED	0
432	7	TARGET TYPE	Government (General)
432	8	REGION	Sub-Saharan Africa
432	9	ATTACK TYPE	Bombing/Explosion
432	10	WEAPON TYPE	Explosives/Bombs/Dynamite
432	11		
433	1	DATE	2/23/2011
433	2	COUNTRY	Nigeria
433	3	CITY	Maiduguri
433	4	PERPETRATOR	Boko Haram (suspected)
433	5	FATALITIES	1
433	6	INJURED	0
433	7	TARGET TYPE	Police
433	8	REGION	Sub-Saharan Africa
433	9	ATTACK TYPE	Armed Assault
433	10	WEAPON TYPE	Firearms
433	11		
434	1	DATE	3/1/2011
434	2	COUNTRY	Nigeria
434	3	CITY	Maiduguri
434	4	PERPETRATOR	Boko Haram (suspected)
434	5	FATALITIES	1
434	6	INJURED	0
434	7	TARGET TYPE	Police
434	8	REGION	Sub-Saharan Africa
434	9	ATTACK TYPE	Armed Assault
434	10	WEAPON TYPE	Firearms
434	11		
435	1	DATE	3/2/2011

435	2	COUNTRY	Nigeria
435	3	CITY	Suleja
435	4	PERPETRATOR	Unknown
435	5	FATALITIES	10
435	6	INJURED	34
435	7	TARGET TYPE	Government (General),Private Citizens & Property
435	8	REGION	Sub-Saharan Africa
435	9	ATTACK TYPE	Bombing/Explosion
435	10	WEAPON TYPE	Explosives/Bombs/Dynamite
435	11		
436	1	DATE	3/2/2011
436	2	COUNTRY	Nigeria
436	3	CITY	Maiduguri
436	4	PERPETRATOR	Boko Haram (suspected)
436	5	FATALITIES	1
436	6	INJURED	0
436	7	TARGET TYPE	Police
436	8	REGION	Sub-Saharan Africa
436	9	ATTACK TYPE	Armed Assault
436	10	WEAPON TYPE	Firearms
436	11		
437	1	DATE	3/13/2011
437	2	COUNTRY	Nigeria
437	3	CITY	Maiduguri
437	4	PERPETRATOR	Boko Haram (suspected)
437	5	FATALITIES	1
437	6	INJURED	0
437	7	TARGET TYPE	Religious Figures/Institutions
437	8	REGION	Sub-Saharan Africa
437	9	ATTACK TYPE	Armed Assault
437	10	WEAPON TYPE	Firearms
437	11		
438	1	DATE	3/20/2011
438	2	COUNTRY	Nigeria
438	3	CITY	Jos
438	4	PERPETRATOR	Unknown
438	5	FATALITIES	2
438	6	INJURED	0
438	7	TARGET TYPE	Religious Figures/Institutions
438	8	REGION	Sub-Saharan Africa
438	9	ATTACK TYPE	Bombing/Explosion
438	10	WEAPON TYPE	Explosives/Bombs/Dynamite
438	11		
439	1	DATE	3/21/2011
439	2	COUNTRY	Nigeria
439	3	CITY	Maiduguri

439	4	PERPETRATOR	Boko Haram (suspected)
439	5	FATALITIES	1
439	6	INJURED	2
439	7	TARGET TYPE	Government (General)
439	8	REGION	Sub-Saharan Africa
439	9	ATTACK TYPE	Armed Assault
439	10	WEAPON TYPE	Firearms
439	11		
440	1	DATE	3/27/2011
440	2	COUNTRY	Nigeria
440	3	CITY	Maiduguri
440	4	PERPETRATOR	Boko Haram (suspected)
440	5	FATALITIES	1
440	6	INJURED	0
440	7	TARGET TYPE	Government (General)
440	8	REGION	Sub-Saharan Africa
440	9	ATTACK TYPE	Armed Assault
440	10	WEAPON TYPE	Firearms
440	11		
441	1	DATE	3/29/2011
441	2	COUNTRY	Nigeria
441	3	CITY	Maiduguri
441	4	PERPETRATOR	Boko Haram (suspected)
441	5	FATALITIES	0
441	6	INJURED	0
441	7	TARGET TYPE	Government (General)
441	8	REGION	Sub-Saharan Africa
441	9	ATTACK TYPE	Bombing/Explosion
441	10	WEAPON TYPE	Explosives/Bombs/Dynamite
441	11		
442	1	DATE	3/29/2011
442	2	COUNTRY	Nigeria
442	3	CITY	Maiduguri
442	4	PERPETRATOR	Boko Haram
442	5	FATALITIES	3
442	6	INJURED	0
442	7	TARGET TYPE	Private Citizens & Property
442	8	REGION	Sub-Saharan Africa
442	9	ATTACK TYPE	Armed Assault
442	10	WEAPON TYPE	Firearms
442	11		
443	1	DATE	3/29/2011
443	2	COUNTRY	Nigeria
443	3	CITY	Maiduguri
443	4	PERPETRATOR	Boko Haram
443	5	FATALITIES	1

443	6	INJURED	6
443	7	TARGET TYPE	Private Citizens & Property
443	8	REGION	Sub-Saharan Africa
443	9	ATTACK TYPE	Armed Assault
443	10	WEAPON TYPE	Firearms
443	11		
444	1	DATE	3/31/2011
444	2	COUNTRY	Nigeria
444	3	CITY	Katsina
444	4	PERPETRATOR	Unknown
444	5	FATALITIES	0
444	6	INJURED	0
444	7	TARGET TYPE	Government (General)
444	8	REGION	Sub-Saharan Africa
444	9	ATTACK TYPE	Bombing/Explosion
444	10	WEAPON TYPE	Explosives/Bombs/Dynamite
444	11		
445	1	DATE	4/5/2011
445	2	COUNTRY	Nigeria
445	3	CITY	Yenagoa
445	4	PERPETRATOR	Unknown
445	5	FATALITIES	0
445	6	INJURED	0
445	7	TARGET TYPE	Business
445	8	REGION	Sub-Saharan Africa
445	9	ATTACK TYPE	Bombing/Explosion
445	10	WEAPON TYPE	Explosives/Bombs/Dynamite
445	11		
446	1	DATE	4/8/2011
446	2	COUNTRY	Nigeria
446	3	CITY	Suleja
446	4	PERPETRATOR	Unknown
446	5	FATALITIES	13
446	6	INJURED	12
446	7	TARGET TYPE	Government (General)
446	8	REGION	Sub-Saharan Africa
446	9	ATTACK TYPE	Bombing/Explosion
446	10	WEAPON TYPE	Explosives/Bombs/Dynamite
446	11		
447	1	DATE	4/8/2011
447	2	COUNTRY	Nigeria
447	3	CITY	Shani
447	4	PERPETRATOR	Unknown
447	5	FATALITIES	8
447	6	INJURED	56
447	7	TARGET TYPE	NGO,Private Citizens & Property

447	8	REGION	Sub-Saharan Africa
447	9	ATTACK TYPE	Armed Assault
447	10	WEAPON TYPE	Firearms
447	11		
448	1	DATE	4/9/2011
448	2	COUNTRY	Nigeria
448	3	CITY	Ife
448	4	PERPETRATOR	Unknown
448	5	FATALITIES	5
448	6	INJURED	0
448	7	TARGET TYPE	NGO
448	8	REGION	Sub-Saharan Africa
448	9	ATTACK TYPE	Armed Assault
448	10	WEAPON TYPE	Firearms
448	11		
449	1	DATE	4/9/2011
449	2	COUNTRY	Nigeria
449	3	CITY	Jere
449	4	PERPETRATOR	Unknown
449	5	FATALITIES	2
449	6	INJURED	0
449	7	TARGET TYPE	NGO
449	8	REGION	Sub-Saharan Africa
449	9	ATTACK TYPE	Armed Assault
449	10	WEAPON TYPE	Firearms
449	11		
450	1	DATE	4/9/2011
450	2	COUNTRY	Nigeria
450	3	CITY	Maiduguri
450	4	PERPETRATOR	Unknown
450	5	FATALITIES	1
450	6	INJURED	5
450	7	TARGET TYPE	Government (General)
450	8	REGION	Sub-Saharan Africa
450	9	ATTACK TYPE	Bombing/Explosion
450	10	WEAPON TYPE	Explosives/Bombs/Dynamite
450	11		
451	1	DATE	4/9/2011
451	2	COUNTRY	Nigeria
451	3	CITY	Maiduguri
451	4	PERPETRATOR	Unknown
451	5	FATALITIES	3
451	6	INJURED	9
451	7	TARGET TYPE	Government (General)
451	8	REGION	Sub-Saharan Africa
451	9	ATTACK TYPE	Bombing/Explosion

451	10	WEAPON TYPE	Explosives/Bombs/Dynamite
451	11		
452	1	DATE	4/15/2011
452	2	COUNTRY	Nigeria
452	3	CITY	Maiduguri
452	4	PERPETRATOR	Unknown
452	5	FATALITIES	0
452	6	INJURED	Unknown
452	7	TARGET TYPE	Government (General)
452	8	REGION	Sub-Saharan Africa
452	9	ATTACK TYPE	Bombing/Explosion
452	10	WEAPON TYPE	Explosives/Bombs/Dynamite
452	11		
453	1	DATE	4/16/2011
453	2	COUNTRY	Nigeria
453	3	CITY	Kaduna
453	4	PERPETRATOR	Unknown
453	5	FATALITIES	2
453	6	INJURED	0
453	7	TARGET TYPE	Business
453	8	REGION	Sub-Saharan Africa
453	9	ATTACK TYPE	Bombing/Explosion
453	10	WEAPON TYPE	Explosives/Bombs/Dynamite
453	11		
454	1	DATE	4/20/2011
454	2	COUNTRY	Nigeria
454	3	CITY	Maiduguri
454	4	PERPETRATOR	Boko Haram (suspected)
454	5	FATALITIES	3
454	6	INJURED	2
454	7	TARGET TYPE	Police
454	8	REGION	Sub-Saharan Africa
454	9	ATTACK TYPE	Armed Assault,Bombing/Explosion
454	10	WEAPON TYPE	Explosives/Bombs/Dynamite,Firearms
454	11		
455	1	DATE	4/24/2011
455	2	COUNTRY	Nigeria
455	3	CITY	Maiduguri
455	4	PERPETRATOR	Boko Haram (suspected)
455	5	FATALITIES	0
455	6	INJURED	0
455	7	TARGET TYPE	Transportation
455	8	REGION	Sub-Saharan Africa
455	9	ATTACK TYPE	Bombing/Explosion
455	10	WEAPON TYPE	Explosives/Bombs/Dynamite
455	11		

456	1	DATE	4/24/2011
456	2	COUNTRY	Nigeria
456	3	CITY	Maiduguri
456	4	PERPETRATOR	Boko Haram (suspected)
456	5	FATALITIES	3
456	6	INJURED	14
456	7	TARGET TYPE	Business
456	8	REGION	Sub-Saharan Africa
456	9	ATTACK TYPE	Bombing/Explosion
456	10	WEAPON TYPE	Explosives/Bombs/Dynamite
456	11		
457	1	DATE	5/12/2011
457	2	COUNTRY	Nigeria
457	3	CITY	Maiduguri
457	4	PERPETRATOR	Boko Haram (suspected)
457	5	FATALITIES	1
457	6	INJURED	1
457	7	TARGET TYPE	Other
457	8	REGION	Sub-Saharan Africa
457	9	ATTACK TYPE	Armed Assault
457	10	WEAPON TYPE	Firearms
457	11		
458	1	DATE	5/25/2011
458	2	COUNTRY	Nigeria
458	3	CITY	Damaturu
458	4	PERPETRATOR	Unknown
458	5	FATALITIES	0
458	6	INJURED	0
458	7	TARGET TYPE	Government (General)
458	8	REGION	Sub-Saharan Africa
458	9	ATTACK TYPE	Bombing/Explosion
458	10	WEAPON TYPE	Explosives/Bombs/Dynamite
458	11		
459	1	DATE	5/26/2011
459	2	COUNTRY	Nigeria
459	3	CITY	Maiduguri
459	4	PERPETRATOR	Boko Haram (suspected)
459	5	FATALITIES	1
459	6	INJURED	0
459	7	TARGET TYPE	Police
459	8	REGION	Sub-Saharan Africa
459	9	ATTACK TYPE	Armed Assault,Facility/Infrastructure Attack
459	10	WEAPON TYPE	Firearms,Incendiary
459	11		
460	1	DATE	5/27/2011
460	2	COUNTRY	Nigeria

460	3	CITY	Unknown
460	4	PERPETRATOR	Boko Haram (suspected)
460	5	FATALITIES	6
460	6	INJURED	0
460	7	TARGET TYPE	Police
460	8	REGION	Sub-Saharan Africa
460	9	ATTACK TYPE	Armed Assault,Bombing/Explosion
460	10	WEAPON TYPE	Explosives/Bombs/Dynamite,Firearms
460	11		
461	1	DATE	5/27/2011
461	2	COUNTRY	Nigeria
461	3	CITY	Unknown
461	4	PERPETRATOR	Boko Haram (suspected)
461	5	FATALITIES	7
461	6	INJURED	0
461	7	TARGET TYPE	Business,Police
461	8	REGION	Sub-Saharan Africa
461	9	ATTACK TYPE	Armed Assault
461	10	WEAPON TYPE	Firearms
461	11		
462	1	DATE	5/29/2011
462	2	COUNTRY	Nigeria
462	3	CITY	Zaria
462	4	PERPETRATOR	Boko Haram
462	5	FATALITIES	0
462	6	INJURED	8
462	7	TARGET TYPE	Private Citizens & Property
462	8	REGION	Sub-Saharan Africa
462	9	ATTACK TYPE	Bombing/Explosion
462	10	WEAPON TYPE	Explosives/Bombs/Dynamite
462	11		
463	1	DATE	5/29/2011
463	2	COUNTRY	Nigeria
463	3	CITY	Bauchi
463	4	PERPETRATOR	Boko Haram
463	5	FATALITIES	14
463	6	INJURED	40
463	7	TARGET TYPE	Private Citizens & Property
463	8	REGION	Sub-Saharan Africa
463	9	ATTACK TYPE	Bombing/Explosion
463	10	WEAPON TYPE	Explosives/Bombs/Dynamite
463	11		
464	1	DATE	5/29/2011
464	2	COUNTRY	Nigeria
464	3	CITY	Abuja
464	4	PERPETRATOR	Boko Haram

464	5	FATALITIES	2
464	6	INJURED	10
464	7	TARGET TYPE	Private Citizens & Property
464	8	REGION	Sub-Saharan Africa
464	9	ATTACK TYPE	Bombing/Explosion
464	10	WEAPON TYPE	Explosives/Bombs/Dynamite
464	11		
465	1	DATE	5/30/2011
465	2	COUNTRY	Nigeria
465	3	CITY	Maiduguri
465	4	PERPETRATOR	Boko Haram (suspected)
465	5	FATALITIES	1
465	6	INJURED	0
465	7	TARGET TYPE	Military
465	8	REGION	Sub-Saharan Africa
465	9	ATTACK TYPE	Armed Assault
465	10	WEAPON TYPE	Firearms
465	11		
466	1	DATE	6/1/2011
466	2	COUNTRY	Nigeria
466	3	CITY	Maiduguri
466	4	PERPETRATOR	Boko Haram (suspected)
466	5	FATALITIES	0
466	6	INJURED	0
466	7	TARGET TYPE	Government (General)
466	8	REGION	Sub-Saharan Africa
466	9	ATTACK TYPE	Bombing/Explosion
466	10	WEAPON TYPE	Explosives/Bombs/Dynamite
466	11		
467	1	DATE	6/2/2011
467	2	COUNTRY	Nigeria
467	3	CITY	Maiduguri
467	4	PERPETRATOR	Boko Haram (suspected)
467	5	FATALITIES	0
467	6	INJURED	0
467	7	TARGET TYPE	Religious Figures/Institutions
467	8	REGION	Sub-Saharan Africa
467	9	ATTACK TYPE	Bombing/Explosion
467	10	WEAPON TYPE	Explosives/Bombs/Dynamite
467	11		
468	1	DATE	6/6/2011
468	2	COUNTRY	Nigeria
468	3	CITY	Biu
468	4	PERPETRATOR	Boko Haram (suspected)
468	5	FATALITIES	1
468	6	INJURED	0

468	7	TARGET TYPE	Religious Figures/Institutions
468	8	REGION	Sub-Saharan Africa
468	9	ATTACK TYPE	Armed Assault
468	10	WEAPON TYPE	Firearms
468	11		
469	1	DATE	6/7/2011
469	2	COUNTRY	Nigeria
469	3	CITY	Maiduguri
469	4	PERPETRATOR	Boko Haram (suspected)
469	5	FATALITIES	2
469	6	INJURED	0
469	7	TARGET TYPE	Religious Figures/Institutions
469	8	REGION	Sub-Saharan Africa
469	9	ATTACK TYPE	Armed Assault
469	10	WEAPON TYPE	Firearms
469	11		
470	1	DATE	6/7/2011
470	2	COUNTRY	Nigeria
470	3	CITY	Maiduguri
470	4	PERPETRATOR	Boko Haram (suspected)
470	5	FATALITIES	5
470	6	INJURED	0
470	7	TARGET TYPE	Religious Figures/Institutions
470	8	REGION	Sub-Saharan Africa
470	9	ATTACK TYPE	Bombing/Explosion
470	10	WEAPON TYPE	Explosives/Bombs/Dynamite
470	11		
471	1	DATE	6/8/2011
471	2	COUNTRY	Nigeria
471	3	CITY	Unknown
471	4	PERPETRATOR	Boko Haram (suspected)
471	5	FATALITIES	1
471	6	INJURED	0
471	7	TARGET TYPE	Police
471	8	REGION	Sub-Saharan Africa
471	9	ATTACK TYPE	Armed Assault
471	10	WEAPON TYPE	Firearms
471	11		
472	1	DATE	6/11/2011
472	2	COUNTRY	Nigeria
472	3	CITY	Yenagoa
472	4	PERPETRATOR	Unknown
472	5	FATALITIES	2
472	6	INJURED	1
472	7	TARGET TYPE	Private Citizens & Property
472	8	REGION	Sub-Saharan Africa

472	9	ATTACK TYPE	Armed Assault
472	10	WEAPON TYPE	Firearms
472	11		
473	1	DATE	6/12/2011
473	2	COUNTRY	Nigeria
473	3	CITY	Maiduguri
473	4	PERPETRATOR	Boko Haram (suspected)
473	5	FATALITIES	4
473	6	INJURED	0
473	7	TARGET TYPE	Private Citizens & Property
473	8	REGION	Sub-Saharan Africa
473	9	ATTACK TYPE	Armed Assault
473	10	WEAPON TYPE	Firearms
473	11		
474	1	DATE	6/16/2011
474	2	COUNTRY	Nigeria
474	3	CITY	Unknown
474	4	PERPETRATOR	Unknown
474	5	FATALITIES	4
474	6	INJURED	0
474	7	TARGET TYPE	Religious Figures/Institutions
474	8	REGION	Sub-Saharan Africa
474	9	ATTACK TYPE	Bombing/Explosion
474	10	WEAPON TYPE	Explosives/Bombs/Dynamite
474	11		
475	1	DATE	6/16/2011
475	2	COUNTRY	Nigeria
475	3	CITY	Abuja
475	4	PERPETRATOR	Boko Haram
475	5	FATALITIES	3
475	6	INJURED	5
475	7	TARGET TYPE	Police
475	8	REGION	Sub-Saharan Africa
475	9	ATTACK TYPE	Bombing/Explosion
475	10	WEAPON TYPE	Explosives/Bombs/Dynamite
475	11		
476	1	DATE	6/20/2011
476	2	COUNTRY	Nigeria
476	3	CITY	Maiduguri
476	4	PERPETRATOR	Boko Haram (suspected)
476	5	FATALITIES	1
476	6	INJURED	0
476	7	TARGET TYPE	Government (General)
476	8	REGION	Sub-Saharan Africa
476	9	ATTACK TYPE	Armed Assault
476	10	WEAPON TYPE	Firearms

476	11		
477	1	DATE	6/26/2011
477	2	COUNTRY	Nigeria
477	3	CITY	Maiduguri
477	4	PERPETRATOR	Boko Haram (suspected)
477	5	FATALITIES	25
477	6	INJURED	30
477	7	TARGET TYPE	Business
477	8	REGION	Sub-Saharan Africa
477	9	ATTACK TYPE	Bombing/Explosion
477	10	WEAPON TYPE	Explosives/Bombs/Dynamite
477	11		
478	1	DATE	6/27/2011
478	2	COUNTRY	Nigeria
478	3	CITY	Maiduguri
478	4	PERPETRATOR	Boko Haram (suspected)
478	5	FATALITIES	2
478	6	INJURED	3
478	7	TARGET TYPE	Private Citizens & Property
478	8	REGION	Sub-Saharan Africa
478	9	ATTACK TYPE	Bombing/Explosion
478	10	WEAPON TYPE	Explosives/Bombs/Dynamite
478	11		
479	1	DATE	7/2/2011
479	2	COUNTRY	Nigeria
479	3	CITY	Maiduguri
479	4	PERPETRATOR	Boko Haram (suspected)
479	5	FATALITIES	2
479	6	INJURED	0
479	7	TARGET TYPE	Private Citizens & Property
479	8	REGION	Sub-Saharan Africa
479	9	ATTACK TYPE	Armed Assault
479	10	WEAPON TYPE	Firearms
479	11		
480	1	DATE	7/2/2011
480	2	COUNTRY	Nigeria
480	3	CITY	Maiduguri
480	4	PERPETRATOR	Boko Haram (suspected)
480	5	FATALITIES	0
480	6	INJURED	1
480	7	TARGET TYPE	Private Citizens & Property
480	8	REGION	Sub-Saharan Africa
480	9	ATTACK TYPE	Armed Assault
480	10	WEAPON TYPE	Firearms
480	11		
481	1	DATE	7/2/2011

481	2	COUNTRY	Nigeria
481	3	CITY	Maiduguri
481	4	PERPETRATOR	Boko Haram (suspected)
481	5	FATALITIES	1
481	6	INJURED	0
481	7	TARGET TYPE	Private Citizens & Property
481	8	REGION	Sub-Saharan Africa
481	9	ATTACK TYPE	Armed Assault
481	10	WEAPON TYPE	Firearms
481	11		
482	1	DATE	7/3/2011
482	2	COUNTRY	Nigeria
482	3	CITY	Maiduguri
482	4	PERPETRATOR	Boko Haram (suspected)
482	5	FATALITIES	1
482	6	INJURED	0
482	7	TARGET TYPE	Government (General)
482	8	REGION	Sub-Saharan Africa
482	9	ATTACK TYPE	Armed Assault
482	10	WEAPON TYPE	Firearms
482	11		
483	1	DATE	7/3/2011
483	2	COUNTRY	Nigeria
483	3	CITY	Maiduguri
483	4	PERPETRATOR	Boko Haram (suspected)
483	5	FATALITIES	8
483	6	INJURED	15
483	7	TARGET TYPE	Private Citizens & Property
483	8	REGION	Sub-Saharan Africa
483	9	ATTACK TYPE	Bombing/Explosion
483	10	WEAPON TYPE	Explosives/Bombs/Dynamite
483	11		
484	1	DATE	7/4/2011
484	2	COUNTRY	Nigeria
484	3	CITY	Biu
484	4	PERPETRATOR	Boko Haram (suspected)
484	5	FATALITIES	4
484	6	INJURED	2
484	7	TARGET TYPE	Government (General)
484	8	REGION	Sub-Saharan Africa
484	9	ATTACK TYPE	Armed Assault
484	10	WEAPON TYPE	Firearms
484	11		
485	1	DATE	7/5/2011
485	2	COUNTRY	Nigeria
485	3	CITY	Maiduguri

485	4	PERPETRATOR	Boko Haram (suspected)
485	5	FATALITIES	1
485	6	INJURED	0
485	7	TARGET TYPE	Government (General)
485	8	REGION	Sub-Saharan Africa
485	9	ATTACK TYPE	Armed Assault
485	10	WEAPON TYPE	Firearms
485	11		
486	1	DATE	7/10/2011
486	2	COUNTRY	Nigeria
486	3	CITY	Suleja
486	4	PERPETRATOR	Unknown
486	5	FATALITIES	3
486	6	INJURED	7
486	7	TARGET TYPE	Religious Figures/Institutions
486	8	REGION	Sub-Saharan Africa
486	9	ATTACK TYPE	Bombing/Explosion
486	10	WEAPON TYPE	Explosives/Bombs/Dynamite
486	11		
487	1	DATE	7/10/2011
487	2	COUNTRY	Nigeria
487	3	CITY	Kaduna
487	4	PERPETRATOR	Boko Haram (suspected)
487	5	FATALITIES	0
487	6	INJURED	20
487	7	TARGET TYPE	Private Citizens & Property
487	8	REGION	Sub-Saharan Africa
487	9	ATTACK TYPE	Bombing/Explosion
487	10	WEAPON TYPE	Explosives/Bombs/Dynamite
487	11		
488	1	DATE	7/11/2011
488	2	COUNTRY	Nigeria
488	3	CITY	Madalla
488	4	PERPETRATOR	Unknown
488	5	FATALITIES	0
488	6	INJURED	0
488	7	TARGET TYPE	Religious Figures/Institutions
488	8	REGION	Sub-Saharan Africa
488	9	ATTACK TYPE	Bombing/Explosion
488	10	WEAPON TYPE	Explosives/Bombs/Dynamite
488	11		
489	1	DATE	7/12/2011
489	2	COUNTRY	Nigeria
489	3	CITY	Maiduguri
489	4	PERPETRATOR	Boko Haram (suspected)
489	5	FATALITIES	0

489	6	INJURED	0
489	7	TARGET TYPE	Government (General)
489	8	REGION	Sub-Saharan Africa
489	9	ATTACK TYPE	Bombing/Explosion
489	10	WEAPON TYPE	Explosives/Bombs/Dynamite
489	11		
490	1	DATE	7/30/2011
490	2	COUNTRY	Nigeria
490	3	CITY	Jos
490	4	PERPETRATOR	Unknown
490	5	FATALITIES	0
490	6	INJURED	0
490	7	TARGET TYPE	Other
490	8	REGION	Sub-Saharan Africa
490	9	ATTACK TYPE	Bombing/Explosion
490	10	WEAPON TYPE	Explosives/Bombs/Dynamite
490	11		
491	1	DATE	7/31/2011
491	2	COUNTRY	Nigeria
491	3	CITY	Jos
491	4	PERPETRATOR	Unknown
491	5	FATALITIES	0
491	6	INJURED	0
491	7	TARGET TYPE	Other
491	8	REGION	Sub-Saharan Africa
491	9	ATTACK TYPE	Bombing/Explosion
491	10	WEAPON TYPE	Explosives/Bombs/Dynamite
491	11		
492	1	DATE	8/7/2011
492	2	COUNTRY	Nigeria
492	3	CITY	Maiduguri
492	4	PERPETRATOR	Boko Haram (suspected)
492	5	FATALITIES	1
492	6	INJURED	0
492	7	TARGET TYPE	Private Citizens & Property
492	8	REGION	Sub-Saharan Africa
492	9	ATTACK TYPE	Armed Assault
492	10	WEAPON TYPE	Firearms
492	11		
493	1	DATE	8/8/2011
493	2	COUNTRY	Nigeria
493	3	CITY	Maiduguri
493	4	PERPETRATOR	Boko Haram (suspected)
493	5	FATALITIES	1
493	6	INJURED	0
493	7	TARGET TYPE	Police

493	8	REGION	Sub-Saharan Africa
493	9	ATTACK TYPE	Armed Assault
493	10	WEAPON TYPE	Firearms
493	11		
494	1	DATE	8/12/2011
494	2	COUNTRY	Nigeria
494	3	CITY	Unknown
494	4	PERPETRATOR	Boko Haram (suspected)
494	5	FATALITIES	1
494	6	INJURED	0
494	7	TARGET TYPE	Religious Figures/Institutions
494	8	REGION	Sub-Saharan Africa
494	9	ATTACK TYPE	Armed Assault
494	10	WEAPON TYPE	Firearms
494	11		
495	1	DATE	8/15/2011
495	2	COUNTRY	Nigeria
495	3	CITY	Maiduguri
495	4	PERPETRATOR	Boko Haram (suspected)
495	5	FATALITIES	1
495	6	INJURED	0
495	7	TARGET TYPE	Police
495	8	REGION	Sub-Saharan Africa
495	9	ATTACK TYPE	Bombing/Explosion
495	10	WEAPON TYPE	Explosives/Bombs/Dynamite
495	11		
496	1	DATE	8/19/2011
496	2	COUNTRY	Nigeria
496	3	CITY	Maiduguri
496	4	PERPETRATOR	Boko Haram (suspected)
496	5	FATALITIES	4
496	6	INJURED	0
496	7	TARGET TYPE	Police
496	8	REGION	Sub-Saharan Africa
496	9	ATTACK TYPE	Armed Assault
496	10	WEAPON TYPE	Firearms
496	11		
497	1	DATE	8/23/2011
497	2	COUNTRY	Nigeria
497	3	CITY	Maiduguri
497	4	PERPETRATOR	Boko Haram (suspected)
497	5	FATALITIES	1
497	6	INJURED	0
497	7	TARGET TYPE	NGO
497	8	REGION	Sub-Saharan Africa
497	9	ATTACK TYPE	Assassination

497	10	WEAPON TYPE	Firearms
497	11		
498	1	DATE	8/26/2011
498	2	COUNTRY	Nigeria
498	3	CITY	Abuja
498	4	PERPETRATOR	Boko Haram
498	5	FATALITIES	24
498	6	INJURED	81
498	7	TARGET TYPE	NGO
498	8	REGION	Sub-Saharan Africa
498	9	ATTACK TYPE	Bombing/Explosion
498	10	WEAPON TYPE	Explosives/Bombs/Dynamite
498	11		
499	1	DATE	8/28/2011
499	2	COUNTRY	Nigeria
499	3	CITY	Maiduguri
499	4	PERPETRATOR	Boko Haram (suspected)
499	5	FATALITIES	1
499	6	INJURED	0
499	7	TARGET TYPE	Other
499	8	REGION	Sub-Saharan Africa
499	9	ATTACK TYPE	Armed Assault
499	10	WEAPON TYPE	Firearms
499	11		
500	1	DATE	8/28/2011
500	2	COUNTRY	Nigeria
500	3	CITY	Bauchi
500	4	PERPETRATOR	Unknown
500	5	FATALITIES	0
500	6	INJURED	0
500	7	TARGET TYPE	Private Citizens & Property
500	8	REGION	Sub-Saharan Africa
500	9	ATTACK TYPE	Bombing/Explosion
500	10	WEAPON TYPE	Explosives/Bombs/Dynamite
500	11		
501	1	DATE	8/31/2011
501	2	COUNTRY	Nigeria
501	3	CITY	Yola
501	4	PERPETRATOR	Unknown
501	5	FATALITIES	1
501	6	INJURED	0
501	7	TARGET TYPE	Private Citizens & Property
501	8	REGION	Sub-Saharan Africa
501	9	ATTACK TYPE	Armed Assault
501	10	WEAPON TYPE	Firearms
501	11		

502	1	DATE	9/1/2011
502	2	COUNTRY	Nigeria
502	3	CITY	Unknown
502	4	PERPETRATOR	Boko Haram (suspected)
502	5	FATALITIES	0
502	6	INJURED	0
502	7	TARGET TYPE	Military
502	8	REGION	Sub-Saharan Africa
502	9	ATTACK TYPE	Armed Assault
502	10	WEAPON TYPE	Firearms
502	11		
503	1	DATE	9/6/2011
503	2	COUNTRY	Nigeria
503	3	CITY	Maiduguri
503	4	PERPETRATOR	Boko Haram (suspected)
503	5	FATALITIES	0
503	6	INJURED	0
503	7	TARGET TYPE	Government (General)
503	8	REGION	Sub-Saharan Africa
503	9	ATTACK TYPE	Bombing/Explosion
503	10	WEAPON TYPE	Explosives/Bombs/Dynamite
503	11		
504	1	DATE	9/6/2011
504	2	COUNTRY	Nigeria
504	3	CITY	Maiduguri
504	4	PERPETRATOR	Boko Haram (suspected)
504	5	FATALITIES	0
504	6	INJURED	0
504	7	TARGET TYPE	Government (General)
504	8	REGION	Sub-Saharan Africa
504	9	ATTACK TYPE	Bombing/Explosion
504	10	WEAPON TYPE	Explosives/Bombs/Dynamite
504	11		
505	1	DATE	9/6/2011
505	2	COUNTRY	Nigeria
505	3	CITY	Maiduguri
505	4	PERPETRATOR	Boko Haram (suspected)
505	5	FATALITIES	1
505	6	INJURED	0
505	7	TARGET TYPE	Religious Figures/Institutions
505	8	REGION	Sub-Saharan Africa
505	9	ATTACK TYPE	Armed Assault
505	10	WEAPON TYPE	Firearms
505	11		
506	1	DATE	9/11/2011
506	2	COUNTRY	Nigeria

506	3	CITY	Jos
506	4	PERPETRATOR	Boko Haram (suspected)
506	5	FATALITIES	0
506	6	INJURED	0
506	7	TARGET TYPE	Private Citizens & Property
506	8	REGION	Sub-Saharan Africa
506	9	ATTACK TYPE	Bombing/Explosion
506	10	WEAPON TYPE	Explosives/Bombs/Dynamite
506	11		
507	1	DATE	9/12/2011
507	2	COUNTRY	Nigeria
507	3	CITY	Maiduguri
507	4	PERPETRATOR	Unknown
507	5	FATALITIES	1
507	6	INJURED	0
507	7	TARGET TYPE	Business
507	8	REGION	Sub-Saharan Africa
507	9	ATTACK TYPE	Armed Assault
507	10	WEAPON TYPE	Firearms
507	11		
508	1	DATE	9/12/2011
508	2	COUNTRY	Nigeria
508	3	CITY	Maiduguri
508	4	PERPETRATOR	Boko Haram (suspected)
508	5	FATALITIES	4
508	6	INJURED	0
508	7	TARGET TYPE	Private Citizens & Property
508	8	REGION	Sub-Saharan Africa
508	9	ATTACK TYPE	Armed Assault
508	10	WEAPON TYPE	Firearms
508	11		
509	1	DATE	9/14/2011
509	2	COUNTRY	Nigeria
509	3	CITY	Maiduguri
509	4	PERPETRATOR	Boko Haram (suspected)
509	5	FATALITIES	3
509	6	INJURED	2
509	7	TARGET TYPE	Private Citizens & Property
509	8	REGION	Sub-Saharan Africa
509	9	ATTACK TYPE	Armed Assault
509	10	WEAPON TYPE	Firearms
509	11		
510	1	DATE	9/17/2011
510	2	COUNTRY	Nigeria
510	3	CITY	Maiduguri
510	4	PERPETRATOR	Boko Haram (suspected)

510	5	FATALITIES	1
510	6	INJURED	0
510	7	TARGET TYPE	Private Citizens & Property
510	8	REGION	Sub-Saharan Africa
510	9	ATTACK TYPE	Armed Assault
510	10	WEAPON TYPE	Firearms
510	11		
511	1	DATE	9/21/2011
511	2	COUNTRY	Nigeria
511	3	CITY	Maiduguri
511	4	PERPETRATOR	Boko Haram (suspected)
511	5	FATALITIES	1
511	6	INJURED	0
511	7	TARGET TYPE	Government (General)
511	8	REGION	Sub-Saharan Africa
511	9	ATTACK TYPE	Armed Assault
511	10	WEAPON TYPE	Firearms
511	11		
512	1	DATE	9/21/2011
512	2	COUNTRY	Nigeria
512	3	CITY	Maiduguri
512	4	PERPETRATOR	Boko Haram (suspected)
512	5	FATALITIES	1
512	6	INJURED	0
512	7	TARGET TYPE	Private Citizens & Property
512	8	REGION	Sub-Saharan Africa
512	9	ATTACK TYPE	Armed Assault
512	10	WEAPON TYPE	Firearms
512	11		
513	1	DATE	9/26/2011
513	2	COUNTRY	Nigeria
513	3	CITY	Port Harcourt
513	4	PERPETRATOR	Unknown
513	5	FATALITIES	0
513	6	INJURED	0
513	7	TARGET TYPE	Business
513	8	REGION	Sub-Saharan Africa
513	9	ATTACK TYPE	Hostage Taking (Kidnapping)
513	10	WEAPON TYPE	Unknown
513	11		
514	1	DATE	9/29/2011
514	2	COUNTRY	Nigeria
514	3	CITY	Suleja
514	4	PERPETRATOR	Boko Haram (suspected)
514	5	FATALITIES	2
514	6	INJURED	0

514	7	TARGET TYPE	Private Citizens & Property
514	8	REGION	Sub-Saharan Africa
514	9	ATTACK TYPE	Armed Assault
514	10	WEAPON TYPE	Firearms
514	11		
515	1	DATE	10/2/2011
515	2	COUNTRY	Nigeria
515	3	CITY	Ilorin
515	4	PERPETRATOR	Unknown
515	5	FATALITIES	0
515	6	INJURED	1
515	7	TARGET TYPE	Government (General)
515	8	REGION	Sub-Saharan Africa
515	9	ATTACK TYPE	Armed Assault
515	10	WEAPON TYPE	Firearms
515	11		
516	1	DATE	10/2/2011
516	2	COUNTRY	Nigeria
516	3	CITY	Maiduguri
516	4	PERPETRATOR	Boko Haram (suspected)
516	5	FATALITIES	1
516	6	INJURED	0
516	7	TARGET TYPE	Private Citizens & Property
516	8	REGION	Sub-Saharan Africa
516	9	ATTACK TYPE	Armed Assault
516	10	WEAPON TYPE	Firearms
516	11		
517	1	DATE	10/3/2011
517	2	COUNTRY	Nigeria
517	3	CITY	Maiduguri
517	4	PERPETRATOR	Boko Haram (suspected)
517	5	FATALITIES	2
517	6	INJURED	0
517	7	TARGET TYPE	Private Citizens & Property
517	8	REGION	Sub-Saharan Africa
517	9	ATTACK TYPE	Armed Assault
517	10	WEAPON TYPE	Firearms
517	11		
518	1	DATE	10/9/2011
518	2	COUNTRY	Nigeria
518	3	CITY	Maiduguri
518	4	PERPETRATOR	Boko Haram (suspected)
518	5	FATALITIES	0
518	6	INJURED	1
518	7	TARGET TYPE	Military
518	8	REGION	Sub-Saharan Africa

518	9	ATTACK TYPE	Bombing/Explosion
518	10	WEAPON TYPE	Explosives/Bombs/Dynamite
518	11		
519	1	DATE	10/12/2011
519	2	COUNTRY	Nigeria
519	3	CITY	Damboa
519	4	PERPETRATOR	Boko Haram (suspected)
519	5	FATALITIES	1
519	6	INJURED	3
519	7	TARGET TYPE	Business
519	8	REGION	Sub-Saharan Africa
519	9	ATTACK TYPE	Armed Assault
519	10	WEAPON TYPE	Firearms
519	11		
520	1	DATE	10/13/2011
520	2	COUNTRY	Nigeria
520	3	CITY	Maiduguri
520	4	PERPETRATOR	Boko Haram (suspected)
520	5	FATALITIES	1
520	6	INJURED	0
520	7	TARGET TYPE	Police
520	8	REGION	Sub-Saharan Africa
520	9	ATTACK TYPE	Armed Assault
520	10	WEAPON TYPE	Firearms
520	11		
521	1	DATE	10/14/2011
521	2	COUNTRY	Nigeria
521	3	CITY	Maiduguri
521	4	PERPETRATOR	Boko Haram (suspected)
521	5	FATALITIES	1
521	6	INJURED	0
521	7	TARGET TYPE	Police
521	8	REGION	Sub-Saharan Africa
521	9	ATTACK TYPE	Armed Assault
521	10	WEAPON TYPE	Firearms
521	11		
522	1	DATE	10/16/2011
522	2	COUNTRY	Nigeria
522	3	CITY	Maiduguri
522	4	PERPETRATOR	Boko Haram (suspected)
522	5	FATALITIES	1
522	6	INJURED	0
522	7	TARGET TYPE	Government (General)
522	8	REGION	Sub-Saharan Africa
522	9	ATTACK TYPE	Armed Assault
522	10	WEAPON TYPE	Firearms

522	11		
523	1	DATE	10/19/2011
523	2	COUNTRY	Nigeria
523	3	CITY	Asaba
523	4	PERPETRATOR	Unknown
523	5	FATALITIES	0
523	6	INJURED	1
523	7	TARGET TYPE	Telecommunication
523	8	REGION	Sub-Saharan Africa
523	9	ATTACK TYPE	Bombing/Explosion
523	10	WEAPON TYPE	Explosives/Bombs/Dynamite
523	11		
524	1	DATE	10/19/2011
524	2	COUNTRY	Nigeria
524	3	CITY	Maiduguri
524	4	PERPETRATOR	Boko Haram (suspected)
524	5	FATALITIES	2
524	6	INJURED	0
524	7	TARGET TYPE	Police
524	8	REGION	Sub-Saharan Africa
524	9	ATTACK TYPE	Armed Assault
524	10	WEAPON TYPE	Firearms
524	11		
525	1	DATE	10/22/2011
525	2	COUNTRY	Nigeria
525	3	CITY	Maiduguri
525	4	PERPETRATOR	Boko Haram
525	5	FATALITIES	1
525	6	INJURED	0
525	7	TARGET TYPE	Journalists & Media
525	8	REGION	Sub-Saharan Africa
525	9	ATTACK TYPE	Armed Assault
525	10	WEAPON TYPE	Firearms
525	11		
526	1	DATE	10/23/2011
526	2	COUNTRY	Nigeria
526	3	CITY	Unknown
526	4	PERPETRATOR	Boko Haram (suspected)
526	5	FATALITIES	Unknown
526	6	INJURED	Unknown
526	7	TARGET TYPE	Business
526	8	REGION	Sub-Saharan Africa
526	9	ATTACK TYPE	Bombing/Explosion
526	10	WEAPON TYPE	Explosives/Bombs/Dynamite
526	11		
527	1	DATE	10/23/2011

527	2	COUNTRY	Nigeria
527	3	CITY	Saminaka
527	4	PERPETRATOR	Boko Haram (suspected)
527	5	FATALITIES	Unknown
527	6	INJURED	Unknown
527	7	TARGET TYPE	Police
527	8	REGION	Sub-Saharan Africa
527	9	ATTACK TYPE	Bombing/Explosion,Armed Assault
527	10	WEAPON TYPE	Explosives/Bombs/Dynamite
527	11		
528	1	DATE	10/29/2011
528	2	COUNTRY	Nigeria
528	3	CITY	Maiduguri
528	4	PERPETRATOR	Boko Haram (suspected)
528	5	FATALITIES	1
528	6	INJURED	0
528	7	TARGET TYPE	Religious Figures/Institutions
528	8	REGION	Sub-Saharan Africa
528	9	ATTACK TYPE	Armed Assault
528	10	WEAPON TYPE	Firearms
528	11		
529	1	DATE	11/2/2011
529	2	COUNTRY	Nigeria
529	3	CITY	Unknown
529	4	PERPETRATOR	Boko Haram (suspected)
529	5	FATALITIES	1
529	6	INJURED	0
529	7	TARGET TYPE	Military
529	8	REGION	Sub-Saharan Africa
529	9	ATTACK TYPE	Armed Assault
529	10	WEAPON TYPE	Firearms
529	11		
530	1	DATE	11/3/2011
530	2	COUNTRY	Nigeria
530	3	CITY	Tabak
530	4	PERPETRATOR	Gunmen
530	5	FATALITIES	2
530	6	INJURED	12
530	7	TARGET TYPE	Private Citizens & Property
530	8	REGION	Sub-Saharan Africa
530	9	ATTACK TYPE	Armed Assault
530	10	WEAPON TYPE	Firearms
530	11		
531	1	DATE	11/4/2011
531	2	COUNTRY	Nigeria
531	3	CITY	Damaturu

531	4	PERPETRATOR	Boko Haram (suspected)
531	5	FATALITIES	0
531	6	INJURED	0
531	7	TARGET TYPE	Business
531	8	REGION	Sub-Saharan Africa
531	9	ATTACK TYPE	Bombing/Explosion
531	10	WEAPON TYPE	Explosives/Bombs/Dynamite
531	11		
532	1	DATE	11/4/2011
532	2	COUNTRY	Nigeria
532	3	CITY	Maiduguri
532	4	PERPETRATOR	Boko Haram (suspected)
532	5	FATALITIES	6
532	6	INJURED	6
532	7	TARGET TYPE	Educational Institution,Private Citizens & Property
532	8	REGION	Sub-Saharan Africa
532	9	ATTACK TYPE	Bombing/Explosion
532	10	WEAPON TYPE	Explosives/Bombs/Dynamite
532	11		
533	1	DATE	11/4/2011
533	2	COUNTRY	Nigeria
533	3	CITY	Maiduguri
533	4	PERPETRATOR	Boko Haram (suspected)
533	5	FATALITIES	0
533	6	INJURED	0
533	7	TARGET TYPE	Government (General)
533	8	REGION	Sub-Saharan Africa
533	9	ATTACK TYPE	Bombing/Explosion
533	10	WEAPON TYPE	Explosives/Bombs/Dynamite
533	11		
534	1	DATE	11/4/2011
534	2	COUNTRY	Nigeria
534	3	CITY	Maiduguri
534	4	PERPETRATOR	Boko Haram (suspected)
534	5	FATALITIES	3
534	6	INJURED	1
534	7	TARGET TYPE	Military
534	8	REGION	Sub-Saharan Africa
534	9	ATTACK TYPE	Bombing/Explosion
534	10	WEAPON TYPE	Explosives/Bombs/Dynamite
534	11		
535	1	DATE	11/4/2011
535	2	COUNTRY	Nigeria
535	3	CITY	Potiskum
535	4	PERPETRATOR	Boko Haram (suspected)
535	5	FATALITIES	0

535	6	INJURED	0
535	7	TARGET TYPE	Police
535	8	REGION	Sub-Saharan Africa
535	9	ATTACK TYPE	Bombing/Explosion
535	10	WEAPON TYPE	Explosives/Bombs/Dynamite
535	11		
536	1	DATE	11/4/2011
536	2	COUNTRY	Nigeria
536	3	CITY	Damaturu
536	4	PERPETRATOR	Boko Haram
536	5	FATALITIES	6
536	6	INJURED	10
536	7	TARGET TYPE	Private Citizens & Property,Religious Figures/Institutions
536	8	REGION	Sub-Saharan Africa
536	9	ATTACK TYPE	Bombing/Explosion
536	10	WEAPON TYPE	Explosives/Bombs/Dynamite
536	11		
537	1	DATE	11/4/2011
537	2	COUNTRY	Nigeria
537	3	CITY	Damaturu
537	4	PERPETRATOR	Boko Haram
537	5	FATALITIES	6
537	6	INJURED	10
537	7	TARGET TYPE	Private Citizens & Property,Religious Figures/Institutions
537	8	REGION	Sub-Saharan Africa
537	9	ATTACK TYPE	Bombing/Explosion
537	10	WEAPON TYPE	Explosives/Bombs/Dynamite
537	11		
538	1	DATE	11/4/2011
538	2	COUNTRY	Nigeria
538	3	CITY	Damaturu
538	4	PERPETRATOR	Boko Haram
538	5	FATALITIES	6
538	6	INJURED	10
538	7	TARGET TYPE	Private Citizens & Property,Religious Figures/Institutions
538	8	REGION	Sub-Saharan Africa
538	9	ATTACK TYPE	Bombing/Explosion
538	10	WEAPON TYPE	Explosives/Bombs/Dynamite
538	11		
539	1	DATE	11/4/2011
539	2	COUNTRY	Nigeria
539	3	CITY	Damaturu
539	4	PERPETRATOR	Boko Haram

539	5	FATALITIES	6
539	6	INJURED	10
539	7	TARGET TYPE	Private Citizens & Property,Religious Figures/Institutions
539	8	REGION	Sub-Saharan Africa
539	9	ATTACK TYPE	Bombing/Explosion
539	10	WEAPON TYPE	Explosives/Bombs/Dynamite
539	11		
540	1	DATE	11/4/2011
540	2	COUNTRY	Nigeria
540	3	CITY	Damaturu
540	4	PERPETRATOR	Boko Haram
540	5	FATALITIES	6
540	6	INJURED	10
540	7	TARGET TYPE	Private Citizens & Property,Religious Figures/Institutions
540	8	REGION	Sub-Saharan Africa
540	9	ATTACK TYPE	Bombing/Explosion
540	10	WEAPON TYPE	Explosives/Bombs/Dynamite
540	11		
541	1	DATE	11/4/2011
541	2	COUNTRY	Nigeria
541	3	CITY	Damaturu
541	4	PERPETRATOR	Boko Haram
541	5	FATALITIES	6
541	6	INJURED	10
541	7	TARGET TYPE	Private Citizens & Property,Religious Figures/Institutions
541	8	REGION	Sub-Saharan Africa
541	9	ATTACK TYPE	Bombing/Explosion
541	10	WEAPON TYPE	Explosives/Bombs/Dynamite
541	11		
542	1	DATE	11/4/2011
542	2	COUNTRY	Nigeria
542	3	CITY	Damaturu
542	4	PERPETRATOR	Boko Haram
542	5	FATALITIES	6
542	6	INJURED	10
542	7	TARGET TYPE	Police
542	8	REGION	Sub-Saharan Africa
542	9	ATTACK TYPE	Bombing/Explosion
542	10	WEAPON TYPE	Explosives/Bombs/Dynamite
542	11		
543	1	DATE	11/4/2011
543	2	COUNTRY	Nigeria
543	3	CITY	Damaturu

543	4	PERPETRATOR	Boko Haram
543	5	FATALITIES	6
543	6	INJURED	10
543	7	TARGET TYPE	Police
543	8	REGION	Sub-Saharan Africa
543	9	ATTACK TYPE	Bombing/Explosion
543	10	WEAPON TYPE	Explosives/Bombs/Dynamite
543	11		
544	1	DATE	11/4/2011
544	2	COUNTRY	Nigeria
544	3	CITY	Damaturu
544	4	PERPETRATOR	Boko Haram
544	5	FATALITIES	6
544	6	INJURED	10
544	7	TARGET TYPE	Police
544	8	REGION	Sub-Saharan Africa
544	9	ATTACK TYPE	Bombing/Explosion
544	10	WEAPON TYPE	Explosives/Bombs/Dynamite
544	11		
545	1	DATE	11/4/2011
545	2	COUNTRY	Nigeria
545	3	CITY	Damaturu
545	4	PERPETRATOR	Boko Haram
545	5	FATALITIES	6
545	6	INJURED	10
545	7	TARGET TYPE	Police
545	8	REGION	Sub-Saharan Africa
545	9	ATTACK TYPE	Bombing/Explosion
545	10	WEAPON TYPE	Explosives/Bombs/Dynamite
545	11		
546	1	DATE	11/6/2011
546	2	COUNTRY	Nigeria
546	3	CITY	Maiduguri
546	4	PERPETRATOR	Boko Haram (suspected)
546	5	FATALITIES	1
546	6	INJURED	0
546	7	TARGET TYPE	Police
546	8	REGION	Sub-Saharan Africa
546	9	ATTACK TYPE	Armed Assault
546	10	WEAPON TYPE	Firearms
546	11		
547	1	DATE	11/9/2011
547	2	COUNTRY	Nigeria
547	3	CITY	Mainok
547	4	PERPETRATOR	Boko Haram (suspected)
547	5	FATALITIES	2

547	6	INJURED	Unknown
547	7	TARGET TYPE	Government (General)
547	8	REGION	Sub-Saharan Africa
547	9	ATTACK TYPE	Facility/Infrastructure Attack
547	10	WEAPON TYPE	Incendiary
547	11		
548	1	DATE	11/9/2011
548	2	COUNTRY	Nigeria
548	3	CITY	Mainok
548	4	PERPETRATOR	Boko Haram (suspected)
548	5	FATALITIES	0
548	6	INJURED	0
548	7	TARGET TYPE	Police
548	8	REGION	Sub-Saharan Africa
548	9	ATTACK TYPE	Bombing/Explosion
548	10	WEAPON TYPE	Explosives/Bombs/Dynamite
548	11		
549	1	DATE	11/11/2011
549	2	COUNTRY	Nigeria
549	3	CITY	Bauchi
549	4	PERPETRATOR	Unknown
549	5	FATALITIES	0
549	6	INJURED	4
549	7	TARGET TYPE	Private Citizens & Property
549	8	REGION	Sub-Saharan Africa
549	9	ATTACK TYPE	Bombing/Explosion
549	10	WEAPON TYPE	Explosives/Bombs/Dynamite
549	11		
550	1	DATE	11/13/2011
550	2	COUNTRY	Nigeria
550	3	CITY	Maiduguri
550	4	PERPETRATOR	Boko Haram (suspected)
550	5	FATALITIES	1
550	6	INJURED	0
550	7	TARGET TYPE	Private Citizens & Property
550	8	REGION	Sub-Saharan Africa
550	9	ATTACK TYPE	Armed Assault
550	10	WEAPON TYPE	Firearms
550	11		
551	1	DATE	11/14/2011
551	2	COUNTRY	Nigeria
551	3	CITY	Maiduguri
551	4	PERPETRATOR	Boko Haram (suspected)
551	5	FATALITIES	0
551	6	INJURED	0

551	7	TARGET TYPE	Government (General),Police,Private Citizens & Property
551	8	REGION	Sub-Saharan Africa
551	9	ATTACK TYPE	Bombing/Explosion
551	10	WEAPON TYPE	Explosives/Bombs/Dynamite
551	11		
552	1	DATE	11/14/2011
552	2	COUNTRY	Nigeria
552	3	CITY	Maiduguri
552	4	PERPETRATOR	Unknown
552	5	FATALITIES	0
552	6	INJURED	0
552	7	TARGET TYPE	Unknown
552	8	REGION	Sub-Saharan Africa
552	9	ATTACK TYPE	Bombing/Explosion
552	10	WEAPON TYPE	Explosives/Bombs/Dynamite
552	11		
553	1	DATE	11/14/2011
553	2	COUNTRY	Nigeria
553	3	CITY	Maiduguri
553	4	PERPETRATOR	Boko Haram
553	5	FATALITIES	Unknown
553	6	INJURED	Unknown
553	7	TARGET TYPE	Military
553	8	REGION	Sub-Saharan Africa
553	9	ATTACK TYPE	Bombing/Explosion,Armed Assault
553	10	WEAPON TYPE	Explosives/Bombs/Dynamite,Firearms
553	11		
554	1	DATE	11/16/2011
554	2	COUNTRY	Nigeria
554	3	CITY	Maiduguri
554	4	PERPETRATOR	Boko Haram
554	5	FATALITIES	0
554	6	INJURED	0
554	7	TARGET TYPE	Unknown
554	8	REGION	Sub-Saharan Africa
554	9	ATTACK TYPE	Bombing/Explosion
554	10	WEAPON TYPE	Explosives/Bombs/Dynamite
554	11		
555	1	DATE	11/18/2011
555	2	COUNTRY	Nigeria
555	3	CITY	Maiduguri
555	4	PERPETRATOR	Boko Haram
555	5	FATALITIES	3
555	6	INJURED	Unknown
555	7	TARGET TYPE	Military,Private Citizens & Property

555	8	REGION	Sub-Saharan Africa
555	9	ATTACK TYPE	Armed Assault
555	10	WEAPON TYPE	Firearms
555	11		
556	1	DATE	11/22/2011
556	2	COUNTRY	Nigeria
556	3	CITY	Maiduguri
556	4	PERPETRATOR	Boko Haram (suspected)
556	5	FATALITIES	0
556	6	INJURED	0
556	7	TARGET TYPE	Military
556	8	REGION	Sub-Saharan Africa
556	9	ATTACK TYPE	Armed Assault
556	10	WEAPON TYPE	Firearms
556	11		
557	1	DATE	11/26/2011
557	2	COUNTRY	Nigeria
557	3	CITY	Geidam
557	4	PERPETRATOR	Boko Haram
557	5	FATALITIES	1
557	6	INJURED	7
557	7	TARGET TYPE	Business
557	8	REGION	Sub-Saharan Africa
557	9	ATTACK TYPE	Bombing/Explosion
557	10	WEAPON TYPE	Explosives/Bombs/Dynamite
557	11		
558	1	DATE	11/26/2011
558	2	COUNTRY	Nigeria
558	3	CITY	Geidam
558	4	PERPETRATOR	Boko Haram
558	5	FATALITIES	1
558	6	INJURED	7
558	7	TARGET TYPE	Religious Figures/Institutions
558	8	REGION	Sub-Saharan Africa
558	9	ATTACK TYPE	Bombing/Explosion
558	10	WEAPON TYPE	Explosives/Bombs/Dynamite
558	11		
559	1	DATE	11/26/2011
559	2	COUNTRY	Nigeria
559	3	CITY	Geidam
559	4	PERPETRATOR	Boko Haram
559	5	FATALITIES	1
559	6	INJURED	7
559	7	TARGET TYPE	Police
559	8	REGION	Sub-Saharan Africa
559	9	ATTACK TYPE	Bombing/Explosion

559	10	WEAPON TYPE	Explosives/Bombs/Dynamite
559	11		
560	1	DATE	11/27/2011
560	2	COUNTRY	Nigeria
560	3	CITY	Maiduguri
560	4	PERPETRATOR	Boko Haram (suspected)
560	5	FATALITIES	1
560	6	INJURED	0
560	7	TARGET TYPE	Private Citizens & Property
560	8	REGION	Sub-Saharan Africa
560	9	ATTACK TYPE	Armed Assault
560	10	WEAPON TYPE	Firearms
560	11		
561	1	DATE	11/27/2011
561	2	COUNTRY	Nigeria
561	3	CITY	Maiduguri
561	4	PERPETRATOR	Boko Haram (suspected)
561	5	FATALITIES	1
561	6	INJURED	0
561	7	TARGET TYPE	Government (General)
561	8	REGION	Sub-Saharan Africa
561	9	ATTACK TYPE	Armed Assault
561	10	WEAPON TYPE	Firearms
561	11		
562	1	DATE	12/10/2011
562	2	COUNTRY	Nigeria
562	3	CITY	Kukawa
562	4	PERPETRATOR	Boko Haram
562	5	FATALITIES	4
562	6	INJURED	0
562	7	TARGET TYPE	Military
562	8	REGION	Sub-Saharan Africa
562	9	ATTACK TYPE	Armed Assault
562	10	WEAPON TYPE	Firearms
562	11		
563	1	DATE	12/10/2011
563	2	COUNTRY	Nigeria
563	3	CITY	Jos
563	4	PERPETRATOR	Boko Haram (suspected)
563	5	FATALITIES	0
563	6	INJURED	4
563	7	TARGET TYPE	Private Citizens & Property
563	8	REGION	Sub-Saharan Africa
563	9	ATTACK TYPE	Bombing/Explosion
563	10	WEAPON TYPE	Explosives/Bombs/Dynamite
563	11		

564	1	DATE	12/10/2011
564	2	COUNTRY	Nigeria
564	3	CITY	Jos
564	4	PERPETRATOR	Boko Haram (suspected)
564	5	FATALITIES	0
564	6	INJURED	4
564	7	TARGET TYPE	Private Citizens & Property
564	8	REGION	Sub-Saharan Africa
564	9	ATTACK TYPE	Bombing/Explosion
564	10	WEAPON TYPE	Explosives/Bombs/Dynamite
564	11		
565	1	DATE	12/10/2011
565	2	COUNTRY	Nigeria
565	3	CITY	Sapele
565	4	PERPETRATOR	Boko Haram (suspected)
565	5	FATALITIES	0
565	6	INJURED	0
565	7	TARGET TYPE	Religious Figures/Institutions
565	8	REGION	Sub-Saharan Africa
565	9	ATTACK TYPE	Bombing/Explosion
565	10	WEAPON TYPE	Explosives/Bombs/Dynamite
565	11		
566	1	DATE	12/15/2011
566	2	COUNTRY	Nigeria
566	3	CITY	Maiduguri
566	4	PERPETRATOR	Boko Haram (suspected)
566	5	FATALITIES	5
566	6	INJURED	0
566	7	TARGET TYPE	Private Citizens & Property
566	8	REGION	Sub-Saharan Africa
566	9	ATTACK TYPE	Armed Assault
566	10	WEAPON TYPE	Firearms
566	11		
567	1	DATE	12/21/2011
567	2	COUNTRY	Nigeria
567	3	CITY	Ibeno (Local Government Area)
567	4	PERPETRATOR	Unknown
567	5	FATALITIES	0
567	6	INJURED	0
567	7	TARGET TYPE	Private Citizens & Property
567	8	REGION	Sub-Saharan Africa
567	9	ATTACK TYPE	Hostage Taking (Kidnapping)
567	10	WEAPON TYPE	Firearms
567	11		
568	1	DATE	12/23/2011
568	2	COUNTRY	Nigeria

568	3	CITY	Mubi
568	4	PERPETRATOR	Unknown
568	5	FATALITIES	0
568	6	INJURED	2
568	7	TARGET TYPE	Business
568	8	REGION	Sub-Saharan Africa
568	9	ATTACK TYPE	Bombing/Explosion
568	10	WEAPON TYPE	Explosives/Bombs/Dynamite
568	11		
569	1	DATE	12/25/2011
569	2	COUNTRY	Nigeria
569	3	CITY	Jos
569	4	PERPETRATOR	Boko Haram
569	5	FATALITIES	0
569	6	INJURED	0
569	7	TARGET TYPE	Unknown
569	8	REGION	Sub-Saharan Africa
569	9	ATTACK TYPE	Bombing/Explosion
569	10	WEAPON TYPE	Explosives/Bombs/Dynamite
569	11		
570	1	DATE	12/25/2011
570	2	COUNTRY	Nigeria
570	3	CITY	Jos
570	4	PERPETRATOR	Boko Haram
570	5	FATALITIES	0
570	6	INJURED	0
570	7	TARGET TYPE	Unknown
570	8	REGION	Sub-Saharan Africa
570	9	ATTACK TYPE	Bombing/Explosion
570	10	WEAPON TYPE	Explosives/Bombs/Dynamite
570	11		
571	1	DATE	12/25/2011
571	2	COUNTRY	Nigeria
571	3	CITY	Jos
571	4	PERPETRATOR	Boko Haram
571	5	FATALITIES	0
571	6	INJURED	0
571	7	TARGET TYPE	Unknown
571	8	REGION	Sub-Saharan Africa
571	9	ATTACK TYPE	Bombing/Explosion
571	10	WEAPON TYPE	Explosives/Bombs/Dynamite
571	11		
572	1	DATE	12/25/2011
572	2	COUNTRY	Nigeria
572	3	CITY	Jos
572	4	PERPETRATOR	Boko Haram

572	5	FATALITIES	0
572	6	INJURED	0
572	7	TARGET TYPE	Unknown
572	8	REGION	Sub-Saharan Africa
572	9	ATTACK TYPE	Bombing/Explosion
572	10	WEAPON TYPE	Explosives/Bombs/Dynamite
572	11		
573	1	DATE	12/25/2011
573	2	COUNTRY	Nigeria
573	3	CITY	Damaturu
573	4	PERPETRATOR	Boko Haram
573	5	FATALITIES	4
573	6	INJURED	0
573	7	TARGET TYPE	Police
573	8	REGION	Sub-Saharan Africa
573	9	ATTACK TYPE	Bombing/Explosion
573	10	WEAPON TYPE	Explosives/Bombs/Dynamite
573	11		
574	1	DATE	12/25/2011
574	2	COUNTRY	Nigeria
574	3	CITY	Gadaka
574	4	PERPETRATOR	Boko Haram
574	5	FATALITIES	0
574	6	INJURED	Unknown
574	7	TARGET TYPE	Religious Figures/Institutions
574	8	REGION	Sub-Saharan Africa
574	9	ATTACK TYPE	Bombing/Explosion
574	10	WEAPON TYPE	Explosives/Bombs/Dynamite
574	11		
575	1	DATE	12/25/2011
575	2	COUNTRY	Nigeria
575	3	CITY	Jos
575	4	PERPETRATOR	Boko Haram
575	5	FATALITIES	1
575	6	INJURED	0
575	7	TARGET TYPE	Police,Religious Figures/Institutions
575	8	REGION	Sub-Saharan Africa
575	9	ATTACK TYPE	Bombing/Explosion,Armed Assault
575	10	WEAPON TYPE	Explosives/Bombs/Dynamite,Firearms
575	11		
576	1	DATE	12/25/2011
576	2	COUNTRY	Nigeria
576	3	CITY	Madalla
576	4	PERPETRATOR	Boko Haram
576	5	FATALITIES	37
576	6	INJURED	57

576	7	TARGET TYPE	Religious Figures/Institutions
576	8	REGION	Sub-Saharan Africa
576	9	ATTACK TYPE	Bombing/Explosion
576	10	WEAPON TYPE	Explosives/Bombs/Dynamite
576	11		
577	1	DATE	12/27/2011
577	2	COUNTRY	Nigeria
577	3	CITY	Sapele
577	4	PERPETRATOR	Unknown
577	5	FATALITIES	0
577	6	INJURED	7
577	7	TARGET TYPE	Religious Figures/Institutions
577	8	REGION	Sub-Saharan Africa
577	9	ATTACK TYPE	Bombing/Explosion
577	10	WEAPON TYPE	Explosives/Bombs/Dynamite
577	11		